FRIENDS *of the*
Livingston Public Library

**Gratefully Acknowledges
the Contribution of**

Judy Silberner and Haim Erder

For the 2020-2021 Membership Year

THE VAPORS

THE *VAPORS*

A SOUTHERN FAMILY,
the NEW YORK MOB,
and the RISE AND FALL *of* HOT SPRINGS,
America's Forgotten CAPITAL *of* VICE

DAVID HILL

FARRAR, STRAUS AND GIROUX
New York

Farrar, Straus and Giroux
120 Broadway, New York 10271

Library of Congress Control Number: 2020934836
ISBN: 978-1-250-08611-2

Our books may be purchased in bulk for promotional, educational, or
business use. Please contact your local bookseller or the Macmillan Corporate
and Premium Sales Department at 1-800-221-7945, extension 5442, or by
e-mail at MacmillanSpecialMarkets@macmillan.com.

www.fsgbooks.com
www.twitter.com/fsgbooks • www.facebook.com/fsgbooks

10 9 8 7 6 5 4 3 2 1

For Jimmy

I got a letter from Hot Springs, tell you how it read.

Lord, you come at once, boy. Your sure enough girl is dead.

—Mississippi Fred McDowell, "Letter from Hot Springs"

Contents

The dialogue that appears in this book has been reconstructed using a variety of sources. FBI transcripts, newspaper reports, personal correspondence, audio recordings, and court documents were used to re-create trials, public gatherings, wiretapped conversations, and other events that are, or have become, part of the public record. The private histories of Hazel Hill, Dane Harris, Owney Madden, and their associates—particularly their modes of speech—are presented based on the recollections of family members and others with memories (either firsthand or secondhand) of Hot Springs during the years 1931–1968.

Books on organized crime must rely on texts and sources that are unreliable. FBI informants, trial witnesses, criminal suspects, and journalists' sources whose accounts are of questionable veracity have over the years become a part of the historical canon. Likewise, the oral histories of Hot Springs, a small and close-knit southern town where many of the families of the people in this book still reside, are often in disagreement with each other or the public record. During the course of my research for this book over the last five years, I encountered several instances of competing accounts from multiple sources. In those cases I made choices about what to present and what to leave out based on my own sense of the facts.

The events of this book took place more than fifty years ago. The impact of those events, however, reverberates in Hot Springs to this day, in ways both large and small. During the time I spent in Hot Springs doing research, many people were willing to share their stories with me. Some, however, refused to participate or would talk to me only if I left their names out of this book, either out of fear of reprisal or distrust of outsiders. I have granted anonymity to those who requested it. Though Hot Springs has changed in many ways from the "sin city of the Bible Belt" it once was, ghosts of the past still linger.

THE VAPORS

Prologue

APRIL 7, 1961

Down in the valley beneath the shadow of Sugar Loaf Mountain, where the hot vapors rise from the healing waters of the springs, L. V. Rowe was on one hell of a roll at the dice table. He was crowded in between the stickman and the other dice players, who were lined up two and three deep at all five tables, making the wide marble-and-crystal-appointed room feel small.

"Five! A no-field five!" yelled the boxman.

The gamblers whooped. The dealers placed the checks down on the felt in front of the winning players. Rowe picked his up and placed them in his stack along the rail of the table. The stickman shoved the two dice along the felt and left them right in front of him, and he picked them up and shook them in his fist. He was on some run indeed.

"We're coming out!" the boxman yelled as Rowe prepared to shoot. He flung the dice across the table, and the crowd roared.

This was the Vapors, the grandest casino in what was once the premier gambling destination in America. Hot Springs, Arkansas, is a very different place today—an anonymous southern city twenty-five miles from the nearest interstate, the gamblers long since run out of town—but late on a Saturday night in April 1961, at the height of the horse racing season at Oaklawn Park, there was no more exhilarating place to be in the entire country. The gaming floor was filled to capacity with revelers after a long day of hollering at the track. Hot Springs was in the middle of a banner season, welcoming five million visitors that year alone—a high-water mark in the city's history.

AS FAR BACK AS the nineteenth century, when Las Vegas was still a dusty smudge on the horizon, Hot Springs had been a popular resort town. They used to call it "America's first national park," because long before there was even a National Park Service, Hot Springs was the first park managed by the federal government. In 1832, before Arkansas was even a state, President Andrew Jackson signed legislation designating the land around Hot Springs where the thermal waters flowed from the mountains as federal territory, with the idea that the government could construct medicinal bathhouses. On March 4, 1921, when the federal government did finally designate Hot Springs a national park, it had the distinction of being the country's smallest. In fact, it was arguably not even a park at all. Not in the traditional sense of one, anyway. The national park was merely a stretch of federal property smack-dab in the middle of the then-bustling small town. The more lush and dense areas of the national park weren't nearly as popular among visitors as the one-block stretch that lined one side of Central Avenue in downtown Hot Springs, which they called Bathhouse Row. The federal government operated a string of eight bathhouses up and down the block, which piped in the naturally hot water that bubbled up from deep below the earth's surface and sprang from cracks in the surrounding mountains. The city's unofficial motto was "We Bathe the World."

The hot water brought visitors in search of the medicinal qualities it was said to possess. They came to soak in scalding hot baths or to sit in so-called vapor cabinets, often on doctors' orders, to treat everything from diabetes to epilepsy. Prizefighters like Jack Dempsey trained for fights in Hot Springs in order to be close to the baths. Baseball players like Babe Ruth would spend the spring months in Hot Springs, recuperating by soaking in the hot water. The popularity among professional ball players was so great that Hot Springs eventually became the official spring training location for a number of major- and minor-league teams, including the Brooklyn Dodgers, the Boston Red Sox, and the Pittsburgh Pirates. As visitors to Hot Springs would disembark from their trains, they would be besieged by doctors advertising their services, such as post-bath mercury rubbings. Some of the more popular ailments that patients came to treat were venereal diseases. Al Capone would "take the waters" in the 1920s to treat his syphilis. These regular and quasi-permanent guests built Hot Springs into one of America's first resort towns, one that aimed to rival the glitziest spas of prewar Europe.

Hot Springs grew into one of the most unusual cities in the country, with an economy that revolved around tourism and employed some of the South's most colorful characters. From carnival folks to musicians and artists, people of all races and religions flocked to Hot Springs for work taking care of the diverse and often international guests. Despite being deep in the heavily Baptist and segregated south, Hot Springs boasted two synagogues and a Jewish hospital, two Catholic churches and a Catholic school, and nineteen black churches that served the city's thousands of African American residents, most of whom worked in the bathhouses or the hospitality industry. On the east side of Malvern Avenue were black-owned hotels, restaurants, and theaters—even a black-owned-and-operated hospital. All this in addition to a growing number of Greek, Italian, and other European immigrant families, all of whom followed paths to Hot Springs to either take the baths or take care of those who did. And taking care of the bathers meant more than just scrubbing them and drying them off. The hospitality business in Hot Springs was full-service. All that a visitor desired was available. They needed only cross the street.

On the other side of Central Avenue, directly across from the federally owned Bathhouse Row, were saloons, brothels, crooked auction houses, and all sorts of bookmaker shops and casinos. The diverse residents of Hot Springs weren't a bunch of Bible Belt simps. Hot Springs was home to card dealers and bookies, jazz musicians and burlesque dancers, prostitutes and con artists, and everything in between. Throughout the years musicians from Duke Ellington to Elvis Presley would visit to perform or simply to vacation. Often these notable visitors to Hot Springs rubbed elbows with some of America's most notorious, as the small southern town's lax attitude toward crime and vice made it a popular hideout for criminals like Sam Giancana, Vito Genovese, Al Capone, and Alvin "Creepy" Karpis. Hot Springs was visited by sitting presidents and presidents-to-be, and even saw one of its native sons, Bill Clinton, go on to live in the White House. Some called Hot Springs the spa. Some called it Bubbles. The ones who took notice of the cloud of mist hovering over Sugar Loaf Mountain—the hot vapor emanating from the natural spring flowing just beneath the surface, like smoke billowing from a chimney that wasn't there—understood why this place was called the Valley of the Vapors. It was all enough to give the God-fearing people of Arkansas—those who didn't live in Hot Springs, at least—a bad case of nerves.

Hot Springs had enjoyed wide-open casino gambling in one form or another since 1870, despite the fact that gambling was then and had always been illegal in Arkansas, as it was in every state in America except Nevada, which legalized gambling in 1931. But in Hot Springs, gambling clubs like the Vapors were open to the public and on full display, the criminal activity inside of them advertised on bright marquees and in newspaper and radio advertisements across the country. In addition to the Vapors there were the Southern Club, a large downtown casino that had been in operation since 1894; the Tower Club, a modest supper club on the outskirts of town; and the Belvedere Club, a stately country club on rolling hills that could hold up to two thousand gamblers. In addition to these four main clubs there were over seventy more casinos, bookmaker shops, and establishments with some form of gambling, large and small, scattered throughout the town of twenty-eight thousand people. On a per capita basis, Hot Springs was perhaps the most sinful little city in the world.

The Vapors club was the newest joint in town, and it was like nothing Hot Springs had ever seen before, as plush as any place in New York or Las Vegas. It was built to accommodate the influx of wealthy gamblers who had flocked to Hot Springs in the years after the war—newly rich oilmen from Oklahoma and Texas, monied Wall Street executives from New York, and well-connected gangsters from Chicago and the East Coast. The Vapors was a place where these men and women of means could feel comfortable. It aspired to be everything the nicest club in Las Vegas was, and to that end its owners spared no expense. By 1961, Hot Springs found itself locked in a competition for tourists, and it could no longer rely on its small-town charm and its scenic beauty to attract gamblers. Americans cared less about healing waters and spa cures than they once had—instead, they were flocking to the arid desert of Nevada, where the sin was shameless and on full display, advertised in looping neon. At the same time, attitudes toward gambling back in Arkansas were hardening. The culture wars of the sixties were about to begin. America was changing faster than the revelers at the Vapors on that April night would have cared to admit.

The Vapors was small in size relative to its counterparts in Las Vegas. It had no hotel attached to it. It was only one story, a squat but modern brick building erected in 1960 near the intersection of Central Avenue, which served as the city's main drag, and Park Avenue, which was the main road out of town toward Little Rock. Despite its physical size, the club employed more than two hundred people, while all the other clubs in town employed seven hundred to eight hundred combined. The payroll at the Vapors was over a million dollars a year. In addition to the casino, the club offered a twenty-four-hour coffee shop, an elegant steak house with the finest chefs from across the South, and a showroom with nightly entertainment worthy of Broadway. So much so that the Vapors developed a reputation as a good place to premiere a new show before taking it to New York. The entertainment budget was over ten thousand dollars a week, with marquee acts like Mickey Rooney, Liberace, and the McGuire Sisters under contract.

In the nine months it had been open, the Vapors had already hosted elected officials, mobsters, and movie stars. A reporter from the *St. Louis Post-Dispatch* wrote, "The Vapors is like a miniature Las Vegas Strip, with top-flight entertainers." The word was out that Hot Springs wanted to fight back against the rise of Las Vegas, competing with the other Sin City for entertainers and for customers. From coast to coast, the upper crust was talking about this little club in a little southern town, and no small number of the five million visitors in 1961 were drawn to Hot Springs by word of mouth. While Vegas could attract visitors with the promise of legal gambling, the Vapors and other casinos like it were forced to walk a fine line between tacit acknowledgment of the obvious and open denial of what was taking place within their walls. In light of this fact, the visitor totals were astounding.

Hot Springs was also bringing in hundreds of millions of dollars in revenue by the early sixties, and construction had begun on over a dozen new luxury hotels. It wouldn't be long, folks figured, until Hot Springs once again surpassed Las Vegas. The future looked bright, at least on a Saturday night at a crowded craps table at the Vapors, and the locals were proud of the town's reinvention. Where else might a good country person like L. V. Rowe enjoy a show from a big-time Hollywood star, play cards beneath Tiffany chandeliers, and roll the dice with boldfaced names from all over America?

Rowe was a doctor—well, a chiropractor, anyway—and a regular at the Vapors. Like a lot of folks who came to live in Hot Springs in those days, he loved to gamble. For many of his fellow dice players, his good fortune at the craps table must have been a happy sight. Who didn't like to see a local boy do well? It also helped that in craps, the players tend to win and lose together. It was everyone against the house. With each successive roll of the dice, the players either celebrated or commiserated together as one.

Hazel Hill was another good country person who loved to gamble. She was forty-two, an attractive brunette, and looking like high society that night in her party dress and shawl. Only she wasn't high society, not by a long shot. On her own dime, Hazel wouldn't ordinarily be in a place like the Vapors. She'd likely be at the Tower Club, with the other down-on-their-luck locals. Or, if it was a special occasion, she might be at the Pines Supper Club, or any number of the more proletarian establishments around town, where the low rollers and hustlers could gamble cheap and drink even cheaper. Hazel worked for the Vapors as a shill player, gambling with house money to keep the tourists interested and the games going. It wasn't a great job as far as the money went, but it was the best job Hazel had ever had, playing with the house's money and blowing on doctors' dice for them. Whatever the pay, it was worth something to her to just be in the Vapors. It put Hazel right at the center of the whole world.

Like Dr. Rowe, Hazel had been drawn to Hot Springs because of the gambling business. She arrived in town at age sixteen and had spent her young life working in and around these clubs, all while trying to raise three children, the youngest of whom, Jimmy, was my father. Jimmy Hill would grow up in the bright lights of the casinos and attend high school alongside Bill Clinton, and yet the town that once seemed so full of promise would eventually rob him of his mother.

Hazel was a street-smart high school dropout. She had become a wife and a mother in Hot Springs, earning her living on her wits and the skills she had picked up in the casinos—how to calculate odds, how to place and take bets, how to deal cards. By 1961, her two older sons were already off on their own and Jimmy was just starting high school. Yet she was still young, still filled with enthusiasm for the pomp and promise of Hot Springs. She still believed, despite how hard and heartbreaking her life had been up to that point, that a better future was possible for her in that town. It was hard not to believe that while sitting in a place like the Vapors. The club was a monument to such magical thinking, the splendor of it intoxicating.

For someone like Hazel, it was hard to resist the lure of all the vice on display around her. At the end of each shift as a shill, she made her way back to the office to turn in what was left of her players' checks, all of which belonged to the house. While her dream was to one day deal blackjack at the Vapors, a job that could pay as much as fifty dollars a night plus tips, for now she was content to pretend to gamble for ten dollars a night. After handing over the house's winnings, she was given two blue five-dollar chips in return. Paying her in chips was smart. It was a good way to make sure the money never left the walls of the club. For someone like Hazel, the walk from the back office to the parking lot could be agonizingly long. Often she went straight from the gambling tables to the bar.

Now, though, it was Dr. Rowe who was pocketing chips. The shills had their eyes on him. One of Hazel's fellow shill players, a buddy of the club owner named Richard Dooley, watched Rowe like a hawk. One of the craps dealers was paying Dr. Rowe more money on each of his winning bets than he actually won. It could have been a simple error, but the fact that Rowe was putting the extra chips in his pocket, rather than in his stack of chips along the rail of the table, told Dooley all he needed to know. Dooley signaled John Ermey, who had once been the chief of police of Hot Springs but now had a more lucrative and powerful position as the head of security at the Vapors. This was how it worked, how the town was able to stay wide open in bald-faced violation of the law for so many years: at one time or another, the whole of the establishment was in on it, from the mayor to the chief of police to the district judge to the county clerk. Many of the bouncers, guards, and even pit bosses and dealers at the Vapors were off-the-clock police officers padding their municipal paychecks. The city government levied fines on the clubs for breaking gambling laws, and then used those funds, which were essentially illicit payoffs, to build a new police station. According to a long line of Arkansas governors, gambling was a local issue, to be handled by local law enforcement. Federal laws applied only to criminal activity that crossed state lines. So it was left to the municipal government to enforce, or not, the state's prohibition on gambling in Hot Springs.

Ermey made eye contact with Johnny Mattison, the casino manager, across the room. Ermey motioned toward Dr. Rowe's table. Mattison nodded. The two men hovered over the table, one behind the stickman and one behind the doctor.

"Eight easy!" the stickman shouted.

The dealer set a stack of checks down; Dr. Rowe picked them up. Mattison saw that there were more checks in the stack than Rowe was owed. Dr. Rowe put some in his stack on the rail of the table and some in his jacket pocket. Mattison had been in the gambling business almost his entire life. He knew a crossroader when he saw one.

Mattison stood behind the dealer who kept putting the wrong number of checks down in front of Rowe, a road gambler they called Slick who had been hired as temporary help during the busy horse racing season. "Come with me, Slick. This gentleman will take your place." No sooner had Mattison and Slick walked away from the table than Dr. Rowe felt a hand on his shoulder.

"Get your chips and come with me," Ermey growled.

"Where are we going?"

"We're going to the office."

"What for?"

"Goddamn, come on and you'll find out." At this hour of the night John Ermey didn't have any patience for dumb. He yanked Rowe by the arm. Rowe yanked it right back.

"If you don't come on you'll have so many knots on your head you can't wear your hat," Ermey barked at Rowe.

Right about then Dr. Rowe felt another man's hands on his other arm, and he was lifted off the ground and carried through the throng and into the adjoining theater, where guests were dancing to the sounds of the Buddy Kirk Orchestra. They dragged Dr. Rowe along through the back hallway and stopped in front of a door. Dane's door.

Dr. Rowe felt his body turn cold. He turned to run. John Ermey blocked his path. The third man, a square-jawed Greek tough named Harry Leopoulos, pulled Rowe forward into the office.

"Get your ass in here or I will smear you from one end of town to the other." Leopoulos picked Rowe up off the ground. Rowe turned toward Ermey, who was carrying a pistol. That tore it. Rowe gave up his fight and let Leopoulos heave him into the office.

Sitting behind the large oak desk was Dane Harris. He had broad shoulders, a round face, a tight crew cut, and the look of a young college professor. He sat with one perfectly creased pants leg crossed over the other, leaning back in his seat and thumbing through a hand of playing cards. He was all of forty-three years old, but his position behind that desk made him the most powerful man in Hot Springs. The latest in a long line of boss gamblers, Dane Harris was the de facto leader of the community of more than forty big-time scofflaws who ran the city's casinos and bookmaking joints. That meant Dane ran all of Hot Springs, the whole combination. His job was to make sure it all functioned like a well-oiled machine, and his was no easy task.

Before Dane there had been other boss gamblers—men who kept the various parties involved in enforcing the gambling laws happy, and who kept the spoils of the business divided fairly between the myriad club owners. Dane, though, had faced the unique challenge of restoring order to a city that had suffered through a number of tumultuous years without a leader. Rival club owners sponsored their own candidates, splitting the combination in two and sometimes three. The police and the governor would shut some clubs down and let others operate. Some judges would spring the bookies when they got pinched, while others would issue warrants for the enemies of their friends. Everyone fought over who should get what, who could operate and who couldn't. Dane was the man who fixed all that. He built a coalition of powerful backers and presented them with a vision of Hot Springs as the next Las

Vegas—scratch that, even bigger than Las Vegas. He built the Vapors to prove it. The gamblers, politicians, even the mobsters lined up behind him. And now he got to sit behind the big oak desk—a boy king, and the last person L. V. Rowe wanted to find himself face-to-face with. Not like this, anyway.

Across the desk from Dane sat Jerry Rosenberg. Rosenberg was the Las Vegas Flamingo's credit man, which meant he worked for Meyer Lansky, who at that time controlled the gambling interests for nearly all of the organized crime families in the United States. He was in Hot Springs that night as the Vapors' temporary credit man, which was a nice way of saying he was the house loan shark. On big nights like Saturdays during the horse racing season, the Vapors hosted scores of high rollers and did considerably more business than usual. That extra volume necessitated access to serious credit, instant and on demand. That wasn't the kind of service you could get from the Bank of Arkansas. Rosenberg approved loans to the Vapors' customers, loans that were in all probability backed by the mob.

In denial of the obvious, folks in Hot Springs liked to say that their gambling combination was homegrown, free of the influence of the mobsters who pulled the strings of the nine-billion-dollar illegal gambling industry across the country. But while the fellows that owned the majority of the bigger clubs in Hot Springs were locals, Hot Springs depended on the mob for much of the gas that fueled the gambling engine, and this was by design. That nine billion dollars was the single biggest source of revenue for the mob in 1961, which had organized itself into a national crime syndicate that coordinated its efforts and divvied up the profits. The money didn't come from directly running craps games and the like. It came from controlling the infrastructure that those craps games and poolrooms relied on to operate. The mob sold the clubs of Hot Springs their slot machines, manufactured their dice tables and chips, and even trained their dealers and pit bosses in mob-run casinos in places like Las Vegas and Havana. Most crucially, the mobsters controlled the race wire, the all-important service that provided sports results to bookmakers from coast to coast. They wielded the wire as a cudgel to extract a percentage of practically every dollar bet in America.

In Hot Springs, the wire service was run by Owney "the Killer" Madden, former owner of Harlem's Cotton Club and onetime New York City crime boss, who upon release from prison in 1931 was urged by Lansky and other leaders in the national crime syndicate to "retire" to Hot Springs. Over the past thirty years Madden had ingratiated himself into the local community, and he served as the mob's ambassador to this small southern town. He had become a powerful entity in Hot Springs, and his power was resented by many and even tested by some.

Dane Harris, however, saw Owney as a valuable ally, and someone who shared his vision for how Hot Springs should be run. And Owney saw in the young Dane a person who was ambitious enough, tough enough, and, most important, smart enough to shepherd Hot Springs toward a bright future. While Owney the Killer had once dealt with his enemies in New York by shooting them down in the streets, in Hot Springs he employed a cool hand. Owney intended to live out the rest of his days in the spa. He did not intend to go back to prison, but neither did he plan to retire. He had spent his life and made his fortune operating some of the most famous nightclubs in New York City. He had launched the careers of Mae West, George Raft, and Duke Ellington. He wasn't about to sit on the sidelines of a cow town like Hot Springs, Arkansas. Not when it held such potential. Owney helped Dane become boss gambler without firing a single shot—he protected Dane from enemies without, and Dane protected Owney from enemies within.

And yet the presence of men like Owney Madden and Jerry Rosenberg in Hot Springs had become the central problem that Dane Harris had to reckon with. By 1961 the public had grown weary of the mob. The U.S. attorney general, Robert Kennedy, was waging war on organized crime with a series of legislative initiatives aimed at curtailing its influence over the gambling business. Before his brother was elected president, the younger Kennedy had been special counsel to the Senate Committee on Investigations, which had probed rackets throughout the 1950s in a series of highly publicized hearings. Kennedy, the Senate, and the Federal Bureau of Investigation had succeeded in shutting down wide-open gambling towns like Hot Springs all across America. Places like Phenix City, Alabama; Newport, Kentucky; Fort Worth, Texas; and even Palm Beach, Florida. As each of those towns closed up shop, Hot Springs grew.

In 1961, Hot Springs remained miraculously untouched by the Senate probe, and still managed to stand shoulder to shoulder with Las Vegas as one of America's capitals of vice. Robert Kennedy's chief organized crime investigator, William Hundley, called Hot Springs "the largest illegal gambling operation in the United States." The town was in the crosshairs, and Dane knew that something had to be done before Kennedy succeeded in shutting down Hot Springs altogether. A lot of folks in Arkansas believed they could stave him off if the clubs would only cut ties with the mob, but it wasn't as easy as that. If it were, they'd have done it long before. Dane and the other club owners needed the mob. They couldn't make book without the wire. They couldn't deal craps without well-trained and trustworthy dealers and pit bosses. They couldn't run a big-money game without any credit for their players. And as the spa's popularity and profits grew, so, too, did the interest of the various crime families around the country. Dane had to work with Owney and the local political machine to keep the mob, the government, and the increasingly agitated locals all at bay while he figured out how to square the circle. What that added up to was that while Jerry Rosenberg and his ilk brought on the heat, there was no way around him. For the time being he was there to stay. And he wasn't someone who suffered fool-ass country chiropractors like Dr. Rowe too gladly.

Ermey pushed Rowe up against a wall while Leopoulos fished chips out of his pockets. "How many goddamn chips do you have?" asked Ermey.

"Tell me what this is all about!" Rowe demanded.

"We have reason to believe you were taking chips that the dealer was putting down for you," said Dane as he continued to play his hand with Rosenberg.

Dr. Rowe expressed his disbelief that anyone could take him for a cheat. After all, he played here every week. They all knew him.

Yes, Dane replied, they knew him well. "You're a small player. You play one and two checks. Yet I've seen you cash out one night seven hundred, six hundred one time."

Ermey and Leopoulos stacked the checks from Rowe's pocket on the desk. There was a knock on the door. Leopoulos opened it for Richard Dooley.

"Is this the guy?" Dane asked him.

Dooley nodded.

"How much did he buy?"

"Fifty dollars."

"That's a lie!" Rowe said. "I bought in for a hundred!" He told them he won the money fair and square and he intended to leave with his winnings.

"I'll splatter your head against that wall," Leopoulos said. "When I get through with you, there won't be any of you left." Dr. Rowe saw a blackjack, a short lead club sheathed in leather, appear in Harry Leopoulos's hand. Dane Harris motioned for Dooley to leave the room.

AT THE END OF her shift that night, Hazel stopped off at the lounge and took a seat at the bar. She had worked for Dane Harris off and on for the past few years at his various nightclubs and other businesses. Sometimes she wore an apron, sometimes at the smaller clubs she dealt cards, sometimes she shilled. But she rarely got to sit at the famous mahogany bar of the Vapors and drink with the Arkansas aristocracy. On this night, however, she would carry no tray. She would deal no cards. The orchestra struck up "Mostly Martha." The dance floor filled with spinning skirts. The bartender greeted her by name.

Hazel told the bartender to fix her a whiskey. It wasn't all nice, being there in the Vapors. There was a darkness to it. What other secrets lurked behind the curtains of the casinos and supper clubs of Hot Springs? How many beaten and bloodied bodies were in the back alleys? How many people got hurt so that these rich people could eat steak and dance the night away? How many top-shelf whiskeys could a young woman get for ten dollars at the elegant bar at the Vapors? She had no idea. How many whiskeys could she even drink? About that question she had some inkling.

Hot Springs might yet be the next Las Vegas. It might yet be the place that, growing up, Dane Harris always believed it could be. It might yet be the place that, upon arriving thirty years before, Hazel Hill and Owney Madden thought it already was—a place where they could have it all. The year 1961 was the most successful year so far for the biggest illegal gambling operation in the United States, and it was fixing to get a whole lot bigger. Getting to this point had not been easy for Dane, Hazel, or Owney. A heaviness lingered. There was, it seemed, a price yet to be paid.

Part I

WATER

1931–1939

Hazel

APRIL 4, 1935

Two hundred dollars and I'll throw in the girl.

Hazel wasn't sure where she was headed. She was barely sixteen years old, sitting shotgun in her daddy's Plymouth. They were driving down Highway 70 on the outskirts of Hot Springs, and they weren't heading back toward Ohio.

Clyde Welch turned off the highway onto a dirt road, the dust kicking up around the car like a brown storm cloud delivering them to their destination, a little farmhouse at the top of a big green hill. Clyde parked the car and looked toward the house. There on the wooden porch waiting for him was a tree trunk of a man, a long white beard draped on top of his dusty overalls. Clyde took a deep breath before he got out of the car, then headed up to meet the old man. Hazel knew this house and this old man. She watched from inside the Plymouth as her daddy shook hands and conversed with the father of Hollis Hill, the young man she had taken up with while she and Clyde were staying in Hot Springs. She was surprised that Clyde even knew about the boy. She couldn't have known what to make of the two fathers having a conversation on the Hill family porch on Clyde and Hazel's way out of town. Whatever it was about, it probably wasn't good.

Hazel and Clyde Welch had come to Hot Springs, Arkansas, from Ashland, Ohio, in that Plymouth four weeks earlier. Clyde was a horse trainer, or tried his damnedest to be one at any rate. The Oaklawn Park racetrack first opened in Hot Springs in 1905, but had been shuttered off and on since the state government banned betting on horse racing in 1907. There had been many efforts over the years to change the law and bring horse racing back, but they had always been defeated.

It was ironic that the racetrack had remained dark, because for many of those years Hot Springs was "running wide open," with casino gambling happening in full view of God and everybody. Horse racing was experiencing a surge in popularity across America, in part a consequence of the phenomenal racehorse Man o' War winning twenty out of twenty-one races in the years after World War I. Across the country, states were lifting their prohibition on horse betting to meet the public demand for the sport. But Arkansas's state legislature, led by conservative Baptists from other parts of the state, didn't follow suit, and Oaklawn's out-of-state owner, the St. Louis real estate tycoon Louis Cella, chose to keep the track closed rather than operate in defiance of the law like the casinos. He also owned racetracks in Memphis, New Orleans, Detroit, Buffalo, and several other cities. He was content to wait for the political winds in Arkansas to shift, however long that might take.

When the Great Depression that had set upon the rest of the country finally made its way to Hot Springs, the casino owners were the ones who took action to get the Oaklawn Park racetrack reopened. Horse racing, they reckoned, would be just what they needed to keep the tourists flowing to Hot Springs through the tough times. It was the casino operators, along with Mayor Leo McLaughlin, who reached out to Louis Cella in 1934, and promised him that if he opened back up they'd make sure he wouldn't get in any trouble. They weren't just blowing smoke. They had clearly figured out how to operate illegally without consequence. But in 1934 their good fortune was a fairly recent development. For many of the years that Oaklawn was closed down, the casinos had plenty of trouble with the law, consistently getting raided and shut down, moving their dice tables from one back room to the next. Louis Cella likely remembered those days. He also likely remembered how back in 1907 the original owners of Oaklawn had said to hell with the law and tried to open up and hold horse races anyway. They were greeted on opening day by an armed state militia.

This, however, was a new day in Hot Springs. In 1928, the voters had chosen as their mayor Leo McLaughlin, a gregarious man who paraded around town in a boater hat with a carnation on his lapel and rode to and from the courthouse in a horse-drawn viceroy carriage. He promised the citizens that if he was elected he'd let the gamblers open up shop, laws be damned, and he'd made good on that promise. He taxed the craps games and the brothels, paved the roads and strung up electric lights, and everyone was happy. McLaughlin handpicked the sheriff and the prosecutors, and he kept the governor at bay. Thanks to the new, more permissive administration, Cella was finally swayed. Oaklawn Park would be open for business for the 1934 season.

Like every other horseman in America, Clyde Welch caught wind that Oaklawn was opening back up at the start of 1934. It was welcome news. The Depression had set upon Clyde Welch, too. He had diabetes and he couldn't afford to see a doctor. Terrible pain in his legs and feet made him limp. Welch didn't have a stable of stakes horses. He was a blue-collar, lunch-pail horse trainer who stayed on the road working a circuit that took him from one end of America all the way to the other, and sometimes even down into Mexico. But lately he hadn't had any horses to train at all. When he heard about Oaklawn, he knew there'd be a lot of excitement—Clyde had been to Hot Springs before and knew it was a wild place. Even the residents used to brag that it was "the sin city of the whole world." He figured he could hustle work away from other trainers with an ace up his sleeve—he'd agree to work on commission, getting paid only when he won. Without a horse or even a promise of one to train, he packed his sixteen-year-old daughter into his Plymouth and headed down south from Ashland, Ohio, to see if he couldn't convince an owner or two to take a chance on a Yankee trainer with only one good foot.

Despite the town's reputation, not everyone in Hot Springs was a sinner. Even the gambling clubs and taverns would close up shop on Sundays. There were more than a few true believers in Hot Springs. One of them was an old-school Baptist minister named Luther Summers. He made his way in the world preaching in Tennessee tent revivals, dunking heads in the water and saving souls at a furious enough rate to get the attention of church leaders throughout the South. He preached fire and brimstone against the ills of society—chief among them liquor and gambling. His crusade eventually brought him to Hot Springs in the late 1920s, where he took over the pulpit at the Park Place Baptist Church—known in its Sunday live radio broadcasts across the South as the "little white church in the valley."

Summers caught wind of the effort to reopen the racetrack, and he tried to organize a united front among the clergy to oppose it. He appealed to Governor Junius Marion Futrell to send in the militia. For his efforts, Summers received a letter in the mail with a crudely drawn skull and crossbones that read "Your church will burn and you will be among the missing." He took the letter to the police. They told him if they were him, they'd leave town. So that's what Summers did. He bid his congregation farewell and moved away from Hot Springs. The little white church in the valley found itself a new preacher, one who was more charitable toward the town's tourist trade.

THE RACES BEGAN ON March 1, 1934, in open defiance of the law. The militia didn't show up, but tens of thousands of visitors did, day after day. Clyde and Hazel were among them. Throughout the twenty-seven-day race meet, Clyde was able to scare up plenty of horses to train for free. Hazel did her part, too. She worked on the backstretch, scurrying around the track collecting zappers, the electric buzzers jockeys would use to cheat by shocking the horse to get an extra jolt of speed out of them. The jockeys unscrupulous enough to use them would toss them into the dirt on the backstretch at the end of the race. Hazel would pick them up and sell them back to the cheating jockeys. On April 4, the final day of the race meet, over fifteen thousand people attended the races—the largest crowd to witness a sporting event in Arkansas history. The most successful race meet in Hot Springs history wasn't much of a success for Clyde Welch, however. Despite finding plenty of horses to work, Clyde didn't make much happen with any of them. Hazel might have made a few bucks hustling zappers, but Clyde was flat busted. After the last day of racing, Hazel and Clyde packed up the Plymouth and headed out of town, making one quick stop on the way at the Hill family's farmhouse.

Richard Hill, the hulk Clyde was gabbing with on the porch, had a sister who owned the café next door to the apartment Clyde and Hazel had rented for the month. Hazel killed a lot of time in that café during those four weeks and eventually met Hollis, Richard's twenty-two-year-old son, who drove a milk truck and made deliveries to his aunt's café every day. Hollis was handsome, charming, and confident. He had a thin mustache and, when he wasn't working, wore a fedora with the brim pushed up in the back in the style of the time. He flirted with Hazel in the café, and before long he was taking her out to the dances at Fountain Lake, a sprawling array of swimming pools, water slides, and beer bars surrounding a small natural spring on the outskirts of town, where many locals, especially the younger folks, liked to hang out when the downtown clubs were filled with tourists.

The whole thing was scandalous as hell, since young Hollis was six years older than Hazel and married to boot. At the time this didn't much matter to Hazel. She was just passing through. When the last race had been run she figured she'd be on her way to the next town. Yet here she was, sitting in her daddy's car outside the Hill house instead of watching Hot Springs disappear in the rear window of the car.

Old Richard Hill shook Hazel's daddy's hand again and then

reached into the pocket of his big overalls. He came out with a wad of cash and peeled off a few bills for Clyde. Richard slapped Clyde on the back and sent him limping back to the car.

Clyde still didn't look directly at Hazel, just stared straight ahead. Hazel was just a girl, but she had a tough disposition, and boy, did she like to boss Clyde Welch around. He was her daddy, but he was a touch afraid of her. Clyde told Hazel he had sold Richard Hill the car for two hundred dollars. How, she asked him, were they supposed to get to the next town without a car?

"I'm goin' to Tijuana," he replied. "You're stayin' here."

Clyde explained to Hazel that Hollis was getting a divorce. Richard Hill said that Hazel could live with the Hill family until the divorce was final; then Hollis and Hazel could live together.

Hazel was stunned. On the one hand, she loved Hot Springs. She loved the energy, the excitement, the bright lights. Ashland was far from the South, but it was as country as any place you'd find. Hot Springs felt like a metropolis. It may as well have been New York City, as far as Hazel was concerned. And it didn't feel like there was any Depression on in Hot Springs. People may have felt it in their pockets, but they didn't show it. People liked to dance and drink and have a good time, no matter what.

On the other hand, Hazel loved her daddy and her brothers and her mother, and she was only sixteen years old. She hadn't finished school yet, not that she ever much cared for school. But was she ready to be on her own, to be grown, to be taken in by a man she just met? Hazel, a wife at age sixteen?

There was also something about the arrangement that looked untoward. *Two hundred dollars and I'll throw in the girl.* But that wasn't really how it was. Clyde had had a hard meet in Hot Springs. He wasn't ready to go back to Ohio empty-handed. He had to follow the horses west in order to earn a living. And Hazel tagging along, whether she sold zappers to jockeys or not, was a drag on his ability to do that. A depression was on. If there was a man with a job who wanted to look after Hazel, then Hazel ought to go with that man. A man with a job was a much better deal for her than an old Yankee horse trainer with a bum foot.

Clyde told Hazel he'd be back for the next year's race meet, and he'd look in on her when he got back. He got out of the car, took his satchel from the back, and set off limping down the big green hill, away from the Hill family farm, the cow and the chickens, the Plymouth, and his baby girl. Hazel turned to face old Richard Hill, still standing on the wooden porch of the little house. There was so much to figure out in that moment between opening the door of the car and everything else that would follow.

Owney

FEBRUARY 13, 1931

**Best of all, gambling was, like alcohol,
a "victimless crime."**

Four years before Hazel Hill arrived in Hot Springs, a long Duesenberg convertible pulled up in front of the Provincial Coffee House and Gift Mart. Even in a town accustomed to rich folks coming to visit, the car turned heads. The driver wasn't someone known around Hot Springs. He commanded attention when he spoke in his English accent. His slender frame, bushy eyebrows, angular nose, and permanent scowl gave him the look of a cartoon villain. But Owney Madden was no cartoon. A villain, maybe, but he was most certainly real.

That day in 1931 was Owney's first visit to Hot Springs. He was accompanying his friend Joe Gould, a former boxer from New Jersey who was traveling to Hot Springs on doctor's orders to treat his arthritis with the hot baths. One of Owney's New York City colleagues, the "Beer Baron of the Bronx," Dutch Schultz, was a fan of the southern resort and had encouraged Owney to tag along with Gould. Schultz also suggested that Owney stop in at the Provincial Coffee House while he was in town. Dutch told Owney that the Brit in him might appreciate the tea and cake, but that the real attraction was the girl who worked the counter.

Visitors from around the country knew about pretty young Agnes Demby, the woman who lit up the dance floor at the Belvedere Club, the popular upscale casino and supper club on the outskirts of town. The attractive thirty-year-old was the postmaster's daughter. She was single, though she had no shortage of potential suitors chasing after her, wealthy bachelors and visitors from faraway places. She wasn't interested in settling down. She liked to go out on the town, eat at fine restaurants, dance, and socialize. Owney wandered the aisles of the shop, loading his arms with the most expensive merchandise from among the gifts and jewelry the store sold in the front. He strutted confidently up to the counter for Agnes to ring him up. The total came to over a thousand dollars. Agnes figured the well-dressed man was trying to make an impression on her, but he wasn't the first rich man to court her in the store. When Owney invited her to dinner, Agnes turned him down.

The rest of the day Agnes fretted about turning down the man with the English accent in the big fancy convertible. Who was this intriguing visitor from New York? She asked around about him. It turned out Owney Madden wasn't some run-of-the-mill hoodlum. He was a hoodlum of great import. Owney ran the Cotton Club, the most popular nightclub in New York City. The club's nightly performances were broadcast over radio stations across America. Like a regular celebrity, Owney was followed wherever he went by magazine photographers. His comings and goings were written about by gossip columnists in New York, Los Angeles, and Chicago. He was best pals with the Hollywood star George Raft. He dated Mae West. He managed Primo Carnera, heavyweight champion of the world. Ed Sullivan once said of him, "When you wanted anything in New York, you saw Owney Madden." Furthermore, Owney wasn't merely a member of the criminal underworld—he was a proper boss. Together with a small fraternity of former Prohibition bootleggers, he helped maintain control of all the vice clubs, rackets, and political machines in New York City. And on his way to the top of the underworld he had killed six, maybe seven people. Maybe even more.

Owney was born in Leeds, England, but he immigrated to New York when he was ten years old. When he was eleven he approached the Gophers, the biggest street gang in Hell's Kitchen, and let them know that he wanted to join. The leaders of the Gophers told the young Owney that if he could beat up a cop and steal his uniform, they'd let him in. They were only teasing the young boy, but Owney brought a police officer's uniform back to them that very same day.

The Gophers were known for muggings, raiding freight train cars, hiring themselves out as goons to break strikes, and extortion. Owney found he was especially good at extortion. He offered businesses in Hell's Kitchen "bomb insurance": they paid him and he didn't bomb them. Over the years Owney rose to the top of the Gophers by showing a unique propensity for killing, including rival Gophers when it suited him.

By the time Owney was twenty-one years old he had everything that came along with sitting atop the hierarchy of a powerful gang, both good and bad. He had money in his pockets, young women at his disposal, important people in his thrall, and enemies who wanted him dead. In 1912 Owney was shot eleven times in an ambush outside the Arbor Dance Hall, on Fifty-second Street, by members of the Hudson Dusters, a rival gang. Owney somehow survived the attack. When the cops asked him who did it, Owney wouldn't talk. "Nothing doing," he said. "The boys'll get 'em." Within a week of Owney's release from the hospital, six of the Dusters were dead. Owney would eventually go to prison on a ten-to-twenty-year sentence for the murder of a fellow Gopher who challenged his leadership of the gang. He served nine years in Sing Sing before he was paroled.

When Owney got out of prison, the Gophers had broken up, and most of his former associates had gone into bootlegging during Prohibition. He quickly organized a gang to rob and hijack bootleggers in

Hell's Kitchen. After Owney stole a shipment from Big Bill Dwyer, one of the top bootleggers in Manhattan, Dwyer opted to put Owney on the payroll rather than go to war. Together the two men, along with Italian gangster Frank Costello, built an operation that ruled "Rum Row," the supply line that stretched from the waterways of the West Indies to New York. Dwyer, Owney, and Costello operated their own private armada of ships that carried rum up the East Coast to New York. The contraband earned them huge returns on their investment, and Owney used the money to build his own brewery and brew his own brand of illicit beer, "Madden's Number 1," which was proudly served at every West Side speakeasy.

It was a time in America, and particularly in New York, when the right combination of toughness and smarts separated the winners from the losers. The city government was corrupt, the people's appetite for booze and vice was insatiable, and an influx of immigrants had created enclaves that operated by their own sets of rules. Owney possessed this special combination—he was more than just tough, more than just a killer. In the early days, before Owney was well known by the New York press, he shied away from the limelight. He didn't spend money garishly and was businesslike in all of his affairs. He made everyone he worked with sign contracts, even other gangsters. He chose businesses to invest in that offered him the greatest return.

As the money continued to roll in, the three kings of Rum Row diversified their income streams. Dwyer bought a professional hockey team. Costello invested in slot machines. Madden was a boxing fan, so he backed a number of professional boxers, including Rocky Marciano and Max Baer. But boxing was largely a hobby for Owney, a way to stay involved in a sport he loved. His smartest investments, and the ones that made him the center of attention in New York, were nightclubs.

Owney had noticed that the customers who purchased his rum and beer, the owners of speakeasy saloons and nightclubs, were making as good a return on their money as he was wholesaling it to them. So Owney invested in some of the clubs he supplied in order to get a piece of the retail side of the action. Some of those clubs, like the Stork Club and the Silver Slipper, grew over the years to become some of the most popular clubs in New York City. But one club, the Cotton Club, would become under his management the most famous nightclub in the entire world.

Owney's nightclubs succeeded not because of his impeccable taste or his hospitality acumen. His clubs succeeded because he was a gangster. Just as he did in the management of his many boxers, whom he would ask to take a dive when the oddsmakers called for it, Owney approached his nightclub business with similar ruthlessness. When the Plantation Club opened in Harlem and hired Cab Calloway away from the Cotton Club, Owney sent them a message. His men walked into the Plantation, broke all the tables and chairs, smashed the glasses, and even dragged the bar out into the street. After that, Calloway returned to the Cotton Club.

Sometimes Owney's thuggishness paired well with his taste and style, to his benefit. A great fan of jazz music, Owney was stunned the first time he heard a young Duke Ellington perform. Owney immediately asked Ellington to come work for him at the Cotton Club, but Ellington was stuck in a long-term contract with a club in Philadelphia. Owney sent a few emissaries to Philadelphia to discuss the issue with the club's manager. Whatever they said, they were persuasive. They returned with Ellington's contract, and the Duke Ellington Orchestra became the Cotton Club's house band.

Despite the fearsome reputation he earned in his younger days, in 1931 Owney was known as someone who, like Big Bill Dwyer before him, preferred to make deals with his adversaries instead of going to war. This quality attracted a number of people who preferred to do business with a cool head. Many considered Owney a gentleman gangster, befitting his English accent and his refined cultural tastes. He was more than just muscle and violence. To most people who met him, including Agnes Demby, Owney Madden didn't seem like a gangster at all. He seemed sophisticated, even nice.

Agnes discovered Owney was staying at the Arlington, a grand old hotel that anchored the downtown district, sitting squarely between the strip of casinos and Bathhouse Row. Agnes got herself fixed up and walked to the Arlington to find him. She spotted Owney sitting in the lobby bar with Joe Gould. She took another look at the English mobster. Could he be as dangerous as people said? He looked so thin, so boyish. Were all the wild stories about him true? She was intrigued, and gave in to her curiosity. Agnes walked over to their table and interrupted them.

"Do you still want to go to dinner?" she asked Owney.

"I'd love to." Owney smiled. So began the unlikely romance of the small-town postmaster's daughter and the big-time New York City gangster. For the next two weeks they spent every moment together. When Owney returned to New York, he realized that he was smitten with the young Agnes. He sent for her, buying her train ticket after train ticket to come and visit him in the city. By August the two of them were an official item, and the daughter of one of the most respected families in Hot Springs was showing up in New York City in the company of America's most notorious criminals. She was seen in speakeasies partying with the film star Texas Guinan. She was ferried through Central Park by the newspaper columnist Walter Winchell. When she was home in Arkansas, she would receive love letters from Owney. My dearest darling, he would address her. In Owney's absence, Agnes grew despondent. "Life is very uninteresting," she wrote in her diary. "Am home alone tonite, reading my old love letters from Owen."

AS OWNEY PINED AFTER Agnes, a storm cloud gathered around his professional life. It started in the Bronx, where Vincent "Mad Dog" Coll, one of Dutch Schultz's hit men, had put his own gang together and demanded to be made a full partner with Dutch in his bootlegging, numbers, and extortion businesses. Dutch refused, and Coll went to war with him, killing dozens of people, including a five-year-old boy named Michael Vengalli, who was struck by a bullet during a shootout in Harlem.

Dutch appealed to Owney for help, and word reached Coll that Owney wanted him gone. Coll kidnapped one of Owney's business partners, Frenchy DeMange, and ransomed him to Owney for fifty thousand dollars. Owney paid the ransom, but he didn't leave it there. As Mad Dog Coll walked out of the Cotton Club with Owney's money, Owney called after him: "That was very unwise, Vincent."

Owney and Dutch met with Frank Costello, Charles "Lucky" Luciano, and a number of the other gang leaders in New York to discuss what to do about Coll, who had gone into hiding. Owney didn't want a war. For one thing, Owney was still on parole. For another, the war between Coll and Schultz had created a lot of negative publicity. The papers were calling the Vengalli killing the "baby murder," and Governor Roosevelt had called it a "damnable outrage." Thousands of people attended Vengalli's funeral, and public anger about the fact that none of the witnesses to the shooting would testify was building. Owney's businesses depended on people feeling safe around him. If he was to get involved in a violent battle with Coll, it might keep people away from his clubs. But when word reached Owney that Coll was planning to kidnap him for a one-hundred-thousand-dollar ransom, he cracked. He would put his reputation for gentlemanliness on hold.

Owney sent word to Coll that he was willing to pay the hundred-thousand-dollar ransom in advance. He asked Coll to wait by a pay phone at the London Chemists drugstore on West Twenty-third Street for a phone call. Coll was no dope. He sent his bodyguard into the drugstore first to check the place out. Satisfied that it was safe, the bodyguard escorted Coll into the phone booth, then took a seat at the soda fountain counter to wait.

Eventually the phone rang. Owney was on the other line. He tried to negotiate the price down with Coll. They argued for a few minutes as a stranger entered the drugstore. Before Coll's bodyguard could get to his weapon, the stranger slid a machine gun out from under his overcoat and let loose a barrage of bullets. The twenty-three-year-old Vincent Coll was shot more than sixty times. Nobody came to his funeral, not even a priest. The undertaker read the Lord's Prayer. Owney and Dutch sent flowers with a card that read "From the boys."

Three days after the shooting, the New York Parole Board convened a meeting and signed an arrest warrant for Owney on charges of parole violation from his 1914 murder charge. The parole board worried Owney might try to flee the country. He did, after all, have a British passport, and had been taking flying lessons. But if Owney did ever plan to escape, in the end he thought better of it. He surrendered himself to the government and went back to Sing Sing to await a ruling on his fate. His former Rum Row partner, Frank Costello, was now a top figure in the Italian Mafia, and he went to work for Owney behind the scenes. After a lot of hand wringing and backroom dealing, the parole board sentenced Owney to a single year in prison.

IT WAS A BEAUTIFUL day outside when Owney Madden was let out of the gates of Sing Sing for the second time, in July of 1933. "I've got a fine day," he told reporters waiting for him outside the prison. "The weather is with me." The wiry forty-year-old's pockets were nearly empty, save for some stomach medicine he used to treat his bullet-riddled guts and nearly fifty dollars that he had earned taking care of flowers in the prison greenhouse. When he stepped through the iron gates to freedom, a long green limousine was waiting for him. It whisked him away to Manhattan, where Owney would attend a meeting that would plot the future of American organized crime.

The world had changed a lot more in that year than Owney could have imagined. Months before his release, Congress had passed the Blaine Act, paving the way for the end of Prohibition and putting an end to the New York mob's main source of income. On top of that, the country was in the throes of the worst financial depression it had ever seen.

While Owney was locked away, there had also been a shakeup in the mobster ranks. New York's underworld was now ruled by a trio of younger gangsters—Meyer Lansky, Ben "Bugsy" Siegel, and Charles "Lucky" Luciano, who had engineered the murders of a number of top Italian Mafia leaders. The three young men were as smart as they were ruthless. Lansky, in particular, had an aptitude for organization. He summoned Owney along with all of the top criminal figures in America to the Waldorf-Astoria Hotel to discuss their collective futures.

Lansky proposed a national crime syndicate, giving each mob its own regional autonomy but creating some rules for national cooperation and control. Lansky believed that the future lay not in drugs or prostitution, but in gambling. Ironically, the poverty of the Great Depression only amplified people's willingness to wager. Best of all, gambling was, like alcohol, a "victimless crime." What made the bootlegging business so lucrative for the mob was that they had sold a product that was popular. During Prohibition, the mobsters who supplied the American appetite for alcohol were treated like folk heroes. Gambling offered the gangsters a chance to build similarly warm—and dependent—relationships with their customers.

In the thirties, there were major illegal gambling operations in every big city from Los Angeles to Dallas to Miami, and even in far-flung towns like Newport, Kentucky, and Phenix City, Alabama. In the barren wastelands of Nevada, work had recently begun on a massive government dam project that had swelled the population of Las Vegas from five thousand to over twenty-five thousand, and mobsters had already swooped in to entertain (and bilk) the captive audience at their casinos. The Nevada state legislature decided it wanted a cut of the profits, and voted to legalize gambling in 1931. The first casino license was issued before Las Vegas even had a post office or a paved road. And then, tucked away on the other side of the country, there was Hot Springs, Arkansas.

Hot Springs would be the toughest nut to crack. Most of the criminal element in America knew Hot Springs as a place where they'd be treated favorably not only by the city's concierges, but even by the local police. But for all that famous southern hospitality the hayseeds in Arkansas liked to lay on the mobsters, the locals weren't letting them move in. Hot Springs was known to withhold judgment on the morals of its visitors, on the men and women on the player side of the tables. But when it came to who was on the house side of the table, the rule was well known and strictly enforced: you had to be a local. Big-city mobsters were welcome to visit, spend their money, maybe even start a fight or steal a car, but that was about the extent of it.

Lansky was familiar with Hot Springs. His son Buddy had been born with spina bifida, though it was misdiagnosed as cerebral palsy. Lansky had heard stories about the healing powers of the hot baths in Hot Springs, and his family took many lengthy trips to the city to see if the waters would help Buddy's condition. The waters worked no miracles, but Lansky found in Hot Springs a power more mortal, but lucrative all the same.

In the person of Owney Madden, Lansky had the perfect candidate to be the mob's ambassador to Hot Springs. New York was finished for him. If he stayed he risked going back to jail or, worse yet, being killed. In Arkansas, Owney's expertise would put him at the forefront of a new and promising market. He had experience running nightclubs, contacts in the entertainment industry, and access to cash that could come in handy to the small town's gambling community. Owney was an English gentleman and an unemotional deal maker. If anyone could charm the locals in Hot Springs, Owney could—and he was already well on his way. He charmed the New York Parole Board into letting him relocate to Arkansas. He charmed Agnes Demby into letting the parole board transfer his care to her family home in Hot Springs. And he charmed the postmaster into giving him his blessing to marry his daughter.

Hazel

The drivers would wildly clap their hands to get the tourists' attention, creating a sound a lot like applause for everyone who got off the train.

Hazel Welch didn't take to life on the Hill family farm. She didn't much care for chickens or cows or hogs. But Richard and Bessie Mae Hill had seven children, and the Great Depression was at its height. The extra eggs and milk and money from the slaughterhouse came in handy. But despite living among animals, the Hills weren't exactly farm people. Richard also worked at Cook's Ice Cream, a popular ice cream parlor on Albert Pike Road not far from the Hill house. Cook's was one of the largest employers in town. In addition to the parlor up front, Cook's had a plant in the back where the ice cream was manufactured, and where Richard Hill worked as an engineer. Cook's delivered dairy products to restaurants and stores across the area, and acted as distributor for the Sealtest milk it used. Richard got Hollis a job driving a delivery truck during the early morning shift, while his fiancée Hazel spent her days roaming the streets of Hot Springs with Hollis's sister Ressie, walking from one end of Central Avenue to the other.

Hazel had missed the lean years, it seemed. The Hot Springs she arrived in was one that, at least on the surface, seemed untouched by the economic calamity that had befallen the rest of the country, and in particular the South. Getting the horse races up and running again had done some real good for Hot Springs. The year after Oaklawn Park took a chance and opened in defiance of the law, the state legislature passed a bill legalizing horse racing in Arkansas again—a bill one Baptist legislator said "smells of the brimstone of Hades." News of the passage of the bill sparked celebrations in the streets of Hot Springs. Oaklawn hired hundreds of new employees, creating desperately needed jobs, but more important, the opening of the track brought an influx of tourists into town—funneling business to Hot Springs' nine major resort hotels, its scores of restaurants and lunch counters, and more than a dozen casinos and bookmaking shops that had become the city's lifeblood.

That jolt didn't come a moment too soon. By 1933, the Depression had caused four of the six local banks to fail and close their doors, and scores of people in Arkansas were out of work. Unemployment stood at 37 percent, and the state's finances were at a "low ebb." The newly elected governor, Marion Futrell, advocated legalizing the sale of liquor by the glass (still prohibited in Arkansas despite the repeal of Prohibition) and the operation of slot machines and other types of gambling in order to grow the state's tax base. While his proposals to legalize slot machines and liquor were voted down, the horse racing measure passed. By taxing ten cents per admission and four cents per dollar bet, Oaklawn would put as much as five thousand dollars a day into the state's coffers.

The next year, the crowds at Oaklawn were just as large. More than twelve thousand people attended the track's opening day on February 22. Those crowds continued throughout the year, and it seemed Hot Springs was back in business. Downtown had come back to life with tourists. The Arlington held regular formal dances. The movie theaters handed out twenty-dollar prizes at every show. The streets were crowded with fancy cars and out-of-state plates. Additional trains from St. Louis,

Chicago, Memphis, and a number of other cities were added. Tourists who got off those trains were accosted by cabdrivers, whom the police tried to control by keeping them behind designated lines and preventing them from speaking to passengers. The drivers would wildly clap their hands to get the tourists' attention, creating a sound a lot like applause for everyone who got off the train.

Those train passengers joined tourists from around Arkansas and surrounding states who sometimes hitchhiked and even walked to Hot Springs to gamble, both at the track and in the clubs, and to drink liquor, both by the "package" and the glass. Vice, it seemed, was a strong economic catalyst. In Las Vegas, where gambling was legal, the workers who built the Hoover Dam were leaving town and heading back home. The ramshackle gambling dens of Las Vegas would lie mostly dormant for another six years before someone would venture to open a proper casino and hotel. But in Hot Springs, where gambling was against the law, rich and poor alike were flocking back to town to try to beat the tough luck of the Depression with a bet on a horse or a roll of the dice.

Even those who didn't work in the "entertainment business" were happy. Hazel, and many like her, found fulfillment in strolling down Central Avenue and taking it all in. For many locals, living in Hot Springs in those days felt like a privilege—there were the fancy dress shops and the glamorous women twirling in front of the mirrors; the big auction houses with their doors wide open and the auctioneers' calls echoing up and down the block, goading the bidders to go higher for an African mask or a pair of pearl earrings; the penny arcades and shooting galleries and the carnival barkers hustling young customers not yet old enough to gamble; the casinos and back rooms and handbooks, their windows wide open and the announcement of the results of the last race or the last number on the roulette wheel carrying overhead; the billiard parlor at Martin's and the teenage boys hanging around shooting pool and the girls sitting at the lunch counter eating candy and drinking sodas; the five different theaters, some with a matinee picture show, some with a tap dancing performance or an amateur boxing match, depending on the day of the week, the tourists throwing quarters and dimes into the ring as the fighters beat on each other—all of this for a young girl from Ohio to take in, and all of it suggesting that a different life lay right behind the doors of downtown.

THE HILL FAMILY LIKED having Hazel around. For one thing, they were excited about the changes they saw in Hollis, whose previous marriage to his high school sweetheart had soured. Their separation had driven him back to his parents and left him dejected. Meeting Hazel had lit a fire under him. She motivated him to finalize his divorce, to double down at work, to start saving up money to get himself and Hazel their own apartment. All of this pleased Richard and Bessie Mae. It also helped that Hazel assisted Bessie Mae with the cooking, even showing her how the midwestern ladies did meat loaf, which all of the kids in the family quite liked. And Hazel was a good sport about being carted off to the Emmanuel Pentecostal Church, a little church on Albert Pike Road that Richard had helped to build. Hazel had never seen anything quite like it before, all that hooting and hollering and speaking in tongues.

After a year on the farm, Hollis and Hazel were properly married on June 20, 1936, at the courthouse by the justice of the peace. Hazel had just turned eighteen years old. Hollis put down a hundred dollars' bond for the license. They moved out of the Hill family home and into an apartment on Rector Street, near Hollis's job at Cook's Ice Cream. In the beginning Hazel enjoyed playing house. She liked feeling like a bona fide adult. But Hollis spent a lot of time working, and she soon grew bored. Hazel found herself back at the Hill house often, spending more time with Ressie and the rest of the Hills than with her husband.

But at night. At night! When Hazel turned eighteen years old she didn't see herself as a teenager—she was a woman with her own apartment and a husband with a good job. For her, the great privilege of being an independent adult was the ability to finally peek at the life that awaited her behind the doors of the dance halls and saloons that had called out to her with stomps and cheers and big brass bands. She often spent her days with the Hills and the cow and the chickens, waiting impatiently for Hollis to come home from work and take her out on the town.

Hollis had to be at work early each morning, but he dutifully took Hazel dancing every night they could afford to do so. Sometimes Hollis would borrow Clyde's old Plymouth from Richard and drive Hazel four miles north of town to Fountain Lake for the nightly dances. It was there that Hazel first tried beer, imploring Hollis to buy her one, since she was still under twenty-one, the legal drinking age in Arkansas. In those days plenty of young women liked to drink beer, though many of them were shy about it. Hollis reluctantly bought them each a beer. They drank and danced under the stars next to the big green lake.

This was how they spent the summer—Hazel kicking around at home or at the Hills' all day, then off to Fountain Lake just as soon as Hollis could wash up, then home so that Hollis could catch whatever sleep he could before he rose at 3:00 a.m. to load the milk and ice cream into the truck and beat the downtown traffic. It was a brutal schedule, but he was a young man with a pretty young bride to keep happy. And what made Hazel happy were the dances, and the shows, and the nighttime swims at Fountain Lake.

IT WAS SOMETIME THAT summer that Hollis and Hazel met Dr. Petty. Though everyone called him doctor, he was actually a pharmacist. He ran the drugstore at the Eastman Hotel. Hazel was impressed by Dr. Petty, and even more so by his glamorous wife, Darla, who was a bit older than the doctor. She wore fine dresses and smoked cigarettes and sported shiny diamond baubles on her ears and neck and wrists, and she spoke with an accent like a Yankee, how Hazel once imagined her own voice sounded but knew that it didn't. Darla's accent was sophisticated, almost European, and when she spoke people hung on her every word: Dr. Petty especially, who was smitten with Darla and let her lead him to and fro like a puppy on a leash.

Late one night, as things were winding down at Fountain Lake, Dr. Petty suggested that Hollis and Hazel take a drive with the older couple. Darla suggested they go to the Southern Club, the city's flagship gambling hall. The sturdy stone building with a black marble facade sat across from the Arlington Hotel. From outside Hazel had often admired the enormous chandeliers that lit up the lobby, though she had never had a proper glimpse of the interior. Darla said that at the Southern they could get a real drink, and they could dance to the orchestra. Hollis reminded her that Hazel was too young to drink. While Fountain Lake was somewhat lackadaisical about serving beer, the sale of liquor was much stricter—especially at a carpet joint like the Southern Club, which already had an illegal gambling room. Prohibition had been repealed eighteen months earlier, but over half of the counties in the state were still dry, and the sale of mixed drinks and hard liquor by the glass was illegal in Arkansas. Liquor was available only in what were called "package stores," and only for personal use in citizens' private homes. Most of the restaurants and bars in Hot Springs served liquor in defiance of this law, and most of those places had to pay someone off for the privilege. There was little reason to jeopardize those arrangements by serving liquor to kids.

Unfazed, Dr. Petty reached across Darla to the glove box and opened it. Darla took out a strange little bottle. She removed the cork and took a long pull of the liquid inside, then passed it to Dr. Petty, who did the same. He passed it back to Hollis. Hollis studied the bottle. It looked like medicine. It was one of the most popular medicines Petty supplied at the Eastman. It was prescription whiskey. Repeal had made a prescription unnecessary, but business was still brisk. For some people, the act of going to the drugstore afforded them some cover, some small amount of dignity, that wasn't granted to those who purchased their bottles in package stores. Prescription whiskey was medicine, after all.

Hollis and Hazel were surprised to see Darla drinking liquor straight from the bottle—it was highly unusual for such a prim lady to drink in this way. But the young couple must have shrugged it off, because it wasn't long before they joined in and traded pulls from the medicine bottle. In good time Hollis and Hazel were regularly getting drunk in the company of the druggist and his wife, whom they knew not as lushes or rascals but as upstanding members of the town's elite. They were adrift in the nightlife of this most mature of little cities, which they knew not as a corrupt and debauched place, but as their fitting and familiar home.

Owney

"But if you do get in trouble and you can't get out of jail, call me. I'll come down and get in with you."

Six months before Hollis and Hazel wed at the courthouse, on a cold December morning in 1935, Owney Madden and Agnes Demby stood in front of the fireplace in the Demby family residence on West Grand Avenue in Hot Springs. They were joined by Agnes's father and Reverend Kincaid, the family minister. The meeting was a surreptitious one. Neither newspapermen, nor FBI agents, nor Paramount Pictures could pry the date and location of the Madden-Demby wedding from those in attendance. The New York *Daily News* wrote that "members of the family today shrouded the affair in utmost secrecy. They wouldn't say when wedding bells would ring, and they insisted none of the principals was 'at home' to reporters. 'No information will be given out,' said a spokesman."

The ceremony was short and the attendees were few in number. When it was all over, the newlyweds drove to Owney's modest room at the Cleveland Manor Apartments, which he had rented while waiting out his parole. Soon he would purchase a home for his new bride, but they would start their life together on their wedding night in his humble bachelor apartment, sharing their first meal together as husband and wife.

Owney had been back in Hot Springs for only two years, but in that time he had drawn a lot of unwanted attention to himself and Agnes. Here in this little apartment in Arkansas lived Owney Madden, king of Rum Row and boss of New York, forty-three years old and in the prime of his life, playing house with the small-town gift counter girl. Hot Springs had grown used to big shots coming to visit, but it wasn't used to those big shots getting hitched and sticking around. And yet Owney would not leave for love or money—for he already had one of these things, and he had a duty to acquire the other. How he'd make his fortune there he had yet to ascertain. But he had been sent to Hot Springs on a deal with Frank Costello—Costello would look after Owney's various business interests back east in exchange for a percentage of whatever Owney could put together down in Arkansas.

Mayor Leo McLaughlin was predictably eager to meet his city's newest resident. McLaughlin invited Owney to his home, a big white mansion at the end of Malvern Avenue, right at the dividing line between the white and black sides of town. McLaughlin's home was incongruous with a humble mayor's salary. Its lavish lawn was encircled by an ornate wrought-iron fence, and the seventeen-room Queen Anne Victorian home had a wraparound veranda on each story. There was even a stable where McLaughlin kept Scotch and Soda, his two horses, which drew the carriage that carried him around town. The residents of Hot Springs didn't question McLaughlin's riches. They knew that their mayor was corrupt, but were confident he wasn't stealing from the public till. McLaughlin had done what he had said he would do as a candidate for mayor: tolerate illegal gambling, and make the gamblers pay for the improvements the city needed. He told the voters of Hot Springs: "Don't worry about giving Leo a raise. Leo will get his one of these days." The house, the horse-drawn buggy, and the fine pinstripe suits were proof enough that he had made good on that promise.

Owney met with the mayor and the municipal judge, Verne Ledgerwood, in the parlor of the stately home. McLaughlin commanded a formidable political machine that depended heavily on poll tax corruption and the support of the city's African American residents. Unlike other counties in Arkansas, where black residents were not allowed to join the Democratic Party and vote in primaries, McLaughlin encouraged it. He paid the one-dollar poll tax required of every voter on behalf of thousands of residents, and he sometimes even filled out their ballots for them. In exchange for political support from the city's black community, McLaughlin permitted the operation of a number of black-owned casinos and nightclubs on the east side of town, where most of the segregated city's black residents lived. McLaughlin used that influence and his poll tax operation to make sure that the right people got elected to office to keep the gambling "combination" intact. Even so, Judge Ledgerwood may have been more powerful than the mayor. The tall and stout Ledgerwood was as reserved as McLaughlin was flamboyant. Where McLaughlin was known for his rousing orations and charisma, Ledgerwood was known for his country-boy wisdom and his ability to think several moves ahead. McLaughlin was the personality, the dealmaker. Ledgerwood was the brains, the strategic thinker. The two had been friends since they were youngsters, and together they had plotted the takeover of the city and county governments in order to open up the town to gambling a full decade before Owney's arrival.

In fact, it was Ledgerwood who had initially recruited McLaughlin to run for mayor, after a dispute with then-mayor Sidney Nutt over the appointment of the police chief. Those were the days of Prohibition, and Hot Springs was inundated with speakeasies. Many of these saloons, places like the Southern Club, the Blue Ribbon, the Ohio Club, and the Citizens, had back rooms where gambling took place. Ledgerwood told McLaughlin that he could get him the support of the back-alley business owners in order to fund a run against Nutt. All McLaughlin had to do was advocate an "open policy" toward liquor and gambling, and he had to let Ledgerwood pick the police chief. McLaughlin agreed to the deal, and he had been mayor for nearly a decade since. During that time, those speakeasy backroom card games had bloomed into full-blown casinos, the patrons entering through front doors beneath brightly lit signs instead of through dark back alleys.

In a sense, this opening of the town was merely a return to its natural state. Hot Springs had been a resort for nearly as long as it had been inhabited. The springs and the bathhouses were on federal land, and their healing powers had been promoted across the country by the surgeon general and the government. Hot Springs was called a "Mecca of the afflicted," and it was (wrongly) claimed that the hot waters could cure 90 percent of all diseases, and that tens of thousands had been healed of incurable ailments by drinking and bathing in the waters. Naturally, a steady stream of visitors beat a path to the valley. And all around them grew a hospitality industry that included hotels, restaurants, saloons, and wide-open gambling and prostitution.

By 1913, however, the town had become lawless, plagued by violence and graft. After a bloody shootout in the streets made headlines in 1910 and a string of major con artist gangs were caught in Hot Springs bilking wealthy visitors out of tens of thousands of dollars, the federal government decided to investigate. In 1913 the Arkansas legislature passed a law making it a felony to operate a gambling house, and the town's dice tables and roulette wheels disappeared into the back rooms. Along with them went the town's municipal budget and a good number of the tourists. It seemed visitors came for more than just the baths. When McLaughlin took over, more than a decade later, the city's residents were desperate for a return to the days when Hot Springs was known as the Carlsbad of America, and bringing back wide-open gambling seemed the only way.

MCLAUGHLIN AND LEDGERWOOD MAY have controlled the levers of government in Hot Springs, but the casinos were run by another man,

W. S. Jacobs. When McLaughlin and Ledgerwood were first elected, Jacobs lived nearly two hundred miles away in Memphis but owned a controlling interest in a few of the backroom gambling clubs. McLaughlin and Ledgerwood summoned Jacobs to Hot Springs and asked him to help them organize the town's gambling combination. Jacobs was reluctant, but he presented them with his conditions: there would have to be a strict limit on the number of clubs allowed to operate, and Jacobs would have sole control over who was allowed to own a share of the action. They agreed, and Jacobs became the boss gambler of Hot Springs, controlling a major share of all the clubs.

Jacobs kept his spot at the top of the action by making sure that all the important people who ran the combination were taken care of. He hobbled around town on his wooden leg and delivered envelopes full of money, including one to Ledgerwood and one to McLaughlin. He loaned money to whoever needed a hand. He hired the local cops and firefighters after hours to work security in his clubs and paid more than what they made at their municipal jobs.

Jacobs was also feared. He squared people's debts and he kept undesirables from returning to town. He even put a scare on Chicago's Capone brothers, who had made Hot Springs a place of respite for themselves and their gang. Once, after Al Capone walked out on an unpaid marker at the Southern, his brother Ralph begged him to make it right. "You know we'll never be able to come back to Hot Springs if we stiff Bill Jacobs," Ralph pleaded. But despite his unforgiving nature and his role as the crime boss of Hot Springs, Jacobs rarely smoked or drank or even gambled. Rather than retiring to a barstool in one of his clubs at the end of each day, he instead took a seat at the lunch counter in the Medical Arts Building and devoured a big bowl of ice cream.

Jacobs didn't hoard all the action, either. He took on partners in each casino to make sure important people were benefiting from gambling. McLaughlin wasn't directly partnered with Jacobs in any of the clubs. Political bosses stayed an arm's length from the casinos for the sake of appearances. There were ways around that unofficial prohibition, however. Ledgerwood's older brother Archie, for example, was offered a 25 percent stake in the Belvedere and the Southern for fifteen thousand dollars—a ridiculously low sum. Despite the bargain, Archie still didn't have that kind of money. He was making fifty dollars a week managing one of Jacobs's casinos. So Jacobs put Archie together with an out-of-town gambler named Ed Ballard to loan Archie the fifteen thousand. The problem, however, was that Ballard actually wanted Archie to pay him back. After Ballard came to town to collect Archie's debt, Ballard was found dead in his suite at the Arlington Hotel, shot three times through the heart.

Ballard's murder was proof of how important it was to make sure the right people were receiving a share of the casino profits. But it was equally important to Jacobs to make sure the right people were kept out of the business, too—especially notorious criminals like Owney Madden. The combination had the local police and courts under control and had a virtual license to kill. A famous New York gangster like Owney, however, could invite the attention of cops and prosecutors from other states or, even worse, the federal government. As far as Jacobs was concerned, if the mob wanted in, it would be better to just shut it all down, because that's what he reckoned would happen anyway.

McLaughlin was smitten with Owney, however. He was excited to have such a well-known person living in Hot Springs. And Owney's connections to so many in the national criminal underworld could be useful to McLaughlin. For many years, gangsters like Al Capone visited Hot Springs to escape violence and controversy. But in recent years that safe haven had been disrupted. Rival gangsters tried to assassinate Al Capone one night as he drove through Hot Springs, riddling his car with bullets. Capone miraculously survived, but the locals were spooked. This kind of shootout was something that happened in places like Chicago and New York, not in the spa. Over time Capone and his gang grew ever rowdier on their trips to town, roughing up caddies on the golf course or stiffing clubs and restaurants for their bills and markers. Capone likely believed that his donations to McLaughlin's political campaigns earned him the right to act as he pleased in Hot Springs, but McLaughlin, Ledgerwood, and Jacobs were worried about just how much these big-city gangsters were beginning to throw their weight around. Having someone like Owney Madden on Hot Springs' side could help. Owney could act as a sort of goodwill ambassador to the underworld, helping Hot Springs enforce the expected level of decorum among gangsters.

McLaughlin let Owney know that he was welcome in Hot Springs, but when it came to the subject of having a piece of the gambling action, that was a nonstarter. Ledgerwood was blunt with Owney: "If it was known you had any interest in the clubs here, we wouldn't be able to operate."

That's how it worked in Hot Springs, they explained to Owney. Jacobs was boss gambler, and no outsiders could own any piece of the clubs. McLaughlin and Ledgerwood could offer Owney their blessing for any other kind of illicit business he wanted to conduct in town, but that's where the hospitality would end for an out-of-town guest. Owney Madden, big shot boss of Hell's Kitchen, would be treated no differently, local address or not.

"Have a good time, stay out as late as you want, spend your money, keep out of trouble," McLaughlin would often say. "But if you do get in trouble and you can't get out of jail, call me. I'll come down and get in with you."

THREE MONTHS INTO THEIR marriage, Owney and Agnes didn't turn any heads as they entered the Southern Club's dining room. This wasn't because they weren't recognized. Far from it. Owney's presence in Hot Springs was something of a spectacle. At the horse races people would crowd around him, strangers would chat him up, people would shove one another just to get a better look at him. The whole town gossiped about his past, about his riches, about his famous friends. Reporters came from around the country to ask questions about him. The New York *Daily News* called him "love smitten" and followed his "bucolic romance with an Arkansas postmaster's pretty daughter." But at the Southern it was different. At the Southern, Owney was treated with discretion, not as if he were anyone else off the street, but not as anything special, either. The staff knew to treat him well but not to make a show of it. The patrons knew to keep their distance. And when he and Agnes entertained famous guests, as they did one night in March 1936, people knew not to stare. In Hot Springs, people had grown used to seeing famous folks out and about, and had learned to act like it wasn't any big deal. In this way the spa had a lot in common with much larger cities, and the famous appreciated it as a form of hospitality. The notorious, even more so.

Owney and Agnes's guests that night were both famous and notorious. The sultry blond showgirl Gay Orlova was certainly famous, but she wasn't interested in any extra attention. The man accompanying her to dinner wasn't her husband, and her husband had no idea she was even in Hot Springs. The man she was with at Owney and Agnes's table was in need of some anonymity himself. Only a few days before, when he departed New York for Hot Springs, the special prosecutor in New York had called for a nationwide manhunt. His name was Charles "Lucky" Luciano, and he was public enemy number one.

The special prosecutor, Tom Dewey, was pulling out all the stops to try to get organized crime in New York under control. To that end Dewey had issued an arrest warrant for Luciano for running a twelve-million-dollar prostitution racket across New York City. Luciano was tipped off and disappeared without a moment's hesitation and with nothing but the shirt on his back. When he stopped off in Philadelphia to pick up Orlova and grab some cash and clothes from Nig Rosen, a fellow gangster and gambler, Rosen suggested Luciano and Orlova head to Hot Springs. Luciano had been there just the year before, for the reopening of the Oaklawn racetrack. Luciano and Meyer Lansky spent a week at the races and soaked in the hot baths. Luciano knew Hot Springs was a place where he could lie low and not worry about the locals dropping a dime on him. And besides, Owney was there now.

Owney introduced Luciano around town, including to the chief of police. Luciano was impressed, but deep down Owney was surely nervous. Luciano's presence in Hot Springs, with every arm of the U.S. justice system looking for him, would worry Jacobs. For the time being, the local law enforcement, judges, and politicians were all playing ball with the gambling leaders. If they started getting calls from cops or judges or prosecutors from other places, if there was a chance that they might personally pay some price for looking the other way, those officials might think twice about supporting gambling. Jacobs had only one priority, and that was keeping the heat off Hot Springs. Lucky Luciano didn't just have heat on him, he was white hot. If Owney wanted to ever find his way into Jacobs's good graces, he had to stop Luciano from becoming a problem for Hot Springs.

Luciano and Orlova stayed in town for two weeks. They spent their days at the racetrack or at the movies, and they spent their evenings dining and dancing at the Belvedere. Luciano stayed out late playing cards at the Southern Club or shooting dice at the Ohio Club. He bought Orlova expensive gifts. Some days they'd stay in bed all day. Luciano got to know everyone in town. He and Orlova dined with Jacobs, McLaughlin, and even Joe Wakelin, the chief of police. It got so they forgot about their troubles back in New York. Eventually even Owney relaxed.

Chief Wakelin and his chief of detectives, Dutch Akers, grew particularly friendly with Luciano. These weren't any ordinary cops. Wakelin, who was Judge Ledgerwood's brother-in-law, was also the head of security at the Belvedere. Dutch Akers had some side jobs, too—like stealing tourists' cars and offering them back to the owners for a reward, or selling confiscated handguns on the black market.

In 1933, two years before Luciano came to hide out in Hot Springs, another notorious gangster, Frank "Jelly" Nash, had chosen the Spa City to hide out from the FBI. Akers used to take payoff money from Nash to give him a heads-up if any cops came around asking about him. It didn't help. The FBI nabbed Nash in front of the White Front Club downtown, and Nash was eventually shot up by his own men when they tried to bust him out of custody in a gunfight with the FBI. Five officers died in that fiasco, and it prompted J. Edgar Hoover to put a target on the Hot Springs Police Department and have his agents look more closely at Wakelin and Akers. "Chicago in its Capone era," said Hoover, "didn't have a thing on Hot Springs."

Still, Akers and Wakelin did some real police work from time to time when things got a little slow. This was the case while Luciano was in Hot Springs on the lam and they received word that police in Yonkers, New York, were searching for a thief named Eli Gersewitz, who was believed to be hiding out in Hot Springs with his tiny Pomeranian dog. Akers saw a man check in to a boardinghouse with just such a dog and decided to bring him in for questioning. Sure enough, Gersewitz confessed. Wakelin put a call in to New York to let them know they could come pick up their prisoner.

On April 1, 1936, Orlova told Luciano she didn't feel like accompanying him to the races. So while Orlova had breakfast at the Arlington, Luciano went across the street to the Ohio Club to play a little craps. There he ran into Dutch Akers, and the two went for a stroll along Bathhouse Row. About halfway down the block they bumped into New York detective John Brennan, who was in town to pick up Gersewitz. Brennan was flabbergasted. Standing before him was the most wanted man in America, walking down a busy street with Hot Springs' chief of detectives.

"Lucky, do you realize that Thomas Dewey has an arrest warrant out for you?" Brennan asked Luciano.

"Why don't you keep out of it?" Luciano replied.

"Look, Lucky. If I act like I didn't see you, and it comes out later I seen you, it would mean my badge." Brennan suggested that it'd be a lot easier for both of them if Luciano just went back to New York with him.

Luciano said to hell with all that.

After considering his options, Brennan opted not to press the issue. He said his goodbyes to Luciano and Akers and headed back to his hotel to phone Dewey's office. He told Assistant Prosecutor Edward McLean he saw Luciano in the flesh, accompanied by the chief of detectives, no less. McLean told Brennan to go back and arrest Luciano right away. "I believe that in view of the friendliness of Luciano and the Hot Springs Police Department that you might consider getting the sheriff or a constable to accompany you," McLean added.

Back at the Arlington, a worried Luciano phoned Owney to let him know he had been spotted. Owney knew that McLaughlin and the Hot Springs leaders would help Luciano. "Don't worry about a thing," Owney assured him. Owney lined Luciano up with a lawyer and rang up the judges to let them know what was happening. If they pinch you, Owney said, "you'll be released this afternoon."

"What about extradition?" Luciano asked.

"You can fight it in Arkansas and you'll win."

Brennan took McLean's advice. He went to the sheriff's office and picked up Deputy Marion Anderson to go with him. The New York cop and the young deputy rolled over to the Arlington and Brennan put his cuffs on Luciano. When Luciano arrived at the courthouse, his lawyer was waiting for him with a writ of habeas corpus. He was taken before the judge, who set bond at five thousand dollars. W. S. Jacobs posted the money. Just like Owney said, Luciano was back on the street before supper.

When Brennan called Dewey to let him know that Lucky had already been released on bond, Dewey couldn't believe what he was hearing. He called up the governor of Arkansas, Marion Futrell, and explained to him that "the most dangerous and important racketeer in New York, if not the entire country," was in Hot Springs, Arkansas, and had just been released on a five-thousand-dollar bond. Futrell was a friend and fishing buddy of Judge Ledgerwood's, and Futrell had been supported by the Hot Springs gambling establishment in both of his campaigns for governor. In exchange, Futrell was happy to defer to the local officials whenever complaints came to him about gambling in Hot Springs. But this was different. This was a national story, and the eyes of the whole country were on him. To make matters worse, Governor Futrell's own attorney general, an ambitious young lawyer named Carl Bailey, sensed an opportunity to make a name for himself amid all the attention, and was fixing to do some good old-fashioned grandstanding.

Futrell called up Ledgerwood and told him they needed to get Luciano back in custody. Bailey had ordered the Arkansas State Rangers to head to Hot Springs to help local law enforcement. Marion Anderson and John Brennan headed back over to the Arlington and broke the bad news to Luciano. They arrested him for the second time that day. This time the judge set the bond at two hundred thousand dollars.

Luciano retained three of the top lawyers in Hot Springs, as well as one of his attorneys back in New York. Attorney General Carl Bailey, Lucky's lawyers, and Judge Ledgerwood went to battle over warrants, petitions, and extradition orders, fighting over whether Luciano would be tried in Hot Springs or in a federal court in Little Rock, where he'd be extradited to New York. Luciano stayed in jail, ordering a feast from Pappas Brothers, a local favorite, to feed all of the prisoners. That night he dined on pasta with all the cops, drunks, wife beaters, and cow stealers in Garland County.

At three o'clock in the morning a ruckus woke Luciano up. The county jail was surrounded by over a dozen Arkansas rangers and Little Rock cops. They demanded Luciano. The jailer bolted the doors and called Garland County Sheriff Roy Ermey to let him know the jail had been surrounded by the out-of-town police. Ermey sent several more sheriff's deputies as reinforcements. The two sides held a standoff at the jail all night long.

Jacobs didn't know how to end the standoff. Governor Futrell had been their ace in the hole. Without Futrell's support, it seemed the gamblers needed to fold their hand and give Luciano up. They phoned Owney late that night to let him know they were out of options and would to have to surrender his friend to the state police. But Owney wasn't ready to give up just yet. Perhaps if he could fix the mess himself, he would demonstrate to Jacobs just how valuable he could be as part of the local gambling combination, and he'd earn the gratitude of Luciano and the rest of the national crime syndicate in the process.

In the wee hours of the morning, Owney sent an emissary to offer Attorney General Bailey fifty thousand dollars to back off and leave Luciano in the custody of the Hot Springs police. That was ten times Bailey's yearly salary as attorney general. Bailey turned the offer down. Owney's Hail Mary pass had come up short.

At eight o'clock the next morning Luciano's lawyers finally relented and allowed state police to take him to Little Rock. When Luciano was brought into court, he was surrounded by a dozen deputies with submachine guns, and even more reporters and photographers were captivated by the spectacle of America's most wanted man being protected by police and judges. The headlines read "New York Vice Leader Wrested from 'Spa' Police," and "'Kidnaped' Cries Vice King as He Is Extradited." Carl Bailey, for one, got to grandstand to his heart's content. He told the gathered press that he had been offered a fifty-thousand-dollar bribe by a prominent Hot Springs resident to release Luciano.

"Every time a major criminal of this country wants an asylum, he heads for Hot Springs, Arkansas," Bailey told reporters. Bailey wasted no time in making his move against Futrell. He started building his case for why he should be the next governor of Arkansas right then and there. "Arkansas cannot be made an asylum for criminals."

LUCIANO HEADED BACK TO New York, where he faced life in prison. Carl Bailey formally entered the 1936 governor's race. Governor Futrell decided not to run for a third term. When Judge Ledgerwood tried to convince Futrell to change his mind, Futrell told him, "I've appointed too many of my relatives to state jobs and they haven't been earning their money." Futrell convinced Ledgerwood that the gamblers in Hot Springs would be best served by Ed McDonald, the secretary of state. Unlike Carl Bailey, Ed was the kind of man who wasn't above accepting an occasional gift. McLaughlin sent the police around to all the local gambling clubs to pick up donations for the upcoming elections.

When all the votes were counted, Mayor McLaughlin won reelection in yet another landslide, as did all of his chosen candidates, including Marion Anderson, the young sheriff's deputy, who at thirty-five was now the youngest county sheriff in the state of Arkansas. It helped that Anderson collected the ballot boxes, which he stuffed with more than thirteen hundred premarked ballots he carried with him in a large sack. But Anderson's ballot-box stuffing wasn't enough to put Ed McDonald over the top. Despite Hot Springs, the eleventh-largest city in Arkansas, putting up the second-highest vote total in the state, Carl Bailey still won the three-way race with a plurality, promising voters he'd do whatever it took to shut down crime and gambling in Hot Springs.

After more than a decade of smooth sailing, Jacobs was finding his worst fears coming true. Luciano and Owney had exposed Hot Springs to the entire country, and at the worst possible time. In 1936, Jacobs employed more than eleven hundred people in Hot Springs, with a yearly payroll of over a half million dollars. After the 1936 election, Jacobs made one additional hire. He paid a man to camp out at Crow's Station, on the highway connecting Hot Springs with Little Rock, to keep a constant lookout for any of Carl Bailey's Arkansas rangers headed into town to raid the casinos.

Hazel

JANUARY 29, 1937

One newspaper described Jacobs as the agents hauled away his equipment as sitting in a chair, holding a little dog, "almost in tears."

Hazel and Hollis were a year into their marriage and still living like newlyweds. They hadn't yet made a decision about children, choosing instead to enjoy the nightlife in Hot Springs as a young couple in love. Their friendship with the Pettys allowed them to graduate from teenage haunts like Fountain Lake, and before long they were regular faces in the bars and clubs downtown. They frequented places like the Blue Ribbon Club, the Pines Supper Club, and the Ohio Club. Their limited means, however, meant they could most often be found at the Kentucky Club.

The Kentucky Club wasn't the fanciest club in town, but it was one of the oldest, built around 1890. Even in the late 1930s it still retained some of that old-world feel. It still had the original ornate wooden saloon-style bar that took up nearly the entire length of the long, narrow room. Upstairs, however, the Kentucky Club was less charming. The second story held the casino, where long card games between Okies and Texans would stretch on for days without breaking up. The third floor served as a brothel, which was periodically shut down by Judge Ledgerwood—not so much out of objection to prostitution, but because competing brothels had paid off the police.

In late January 1937, Oaklawn was preparing to kick off its fourth season since reopening. The track owners were anticipating crowds of more than fifteen thousand to show up for the "Mayor Leo P. Mc-Laughlin Inaugural Handicap." The mayor had declared the day a city holiday, and visitors had already started showing up in the weeks before opening day, with hotels full and clubs like the Kentucky packed with patrons. One night at the end of January the crowd was particularly boisterous, which likely made it difficult to hear when someone shouted out:

It's a raid!

At the rear of the building on the second floor was an emergency exit that emptied out onto the side of West Mountain. Dozens of drinkers and gamblers carefully eased their way down the side of the mountain and back to Central Avenue, joining the crowd that had gathered outside the Kentucky Club to see what was going on. A large van was parked on the sidewalk, surrounded by a couple of squad cars. Men in moving company uniforms carried a roulette wheel out of the club and tossed it carelessly into the back of the van. Down the block the same thing was happening at the Ohio, the Blue Ribbon, even the newly opened Citizens Club. All of Hazel and Hollis's usual haunts were being turned upside down.

A car driving down Central Avenue slowed down to a crawl to gawk at all the craps tables and slot machines being hauled out of the clubs. It slowed so much, in fact, that the car behind it smashed into the rear bumper, causing a chain reaction. Soon the city's main thoroughfare was at a standstill in both directions, and the crowds on the sidewalks swelled to hundreds of people. The day had finally come. Owney's efforts to protect his friend Lucky Luciano had cost Hot Springs dearly. Carl Bailey's promise to clean up Hot Springs turned out to be more than just campaign rhetoric. It was the first raid in over a decade.

Across town at the Belvedere, the guard in the tower at the entrance gate got a phone call that the raiders were on the way. He flashed the lights on top of the clubhouse, then closed and locked the front gate and lit out. When the squad cars and moving vans arrived at the Belvedere, they had to bust the gates open to get inside. By the time they entered the club, there were only a handful of guests, as well as the club's manager, Otis McGraw, and the boss gambler himself, W. S. Jacobs.

Jacobs was surprised to see that none of the raiding party were wearing the uniforms of Arkansas rangers, but were instead dressed in business suits. These men were agents from the Arkansas Department of Revenue, the rangers having been dispatched to help with flood rescue efforts on the Ohio River. The revenue agents had a court order that allowed them to search, seize, and burn all gaming paraphernalia found on the premises. What they didn't have, however, were arrest warrants.

The revenue agents told the men from the moving company what equipment to take and load onto their trucks. They hauled out slot machines, craps tables, everything not bolted to the floor. Concerned, Jacobs went to pick up the phone.

"Sorry, Mr. Jacobs, I can't let you do that." The revenue agent stepped in his path.

"I'm calling my lawyer. You can't take this equipment. Do you know what this is worth?"

The agent did know what it was worth. That was the whole idea. Governor Bailey's aim was to destroy the equipment. Arresting the proprietors would stop gambling only temporarily, since they would make bail and be back in action the next day. Burning the roulette wheels, on the other hand, would at least keep the clubs closed until the gamblers could order new ones. At any rate, Jacobs was rattled. One newspaper described Jacobs as the agents hauled away his equipment as sitting in a chair, holding a little dog, "almost in tears."

As the officers departed after loading up everything they could fit in the van, one of them stopped and said to Jacobs, "You can use your own judgment about opening up tomorrow."

The following day the equipment seized in the raids was piled up high at the state fairgrounds in Little Rock. A crowd had gathered to watch what promised to be a huge bonfire of green felt and polished wood. But when it came time to strike a match, nobody wanted to do it. The Little Rock police had all stayed away. None of the members of Governor Bailey's House committee to investigate Hot Springs had shown up. Nobody who was there wanted to accept responsibility for burning W. S. Jacobs's property. Someone finally ran to the Capitol and fetched John Thompson, a lawyer for the committee. He was irritated to be called away from his work to do something so trivial. But he dutifully lit the match and let it drop. The tables went up in flames.

The raid cost the Hot Springs combination dearly. Much of the equipment seized and burned was new. Jacobs called McLaughlin and Ledgerwood to a meeting. It was their job, he explained, to figure out how to get the governor to back off. But what could they do? Owney had offered Bailey a fortune to lay off Luciano and it didn't work.

Owney, however, was precisely why Jacobs believed they were in this predicament to begin with. Jacobs was frustrated that they had bet on the wrong horse time and time again. Their support of Luciano was a mistake, and it had put them in the position of having to support Ed McDonald against Carl Bailey, another mistake. Now all of their futures hung in the balance. McLaughlin and Ledgerwood were supposed to be the political fixers. Looking to Owney for a solution was like trying to put out a fire with gasoline. McLaughlin and Ledgerwood needed to fix the problem themselves.

The mayor and the judge did as they were told and traveled to Little Rock to speak with the new governor. McLaughlin explained how the fines the city government levied on the casinos made it possible to keep taxes low and added tens of thousands of dollars every month to the public coffers. Ledgerwood pleaded with Bailey that gambling was essential to the city's core economy, which was tourism. Everyone, not just the casino owners, depended on the gambling business. Without tourists, there were no restaurants, no shops, and even the churches would feel the pinch. Gambling was the lifeblood of the town. Without it, many thousands of registered voters would likely move away.

"Our friends in the gambling industry are willing to provide campaign support for a candidate who is friendly to Hot Springs," Ledgerwood told the governor.

"And we can guarantee delivering the vote in Garland County in your next election. You wouldn't want to throw that away," McLaughlin added. All they were asking was for Bailey to maintain the same deal they had with Governor Futrell. Bailey could say all he wanted about how gambling was terrible and illegal and how much he abhorred it, so long as he also said it was a matter to be dealt with by the local police and courts. And for that one simple sentence, he would be rewarded with an anonymous envelope full of cash and the full-throated support of the Garland County Democratic Committee and their many thousands of poll tax receipts on Election Day.

Bailey considered this. He had won a tight race against two other opponents. It was unclear if he could win another term with an outright majority. His political future was still uncertain. He surely worried about being a one-term governor. There were rumors he might run for Senate one day.

Two days later the trucks rolled into town from Chicago and unloaded brand-new dice tables in front of the clubs. Another truck, filled with slot machines, arrived from Louisiana. Hot Springs was back in business. In the days after the raids, a number of local ministers and anti-gambling citizens had been tasked by the governor and the House committee investigators to keep an eye out for any sign the clubs might try to open back up. They immediately contacted Bailey to let him know what was happening.

"You should appeal to your local courts," the governor told them. The ministers knew right away what that meant. Governor Carl Bailey, the great reformer, was now on the take.

It all happened so fast that Hazel and Hollis hardly knew it had happened at all. One night the Kentucky Club was closed, the next night it was back open for business. The word reached the locals at the American Legion, where many of them had taken up residence on barstools while the gambling clubs were closed. Like everyone else, Hazel and Hollis made their way back to the Kentucky to see for themselves. Owney, too, came wandering back downtown to take his usual seat at the Southern Club coffee shop. All up and down Central Avenue, as the club owners opened the shutters to let in the early light, the sound of the bookmakers calling out the morning line odds once again echoed through the streets, and saints and sinners alike understood that the house had won yet again.

Dane

"If either of you can eagle this next hole, I'll send the entire high school golf team to the U.S. Open."

Two years passed without another raid. As the casinos came back to life in Hot Springs, the Black Cat liquor store stayed open late to re-supply the local bars with alcohol. The little liquor store wasn't much, but it was worth a whole lot more than it appeared on its face. Five years after the repeal of Prohibition, Arkansas still didn't allow businesses to serve liquor by the glass. Anyone who wanted a drink stiffer than beer or wine had to go to a "package store" like the Black Cat to buy a bottle. Hot Springs, however, didn't play by the same rules as everyone else. When McLaughlin and Ledgerwood convinced Governor Bailey to look the other way on gambling two years before, they were opening the door to much more than just casinos. The clubs served their patrons liquor by the glass, and most of them bought that contra-band liquor from one of the only places in town that would break the law and sell it to them wholesale, the Black Cat.

The Black Cat was owned by a short, muscular man with dark ruddy skin and bright white hair named Sam Orick Harris. Harris was forty-six years old and a father of two. He was half American Indian, the son of a white man and a Choctaw woman, and had been born on the reservation. When Sam was still very young, he and his sister ran away and were eventually found and adopted by a white couple named Harris, who raised them in Oklahoma. Sam grew up to become a bootlegger, and a bold one at that. He once took an order for a case of booze from a group of prisoners, then broke into the jail to deliver it to them. He operated a notorious still in Hughes County, Oklahoma, that was well known to the thirsty and the police alike, and he was arrested three times for charges that ranged from transporting liquor to conspiracy.

Sam Harris teamed up with Harry Hastings, one of the biggest liquor distributors in Arkansas, to move Hastings's inventory across the border into Oklahoma, where Sam distributed it in the Choctaw Nation. Because Sam had been born in Oklahoma on the Choctaw reservation, he had useful contacts in Indian country. Hastings and Harris's relationship worked well for a while, and soon Hastings wanted to expand the operation. Hastings had a contact in Canada who could supply him with liquor at cheap prices. The quantities were too large and the logistics too difficult for Hastings to easily move across the border, however, so Hastings asked Harris for help. Harris refused, choosing instead to stay close to home and keep his operation simple and small. But before long his eye wandered, and Harris lit out for California to follow another woman, leaving his wife, Hattie, all alone with their two children, Hubert Dane and Wilma Lorraine.

Hattie was despondent. She wanted to follow Sam out to California to bring him back home. Dane wouldn't let her. "Let him go," the young Dane told his mother. "I can take care of you." Dane was thirteen years old, much too young to care for his mother and older sister. Hattie didn't like so much pressure being put on her son. When he was little and the family lived on a farm in Saline County, Dane had come down with rheumatic fever, which left him so weak he couldn't leave his bed. Hattie and Sam had already lost a child, their first son, Jesse, months before Dane was born in 1918. It was nothing short of a miracle that Hattie had seen Dane recover from his illness. And now the boy was forced to help support his family at such a young age—it just wasn't right. But Dane did all he could to be the man of the house. He mowed lawns and looked for any odd jobs he could find. Through it all he developed a close bond with his mother, one that would endure for the rest of their lives.

Dane was a studious young man, and in high school he joined the debate team and found he had a flair for crafting persuasive arguments. He was the star of the team by the time he graduated in 1935. Dane continued his studies in Fayetteville, at the University of Arkansas. He excelled there, too, and dreamed of enrolling in law school, putting his argumentative skills to practical use. He was popular on campus. Though he didn't come from a family with money, he was able to keep company with those who did. He had a rarefied accent—no country twang in his voice, no long syrupy vowels. People told him he sounded like a Yankee. They usually meant it as a compliment, and he took it as one. College was his opportunity to outgrow his country boy roots, but in 1939, as Dane looked forward to his final year of university, Sam Orick Harris returned to Hot Springs and changed the course of Dane's life.

Sam Harris was an ornery man with a hot temper. Once, when Dane's older sister was three years old, Sam punished the child for misbehaving by locking her outside the house for an entire night. The family feared Sam, which is why when Sam ordered Dane to leave the University of Arkansas and come work for him at the Black Cat, Dane put up no resistance. He put his dreams of becoming a lawyer on hold, hopefully temporarily, perhaps forever.

Dane learned the liquor business pretty quickly, managing price controls and inventory. He found he actually liked the work, and discovered he had a knack for numbers. He decided to take an accounting course he saw in an advertisement, hoping to parlay his job at the Black Cat into a career in accounting. Accounting wasn't bad money, and it was honest work.

———

ONE DAY IN THE spring of 1939 Dane met up with his friend Walter Ebel at the golf course. Ebel was still in high school, but he and Dane had become fast friends out on the fairway. They called Ebel "Bookie" because everyone thought he loved to gamble, but Bookie would never refer to himself as a gambler. He'd say he liked to bet only when he had the best of it, when the odds were in his favor. Like Dane, Bookie was a wiz with numbers, particularly when it came to figuring out probability and odds. Bookie's dad, Walter Sr., was a newspaperman. He wrote columns for the local paper, but he also wrote the horse racing morning line, a skill he passed on to his son.

Dane and Bookie were preparing to head out on the course when they were approached by a skinny little man in a white linen cap. "Would you boys be willing to let me join you today?" Though they had never met the man, they knew from his accent who he was. There was only one English accent in this town, and it belonged to Owney Madden. The two young men couldn't have known everything about Owney's presence in their town, but like most folks in Hot Springs they knew he was an important person. Movie stars came to Hot Springs just to visit him. The heavyweight champion of the world had been seen staying at his house. But Dane and Bookie also knew Madden was a big-city mob boss. People said his nickname was "the Killer." The two boys agreed to join him, perhaps with some trepidation, perhaps with some excitement.

Owney had taken an interest in these two boys, particularly Dane, who despite his young age ran the liquor store for his father with aplomb. Dane was responsible and smart. But the question remained—could he golf? Owney offered Dane and Bookie a wager, and the cocky young men agreed. As they traversed the country club golf course, the two teenagers made short work of the big shot gangster. Owney couldn't have seen it coming. Dane had a fluid swing and could send the ball soaring farther than men twice as strong. And Bookie was an ace on the green. When they got to the eighteenth hole, Owney offered one last proposition.

"I tell you what. If either of you can eagle this next hole, I'll send the entire high school golf team to the U.S. Open in Philadelphia." The boys just laughed. The offer wasn't nearly as ridiculous, though, as the fact that Bookie eagled the eighteenth hole.

IT SURELY PUZZLED DANE how so many others could make enough money to have what they needed, to do what they wanted, and not have to risk going to prison for it. Each day as Dane passed by the Belvedere Club, its rolling manicured hills, its lush green pastures, he'd wonder what separated him from the men who owned it. He vowed that one day he'd own a place like Belvedere. He would make his own fortune, but he would do it on the square.

Little did Dane know that the Belvedere, for all its pastoral beauty and bourgeois trimmings, had long hidden a massive distillery supplying bootleg alcohol to the Capone mob in Chicago. Little did he know that everything he saw and coveted in Hot Springs was bought and paid for through the same business that had landed his father in jail and made Owney Madden rich and powerful. Little did he know that there was no square way to make your fortune in Hot Springs.

Later that year, Owney kept his promise to send the boys to the U.S. Open, all expenses paid. Dane wasn't with them. He was down at the Southern Club, as on most mornings that summer, waiting to see what Owney might need him to do that day.

Hazel

JUNE 1939

**"He drinks it out the back of the commode, Mama.
Right out of the commode."**

Hazel's parents had split up, and it wasn't the first time. Even when they were together, Clyde stayed on the road most of the year. When he wasn't away, he and Hazel's mother, Edna, fought like cats and dogs. Hazel had no idea what a happy married life looked like, so it was easy to convince herself that what she had going in Hot Springs with Hollis was as good as it got. Not that it was bad. It just wasn't much of anything, really. They had settled into the monotony of a responsible adult existence. Hollis was up each morning at three o'clock to load the dairy truck. He spent the rest of the morning hours making deliveries around town. It was tough, working those hours, back when he and Hazel spent so many nights out drinking with the Pettys. But they had slowed down, stopped seeing the Pettys as often, and Hollis still struggled with the early shift. Hollis needed to work more hours. He'd come back from his delivery route and spend a few hours in the production plant with his father working on machines or on the assembly line putting together pints of ice cream. Some days he didn't make it home until after supper. And he rarely ate even when he made it home on time. He just hit the bed face-first. Didn't wash up or change, just rushed off to sleep to be ready for the three o'clock alarm.

The way Hazel saw it, Hollis had a good job. He just happened to have bad hours. This was a time when a lot of men were out of work, or working on farms or railroad crews or other jobs that would take them out of town for weeks or months at a time. Having a good job was something to be thankful for, early shift or not. Sure, occasionally Hollis would finish work early and sneak off to the racetrack to bet a couple dollars before he came home and went to bed, but Hazel didn't mind, really. He worked hard—he deserved to relax.

Still, she couldn't deny the feeling of loneliness that settled over her and that apartment like a layer of dust. Even though she could sometimes brush it all away—with a night out with the Pettys, or an afternoon shopping with Ressie, or even a day at that wild Pentecostal church—it would settle right back down over everything just as quickly. What she needed, Hollis's folks told her, was a child.

So Hollis and Hazel set out to have a child. Hollis seemed excited about the prospect. It was the first spark Hazel had seen in him in some time, especially when they discussed where the baby would sleep and how they'd name him Hollis Jr. and how the three of them could get their picture taken by one of the photographers downtown. *Wouldn't that look nice on the wall there?*

The prospect of a child was surely on Hollis's mind each morning when he woke up at three o'clock and shuffled out of the apartment to his truck. As he drove to Cook's Ice Cream each morning, he likely wondered what he'd need to do to be ready for a child, how his life might change, for better and for worse. As he took the bottle of Old Taylor from beneath the seat of the ice cream truck and broke the seal each morning, he may have worried whether he could be a good father to a little girl or boy.

DRINKING SNUCK UP ON Hollis. What started off with sips of a friend's prescription whiskey had turned into a real habit, into bottles of Old Taylor stashed under the seat of his truck or out behind his apartment building. Hazel didn't have a clue, and why would she? Hollis was spending as much time figuring out how to hide the bottles from her and his boss and his family as he was doing anything else. The hiding and the sneaking had become a second job for him, weighing on him as heavily as his work, his wife, his worry.

Hollis often dreamed about his son. He hoped it'd be a son, anyway. A fat baby boy with big hanging cheeks like the jowls of a hog and chubby, stout legs that would grow powerful and strong. He woke from one of those dreams with a start—he was behind the wheel of the Cook's truck flying down the highway. The shock of it straightened him right up. How long had he been out?

The adrenaline from the scare eventually wore off and his eyelids grew heavy again. He decided to knock off early. He needed to rest. Perhaps he could tell his boss, Dale Cook, he was feeling sick. He pulled the truck in to the Eastman Hotel and went inside to see Dr. Petty at the drugstore. Hollis came out with a paper sack, a bottle of medicine tucked away inside, hidden from view.

When Hollis returned to Cook's Ice Cream, Dale was surprised to see him back so early. Hollis told him he couldn't finish the route. He wasn't feeling so great. He thought he needed to go home and lie down. Dale said he thought that sounded like a good idea. Dale was a good man. He said he'd finish up Hollis's route, and if Hollis needed another day to go ahead and take the next one, too. Hollis thanked him and walked back home, his bottle of medicinal whiskey in his back pocket. By the time he got back to his apartment he'd drunk the whole thing. He walked right past Hazel to the bedroom and collapsed onto the bed. Hazel didn't rise from her seat. She bit at her nails.

———

IN JUNE 1939 HAZEL gave birth to a baby boy. They named him Hollis Jr. Richard and Bessie Mae could sense that things weren't right with Hollis and convinced the young couple to move out of the apartment and back in with them. Hazel was of two minds about the whole thing. On the one hand, she was twenty years old and now a mother, and didn't like the idea of being looked after by Hollis's parents. On the other hand, she could use some extra help, and Hollis didn't appear to be fit for much. Hazel still knew little about his drinking, but she did begin to worry about his moods, his listlessness. Being around some family might be good for everyone.

Bessie Mae and Hollis's sisters, Ressie, Josie, and Almagene, were a big help with Hollis Jr., calming the baby or simply giving Hazel a break from time to time. And Bessie Mae and the girls were over the moon to have the little baby in their home. Even Hollis Jr.'s crying and caterwauling were welcome, the ladies competing to see who could soothe the child best.

Hollis's older brother, Edward, and his father, Richard, were also helpful in their own way, but not with the baby. They were more helpful with Hollis Sr. Hazel may have been in the dark about Hollis's condition, either through denial or naïveté, but even though Hollis went to great pains to hide his drinking, it was undeniable to his family what was going on.

Richard took a firm tack with Hollis, kept him close at home and at work. Whenever they found a bottle hidden somewhere, and they often did, they would pour it down the drain. Once Almagene found a bottle in the tank above the toilet. "Can you believe this?" she asked Bessie Mae. "He drinks it out the back of the commode, Mama. Right out of the commode."

Part II

FIRE

1940-1949

Dane

Stover acted like there was nothing to it. After all, he had learned to fly in a three-hour lesson from a doctor over in Stuttgart.

When he wasn't running errands for Owney Madden, Dane tried to enjoy life in the spa. He would play golf or gin rummy, or hang around Cook's Ice Cream or the pool hall after school let out. On the weekends he would go to the parties out at Fountain Lake, big soirees with swimming and dancing. He was a mature and serious young man, but he was in no hurry to escape this part of being young. And a social life in Hot Springs helped keep him from resenting what he might have been missing in Fayetteville at the university. Above all, parties on the lake were an opportunity to see Marcella Sellers.

Marcella was seventeen when she and Dane first met at Fountain Lake. She was a handsome brunette, hair in curly locks, with soft skin and full lips. She had a gap in her teeth that some men found alluring but that made her feel insecure. Whatever her feelings about her appearance, Marcella was a confident and mature young woman. She could more than keep up a conversation with Dane. She was as outgoing as he was introspective. They complemented each other in that way.

Marcella's family had moved to Hot Springs from the tiny rural town of Glenwood a year before. Her people were country folks just like Dane's, but she didn't carry herself like a small-town girl. Just like Dane, Marcella had swallowed her Arkansas accent and tried to speak more formally. Even before her family moved, she'd sneak away from home to go to Hot Springs and listen to jazz music on the black side of town. She loved music, played the piano by ear, and was never happier than when she was twirling on the dance floor. Dane had never met anyone like her. They would swim and dance together at Fountain Lake on the weekends. The affair caught hold of both of them tight. The summer after she turned eighteen, they married in secret. It was six months before either of them told their folks.

THOUGH THE OUTBREAK OF war did little to put a damper on the good times, big changes had come to Hot Springs the year before. One of W. S. Jacobs's duties as boss gambler was to shuttle envelopes of money around to his various employees, partners, and people on the take, and this meant taking envelopes to Little Rock to make sure the various politicians got theirs as well. One day while Jacobs was driving back from Little Rock, his car careened off the highway and crashed. He survived for a few months, but on Christmas Day of 1940 he passed away peacefully at home. His funeral was held two days later. Every police officer in Hot Springs was assigned to work traffic to accommodate the three-hundred-car funeral procession through town. Every casino closed down for the day.

As soon as Jacobs was put in the ground, things began to unravel in Hot Springs. Mayor McLaughlin took over Jacobs's estate, which included a majority share in six of the eight largest gambling clubs in Hot Springs. It fell to McLaughlin to divide up those interests and decide who would get what. Rather than appoint a replacement boss gambler, McLaughlin added new faces into the mix, and tried to use his new-found power to curry favor with people by cutting them in on the action. He put together a partnership of six men to manage Jacobs's former interests in the Southern Club and Belvedere. It lasted nine months before petty jealousies and disagreements forced the partnership to dissolve.

Despite the chaos in the gambling business, the Black Cat's receipts were growing. This was helped by renting out the top floor to bookmakers, but the Harris family was also aided by their relationship with Harry Hastings. Hastings had become one of the most wealthy and powerful men in the state of Arkansas in the years after repeal. He had his fingers in much more than just the liquor business. He was involved in the trafficking of all kinds of contraband through Arkansas and the Mid-South. He was said to fence stolen goods, to help out drug smugglers. They called him "the crime czar of Arkansas." He had bragged that he had personally killed six or eight men. More important, he had friends in high places. Hastings spread his wealth around among the political establishment and was known to hunt and fish with a governor or senator or two. It was this connection that kept the Black Cat as the main supplier for restaurants and bars choosing to serve illegal hard liquor.

Just as Owney Madden had taken a shine to Dane Harris, so too did Harry Hastings. Hastings still utilized Sam Harris's contacts across the border in Oklahoma, which remained a dry state even into the 1940s. Hastings wanted to sell more liquor to the poor, thirsty Okies, but the risk of crossing the state line was a great one. The risk, however, was what made it such a great opportunity. It was why they could charge a premium for their product. All Harry Hastings needed was someone he could trust to do the smuggling. He asked Sam Harris if his son was up for the job. Sam was all too willing to put Dane into service.

The first few times Dane drove the whiskey to Oklahoma, he just had enough to fill his trunk. The idea was to get his feet wet. He'd fill up his car at Moon Distributors in Fort Smith on the Arkansas side of the border, then drive across the bridge and deliver the bottles to a little store on Cherokee Nation land that was run by a man named George

Gunter. George was part Cherokee and an elected county commissioner in Sequoyah County, so he was a good contact to have on the Oklahoma side of the border. So much so that when Dane got pulled over by a county constable as he crossed the Arkansas River with a trunkful of whiskey and was thrown in jail, George Gunter was likely helpful in making sure he got out and the paperwork got lost. After all, it was just a few bottles of booze. Harmless, really.

At that time, liquor wasn't only prohibited in Oklahoma by state law—it was also illegal to sell or possess on tribal land, by an act of the U.S. Congress. Native Americans all across the country weren't even legally allowed to purchase liquor when they were off the reservations. Despite these prohibitions, however, alcohol consumption on tribal lands remained high. The law against Native Americans buying alcohol became a much-debated topic during World War II, when tens of thousands of Native American enlisted soldiers were denied the right to even drink beer on military bases along with their fellow servicemen. With the help of the American Legion, Native Americans were able to get the law repealed in 1953 and open the door for the sale and possession of liquor on reservations.

George Gunter had a son a few years older than Dane named Jack. Jack Gunter was a tall young man, sturdy and strong, with jet-black hair and a handsome face. He and Dane started working together, and Dane would regale him with stories about Hot Springs. Dane invited Jack Gunter to come visit, and he did often. The two young men were fast friends, and Gunter became a part of Dane's circle. Gunter was a fearsome combination of smart and tough, a good guy to have on your side in a less-than-legal business.

Driving whiskey into Oklahoma one trunkful at a time was never the idea. To step things up, Dane went to talk to John Stover, who ran the airfield in Hot Springs. In his time, John was a barnstormer, putting on air shows for farm folks all over the state. He was a daredevil in the sky and a crack mechanic on the ground, and he could build an airplane from the wheels up. He now ran the only air service in Hot Springs. If someone was sick and needed to get to the hospital in Little Rock in a hurry, John Stover would fly them. If someone passed away while in Hot Springs but their loved ones were all still back in Texas, John Stover could get the body home. If someone wanted to make a weekend getaway to the horse races and dice tables but be back in Memphis for work Monday morning, John Stover could pick them up and drop them off. And if someone was being closely watched by the FBI, or maybe wasn't allowed to leave their state without checking in with a parole officer, but needed to get to Hot Springs for a meeting with Owney Madden, well, John Stover could help them out, too.

Stover thought Dane would have an easier time just flying everything back and forth himself. The only trouble was that Dane didn't know how to fly an airplane. Stover acted like there was nothing to it. After all, he had learned to fly in a three-hour lesson from a doctor over in Stuttgart. He could teach Dane everything he needed to know. Soon Dane was carrying Harry Hastings's whiskey from Fort Smith over to Oklahoma through the air. Though the state remained dry, the servicemen from around the country stationed there on military bases were not all accustomed to life without drink. Dane and Harry Hastings would satisfy them by loading a small plane at Moon Distributors in Arkansas with bottles of Heaven Hill, Quality House, and Evan Williams, then landing it at a small airfield nearby on the Oklahoma side of the border. There the crates of booze would be loaded right onto U.S. military vehicles, and the GIs would drive it around to the other bases and distribute it to the troops. With American resolve to support the boys in uniform at such a fever pitch, no Oklahoma state trooper dared pull them over.

Owney

JUNE 1942

"One of our partners is giving dope on you. They want to get rid of you. I am telling you as a friend."

The ballroom was packed with dancers, black and white alike, with a line to get in that stretched halfway down Malvern Avenue. It was strange to see so many white people on Malvern Avenue, which was known around the country as "Black Broadway." Hot Springs was considered a premier location for large gatherings and conventions of black Americans, from the national Baptist and African Methodist Episcopal conventions to meetings between black underworld leaders from Chicago and New York. Scores of black tourists regularly visited Hot Springs, including celebrities and members of Congress. They came to watch baseball spring training, to take baths at the Pythian Bathhouse, to gamble in clubs like the Cameo, or to watch performers like Cab Calloway and Ella Fitzgerald. But this performance was something special. This was the Duke Ellington Orchestra, in town for one night only. And since Ellington had a policy against playing shows to white-only audiences, even in the segregated South, he chose to play a ballroom on Malvern Avenue.

It was Ellington's former boss Owney Madden who had arranged for the orchestra to fly to Arkansas and play. Owney had made Ellington's orchestra the house band at the Cotton Club, and the club's weekly national radio broadcast had built Ellington's renown. But like Owney, Ellington had moved on. His orchestra was in high demand, and getting them for one night in Hot Springs was no small feat.

The war had taken a lot of young men away from Hot Springs, but many more wounded men arrived to take their place. The federal government's Army and Navy Hospital, the only one of its kind in the United States, stood above Bathhouse Row on Central Avenue. Before World War II, the hospital mostly treated aging veterans with arthritis. But the latest conflict sent a steady stream of injured and shell-shocked veterans to Hot Springs, and the hospital upgraded its facilities to meet the needs of the wounded, including a rare X-ray ward and a state-of-the-art refrigerated morgue, at a cost of two and a half million dollars. The hospital was one of the finest medical facilities in the country, but it was soon pushed to its limits. The number of patients jumped from four hundred a month to more than fifteen hundred during the course of the war, and the government purchased the nearby Eastman Hotel for more than five hundred thousand dollars and converted it to a wing of the hospital. Once that filled up, the government started renting rooms for servicemen in the Arlington Hotel.

Eventually, the military decided to use the hospital and Hot Springs as the redistribution center for all soldiers returning to the west-central states. For two weeks, every returning soldier stayed in Hot Springs to have their medical records updated and receive any needed treatment. About twenty-five hundred troops rotated through the program every month. Among the thousands of patients treated at the Army and Navy Hospital were boldfaced names like Al Jolson, Joe DiMaggio, and General John Pershing. As a result, the war years turned out to be a boom time for Hot Springs, particularly for the gambling halls and brothels a stone's throw from the hospital at the top of the hill.

THE WAR AND A run for the Senate had distracted the governor enough that the casinos were able to get back to business in time to take advantage of the influx of veterans. Mayor McLaughlin knew he couldn't keep trying to run things on his own, but he wasn't eager to relinquish the new power he had gained after the death of W. S. Jacobs in 1940. Though he couldn't be both mayor and boss gambler, he could install someone who was more agreeable to him than Jacobs had been.

McLaughlin gave part of Jacobs's share of the Southern Club to his former driver and Southern Club doorman, Jack McJunkins. He also gave him shares in most of the other casinos in town. McLaughlin put the word out that McJunkins would be the new boss gambler. It was surprising, since most folks thought McJunkins wasn't the brightest bulb on the bush. Dutch Akers, the former chief of detectives, who had been arrested in 1938 for helping hide FBI public enemy number one Alvin "Creepy" Karpis, suggested to the FBI that they should try to turn McJunkins into an informant because he was a "rather dumb individual."

The selection of McJunkins sent a message that the paradigm had shifted in the gambling combination. The boss gambler was no longer the boss of the town. From now on the buck would stop with the mayor. Jack McJunkins started wearing a top hat and tails around town to signify his new status. But everyone knew that McLaughlin was pulling all the strings.

THE END OF W. S. Jacobs's reign had initially been a good thing for Owney Madden, too. The mayor still liked Owney, and he wasn't opposed to his owning a little piece of the action. When Owney approached McLaughlin and offered to spread some of his millions around town, McLaughlin welcomed his generosity. The Southern Club was in need of renovations, and McLaughlin arranged for Owney to buy a 25 percent stake so that the place could be fixed up.

Owney also purchased the Kentucky Club, which had fallen on

hard times, and turned it over to a local disabled man named Jimmy Jones who was well-connected but had no means of income. Owney assigned Don Zaio, a gangster from Chicago who worked for Owney as a bodyguard, to lend Jones a hand in getting the Kentucky back up and running again.

Instead of restoring the Kentucky Club to its former stature, however, Zaio and Jones leaned heavier on the prostitution business. The move ruffled some feathers. There was always going to be prostitution in Hot Springs, since tourists expected it, but the combination endeavored to keep it quiet and, most important, maintain a certain level of respectability. The leaders of Hot Springs preferred that their brothels be housed in mansions, run by madams draped in pearls, with young women dressed in satin and lace. The Kentucky Club had none of that. Just rows of small rooms, big enough only for a bed, many without any doors. The women worked fast and cheap. The whole operation attracted an undesirable clientele, bolstered by the influx of wounded and infirm veterans now populating the town.

The police turned the Kentucky Club over one night in a prostitution raid and discovered that in addition to women, Zaio and Jones were running pills out of the club. The revelation didn't sit well with the combination. Selling drugs and running a low-rent brothel not only made the rest of the city look bad, it opened the door to even more serious crimes. Assaults, maybe even murders. Embarrassed, Owney sold the club.

When word got out that Owney had gotten into the casino business, the FBI took notice. J. Edgar Hoover had been frustrated that his agents couldn't prove Owney's involvement in any of the local rackets. Now that Owney was purchasing shares of illegal casinos in Hot Springs, however, Hoover ordered his agents to act. A couple of FBI agents dropped in on city hall one day in 1941 and asked if Owney had filed any paperwork registering as a resident alien. He hadn't. When Owney heard that the FBI was asking questions about his citizenship, he got nervous. Perhaps they were thinking of deporting him back to England.

His marriage to Agnes wouldn't help him if it turned out he had never been in the United States legally to begin with. He acted swiftly.

Owney took some of the money out of his floor safe and started making payoffs around the state. Judges, lawyers, even a senator all got envelopes of cash. In all he spent nearly a quarter of a million dollars preparing for his immigration and naturalization hearing. It may have been the money. It may have been the witnesses who all testified to what a generous, philanthropic individual Owney Madden was, what a pillar of the community he had become. Whatever it was, the judge signed Owney's papers and made him an American citizen. Soon after the news broke, a note appeared under Owney's front door.

Friend Owen—The preachers had a meeting and they are going to prove you lied when you got your papers before Judge Miller. They know you are a partner in the Southern gaming house. One of our partners is giving dope on you. They want to get rid of you. I am telling you as a friend.

Hazel

They found Hollis next to the mass of straw, blacked out and stark naked, two empty bottles of rye whiskey nearby.

The plains of Texas in July are hot. Here's how hot: there were young boys whose job it was to fetch water from the well and bring it to the threshing crew as they ambled alongside the horse-drawn carts in the fields. The well was maybe a few hundred yards away at the farthest point. By the time the boys would get the cool well water to a cart, it would be as warm as a cup of coffee. They'd wrap the buckets in burlap to try to keep it cool, but it didn't matter. It was just that hot. It could make a man wish for death.

Hollis would just as soon go thirsty as drink that hot water sometimes. He'd hold out until evening, when the sun went down a little, and then the water would be a little cooler. By that point he'd be begging for a drink.

Hollis had been on the threshing crew for a few weeks. He started in June back in Northwest Arkansas and rode along with them as they moved their way across Oklahoma and into the Texas Panhandle. Because the war was on, the crew he was working with was made up mostly of Mexicans, young boys, and even a few women. Hollis was the exception—an able-bodied white man spared from the war because the doctors told him he had a weak heart.

Hollis had learned a few things in that short period of time. You needed to keep the grain end in the middle when you bailed the bundles on the cart, unless you wanted to unload the whole thing by hand and restack it when you got to the thresher. You could plug up a thresher if you unloaded the bundles too fast—which is why the combine operator offered twenty dollars to anyone who could manage to plug up the machine, figuring their effort to jam it would get them working faster.

WHEN THE DEPRESSION was on, Hazel had thought so highly of her husband. He worked hard with his father at the dairy, making the buttermilk and the ice cream during the day and driving the truck in the hours before dawn. He helped out around the house, caring for the animals and looking after his folks and brothers and sisters. He doted on and took good care of her, his youthful bride. He seemed excited about becoming a father.

But drink took away the Hollis that Hazel had fallen in love with. Little by little at first, and then all of a sudden in a great, gushing flow, everything about Hollis that was worth a damn just disappeared. One time his brother-in-law found him drunk at the racetrack after work and had to carry him home. He was surprised that Hazel wasn't surprised. "Just put him on the bed," she told him.

Things really went sideways for Hazel and Hollis the morning the cook down at Martin's lunch counter smelled whiskey on Hollis as he unloaded ice cream from the truck. The cook told Dale Cook about it. Dale wasn't surprised. Two days later Hollis came strolling out of the Citizens Club downtown after making a delivery and Dale was sitting in the truck waiting for him. Hollis looked in Dale's lap and saw the nearly empty bottle lying there.

"Hollis, you're the best route man we've ever had," Dale said. "And everybody likes you."

"I know I'm fired," Hollis said. He knew it the second he saw the bottle in Dale's lap.

"Now slow down. I didn't say all that. I want you to promise me you'll sober up. You go on home and get yourself sobered up. If you can go six months without taking a drink, you can come on back here and work. You think you can do that?"

"Hell, I can try."

The two men shook on it. Hollis made it nearly two weeks.

Hollis getting let go from Cook's really tore it for Hazel. By that point they had moved out of the Hill family home, and they had two children to care for. Their second child, Harold Lawrence, was only a few months old. Hazel had no job. They were on their own, with rent and bills to pay, and no money saved up. They needed that paycheck from Cook's. It was a good job, and it was difficult enough for a man who wasn't drunk all the time to find work. When Hazel and Hollis spoke at all, they usually argued. Hollis would disappear frequently. After a while he found himself waking up outside in strange places. He'd find welts and bruises on Hazel and question her about them. It shocked him when she'd tell him they were his doing. Everyone in his life was embarrassed by him or afraid of him or both. His father tried to intervene. He offered to give Hollis a few head of cattle and a place to live on the farm while he dried out. It didn't work. Every time Hollis had a dollar in his pocket he was off in search of a drink.

Hazel was lost. She busied herself with her children as best she could, and in doing so she tried to hide Hollis's demons from the world. "Those boys look like they're clean out of a band box," folks would tell her when she'd bring them to town to run errands or to church with Richard and Bessie Mae. She'd press their clothes until you could prick yourself on the sharp corners. She dug under Hollis Jr.'s fingernails with a toothpick.

FIELDWORK WAS RESSIE'S IDEA. She'd read in the papers that there was a shortage of hands on the farms across America because of the war, and that women and children were following the wheat harvest. The government was giving farmers money to pay for more laborers. Ten dollars a day plus room and board. Hollis could make more working in a factory making airplane parts for the war, but Ressie told Hazel that a normal job wouldn't cut it. Harvesting wheat, he'd have no opportunity to wander off and get a drink. This was the answer to what ailed him, Ressie figured: outdoors in the fields, far from any tavern, with fresh air and sunshine to help him dry out.

Hazel didn't give Hollis a chance to say no. He stumbled into the house one day and there were Ressie and Hazel and Bessie Mae waiting for him like three hens ready to peck. His suitcase was already packed. His sister even paid for the bus ticket.

In the beginning Hollis started on the crew gathering up the wheat and tying it up in bundles. It was backbreaking work. But those were the poorest farms, the ones that had no money for a combine that could do the worst of the work. When his crew moved on to farms with combines, he usually carried a pitchfork and pitched the bundles on the cart. The others on the crew must have been awfully suspicious of what Hollis's story might be. If a young white man, strong enough to pitch hay in a field all day long in excruciating heat, wasn't off fighting in the war, what was his excuse? Hollis must have had a story, and it couldn't be a good one.

Hollis's first month on the wheat harvest was his first month without a drink. The work was a distraction. His thirst now was for cold water, nothing more. There wasn't a bottle of liquor in sight, and he didn't have any money in his pocket to buy one even if there was. At the end of each month when they got their pay, Hollis would send it home to Hazel. He had no need for it out on the road. The men and boys on the crew bunked in barns on straw mattresses. The families on the farms, grateful for the free labor, would cook them fried chicken, roast beef, biscuits with hand-churned butter, peas and carrots. Sometimes they'd even get pie. They needed every bite. That one meal a day had to fuel them for ten or more hours.

They ended the summer in Kansas. After the last of the bundles went on to the thresher, Hollis and the others took a seat. They reclined in the field, drinking their warm water and watching as the straw shot out of the thresher like a fountain into a pile on the ground. They watched as the pile grew larger and larger, until it became a mountain of straw, tall enough to cast a shadow that shielded them from the setting sun. It was a sight Hollis had seen every day for months now, but this was his last day, the last time he'd see it, this physical manifestation of his labor, this totem of the time he had spent out there hidden away from the rest of the world, and from the wickedness that awaited him back home.

There were no heartfelt goodbyes. The men and women lined up, were handed their final paychecks, then went their separate ways. Hollis and a few of the others hopped in the back of the boss man's truck for a lift to the bus station in Dodge City. He couldn't mail this paycheck home. He'd need to find a bank to cash it to pay the bus fare back to Arkansas.

The next morning the boys on the farm outside of Dodge City woke up early to go out and gather up the straw from the mountain the thresher had left behind. They would feed it to the horses, use it in their mattresses, or sell it in town. When they got to the field they found Hollis next to the mass of straw, blacked out and stark naked, two empty bottles of rye whiskey nearby. He told the sheriff he couldn't remember what happened to him, what happened to his clothes, to his suitcase, to his money. When they asked him who they could call to come get him, he gave them Ressie's number. He couldn't bear Hazel's shame.

Dane

1946

**If they belong to the police, the drunkard argued,
then it can't be illegal to play 'em.**

One night in 1946, a tourist who had had a bit too much to drink stumbled upon a row of five slot machines on the sidewalk downtown. He dropped in a quarter, pulled the arm, and the wheels whirred. *Cachunk, cachunk, cachunk,* they lined up three bells in a row, and eighteen more quarters tumbled out of the machine. The sound caught the attention of the police, who had just dragged the machines out of a club. They grabbed the jackpot winner and demanded he give up his quarters. The machines, they argued, had just been seized and were the property of the police.

If they belong to the police, the drunkard argued, then it can't be illegal to play 'em. The police had no retort. They let the man go with his loot.

The five slots belonged to the Army and Navy Hospital, which by the end of the war was filled with twelve hundred patients. Soldiers came to the hospital from every part of the United States, and they quickly assimilated to the freewheeling way of life in Hot Springs. At one point the higher-ranking officers in the hospital decided they needed their own officers' club, just like they would have had on a proper base. In true Hot Springs fashion, the officers stocked their club with slot machines.

When George McLaughlin, the mayor's brother, heard that the soldiers had acquired their own slot machines, rather than leasing them from him, he called the mayor and complained. Leo McLaughlin sent the police to raid the officers' club and seize their five renegade slot machines. The surprised servicemen asked the sheriff why their slots were being confiscated. He told them slot machines were illegal.

The confiscation of five slot machines from a little club for decorated servicemen grew into a major scandal. For many in Hot Springs it represented the greed and corruption of the McLaughlin machine in the wake of W. S. Jacobs's death. There had never been more gambling in Hot Springs. While Jacobs had never permitted more than seven clubs to operate, McLaughlin allowed anyone willing to pay his fee to open up shop. Gambling clubs and horse books now dotted the city, on both the white and black sides of town. McLaughlin's decision to confiscate the soldiers' slots was not only overreach, it was disrespectful to the veterans who had just returned from war. McLaughlin had grown used to being feared and respected in Hot Springs. What he didn't understand was that the veterans were legion in Hot Springs. They extended beyond the wounded visitors. They were also the grown children of his contemporaries, his own constituents of voting age who were filled with a sense of duty. They didn't respect him, and they damn sure didn't fear him.

Dane had volunteered for the war by signing up for the air force, eager to put his flying skills to use flying fighter planes. He was rejected, however, because he was color-blind. Fortunately, the air force was in no position to let a capable pilot sit the war out completely. Dane was assigned to Arkadelphia, Arkansas, to work as a flight instructor. He helped train dozens of men to fly, then sent them off to fight.

Marcella would come visit Dane at the air force base in Arkadelphia every weekend. She'd always put on something nice, pack herself and Dane a picnic lunch, and then stuff the trunk of the Lincoln with as many bottles of whiskey as it could fit. Arkadelphia was in Clark County, which was one of Arkansas's thirty-three dry counties. The boys on the base were always thirsty, and Dane was their man. He sold whiskey to the grunts and gave it away to the officers. He made a lot of friends.

IN ADDITION TO THE armed services and the liquor business, one of Dane's old college fraternity brothers back in Hot Springs had enlisted him to do some flying for a political campaign he was planning. Sid McMath was everything Dane had once hoped to be—a brilliant young lawyer and a decorated and celebrated war hero. McMath grew up in Hot Springs. His father was a barber and his mother sold tickets at the Malco movie theater. McMath was a Golden Gloves champion boxer and a model pupil at Hot Springs High. He went on to attend law school at the University of Arkansas, where he was elected president of the student body. After getting his law degree he practiced briefly as a public defender before being swept away to fight in the Pacific Theater as commander of the Third Marine Regiment. He led his troops in heavy jungle combat, receiving a battlefield promotion to lieutenant colonel. Upon returning home, McMath was awarded the Silver Star and the Legion of Merit for heroism, disregard of his own safety beyond the normal call of duty, and inspiring his fellow soldiers in battle.

When McMath returned to Hot Springs, he wanted to continue to lead. He believed he had a future in politics, and dreamed of one day being governor. Upon McMath's return to Hot Springs, however, his friend Raymond Clinton, the owner of the local Buick dealership and the uncle of the future president of the United States, told McMath that McLaughlin's machine had squashed every potential opponent in the last twelve years. In order to hold any public office at all you needed to be in with Leo McLaughlin's political machine, which meant you needed to be in with Owney Madden and the gambling combination. McMath didn't want to play that game. He didn't want to beg for a spot on a ticket in a rigged election. And McMath knew that McLaughlin was vulnerable. His image as the savior of Hot Springs had waned over his two decades in office. McLaughlin was beset by scandals, and many now saw him as more a dictator than a savior—particularly those who had recently returned from the war. McMath believed he could win a fair contest against the McLaughlin machine, if only a fair contest could be had.

One blustery February evening in 1946, McMath invited as many fellow veterans as he could to a meeting at Hammond's Oyster Bar on Central Avenue in Hot Springs. It was late, but Hammond's was open all night. The young men crowded around a booth in the corner. They might have all been veterans, but that wasn't all they had in common. Dane was one of the few men in McMath's group who wasn't a lawyer.

McMath gave the veterans his pitch: Why should Leo get to pick who served in every office from municipal judge down to dogcatcher? How long were these old men going to run this town? McMath reminded the young men at Hammond's that they had all just risked their lives fighting to bring democracy to people living under fascist dictatorships. Didn't it just burn them up that they returned to a dictatorship at home?

McMath believed it was their turn to run the show in Hot Springs. They had served their country with bravery and now they wanted to serve their community, and they didn't want to wait until they were old men to do it. The boys were nodding their heads in agreement, but looking over their shoulders to see who was listening in. McMath had picked each of these young men for a reason. He knew they were smart, responsible, and up to the task of serving in government. But he also knew that they were each ambitious in some way. Some wanted to serve in politics. Some wanted in on the gambling action. He chose the smartest, but also the hungriest. Appealing to their general sense of fairness wouldn't be enough. He needed men who wanted to be in political office bad enough to fight for it. Because a fight was what it was going to take.

"Go home. Discuss with your wives and family what's at stake. Be thinking about if you are willing to put your name on the ticket and run for office," McMath told the group. "And let's keep what we discussed between us until we are ready to announce our intentions. You know the score."

Q. BYRUM HURST DIDN'T need to do much thinking about it. Hurst was the son of a local Church of God minister, himself active in Democratic Party politics. Ever since Hurst was a little boy, tagging along with his father to political meetings, he had wanted to hold public office. Unlike McMath, Hurst didn't win any medals for jungle missions. He served stateside as a counselor to soldiers preparing to deploy. But Hurst could see how his status as a veteran was an important qualification. He understood the optics of a group of uniformed veterans running for office, how they could capitalize on the public's feelings about the boys come home from war. It was their best and perhaps only chance to elbow their way into the local political establishment. But to capitalize on it, they'd need to make their move now. They couldn't wait until public sentiment about the war had faded.

Hurst wasn't completely on the outside looking in. He was friendly with many in the gambling combination, including Owney Madden. While some of the veterans saw gambling as the engine for the corruption they wanted to overthrow, Hurst was unapologetically pro-gambling. He refused to participate in the campaign if it was going to call for putting the lid back on the town. Where would Hot Springs be without gambling? And what's the point of fighting these bastards to get in power if you weren't going to get a piece of the action as your reward?

Like Hurst, Dane Harris understood that there was something brilliant about Sid McMath's plan. But while Hurst and McMath had dreamed of holding political office since they were little, Dane wasn't interested in politics. He wasn't cut out for it. What Dane was interested in was getting a cut of the action in Hot Springs. Like everyone else who grew up in the spa, Dane knew that the gambling business was the surest way to wealth and power, and he knew if he could get his foot in the door, he could do something big. Dane believed that Hot Springs had the potential for so much more than folks realized. There was plenty of money in Hot Springs, and even more sitting with out-of-town interests anxious to invest. There were thousands of visitors returning from the war in Europe, resting up in Hot Springs before they went home. There were tourists from all over the world coming to take baths. Why couldn't Hot Springs be a world-class city, a national capital of entertainment and leisure?

But if Hot Springs was going to beat Las Vegas and become the American capital of gambling, it would need some new leadership, both at city hall and behind the green felt tables. Leo McLaughlin and Jack McJunkins weren't leading Hot Springs—they were too busy helping themselves. Dane didn't agree with Sid McMath's opposition to gambling, but he knew him and respected him a great deal. Dane believed it was time for a change in Hot Springs. He decided to throw his lot in with the GIs. He would volunteer for McMath, as would Bookie Ebel. They enlisted the help and support of their friends. One of those friends, Leonard Ellis, would even join the ticket and run for the down-ballot office of chancery court clerk. If they were successful, perhaps this would be a way into the center of the action.

ON THE MORNING OF July 4, 1946, the residents of Lonsdale, a little town about fifteen miles outside of Hot Springs, awakened to the sound of a low-flying airplane circling the town. Hundreds of pieces of paper fell from the airplane onto the streets of Lonsdale like confetti. Folks came out of their houses, out of the cafés and businesses, out into the streets to see what was falling from the sky.

On one side of the papers was an invitation to a political meeting that night at the Colony House Theater. The other side had a cartoon of Leo McLaughlin riding a horse and giving the Nazi "Sieg heil!" salute.

According to the leaflet, the meeting was organized by something called the Government Improvement League, which they cleverly shortened to the "GI League."

About eight hundred people showed up that night, curious about these leaflets dropped from the sky. Standing on the stage of the theater were a dozen young men in full military dress, medals and ribbons dangling from their chests. Their leader, Sid McMath, stood in front. He paced the stage, finger held aloft, and gave a barn burner of an address.

"I will protect you against the violation of your civil rights," he hollered. "I will champion the rights of the people against all opponents—yes, against his majesty Der Fuehrer of Hot Springs." McMath, against all odds, was running for prosecuting attorney of Garland County—a position that would put the gambling combination squarely in his sights.

They had chosen Lonsdale to kick off their campaign because it was far enough outside of Hot Springs that people there didn't live in fear of Leo McLaughlin. Lonsdale wasn't so far, however, that McLaughlin couldn't get to them. As Sid McMath held forth, outside the theater two Hot Springs police officers scattered roofing tacks throughout the parking lot. After the rally, Sid McMath, Q. Byrum Hurst, Leonard Ellis, and the other GIs stayed at the Colony House until they had changed each and every flattened tire.

The newspapers called the campaign "the GI Revolt." The GI League held campaign rallies in every single ward and precinct. They campaigned day and night, handing out literature and greeting voters door-to-door and on the streets. In the weeks leading up to the primary, members of the GI League ticket were encouraged to drop out of the race with bribes, or offered positions to come over and serve on the McLaughlin ticket. When it was clear none of them would accept, the bribes turned to threats. Q. Byrum Hurst received phone calls threatening to hurt his wife and infant daughter.

Two of the GIs' most vocal supporters were Earl Ricks, a retired air force colonel, and Raymond Clinton. Ricks and Clinton let the GIs use their Buick dealership garage as a headquarters, and by Election Day the place looked more like an armory than a political field office. The GIs prepared for Election Day by rounding up shotguns and ammunition. There were rumors that people would be muscled and intimidated at the polls, so the GIs offered to escort people to vote. They drove around town on primary day in teams of four, a shotgun in each of their laps.

As the reports from around the county came in to McLaughlin's office, he felt pretty good about his chances. He had his own army out on the streets, but they weren't armed with shotguns. Jack McJunkins was armed with two thousand poll tax receipts, each attached to a two-dollar bill. Saloon owners, liquor store clerks, pool hall attendants, bookies, and gamblers all carried around pockets full of poll tax receipts. They'd find someone thirsty for a drink, or in need of getting a bet down, and they'd hand them a receipt and tell them to come back after they voted. It didn't matter if they had already voted, or if they were even eligible to vote. Nobody in a Garland County polling precinct was going to ask any questions. That was how Leo McLaughlin had stayed mayor for twenty years.

McLaughlin picked up the telephone to check in on the vote count in neighboring Montgomery County, where some of the judicial districts extended. He didn't control the count in Montgomery, but he needed to know how many votes they had so he could make up the difference by stuffing ballot boxes in Garland County. He couldn't get through; the line was dead. All day long he tried to reach his poll watchers in Mount Ida, but he never got a line to connect. The night before the primary someone had taken it upon themselves to sever all the phone lines connecting Mount Ida and Hot Springs.

In the end nobody had to use their guns. Despite the fever pitch of the campaign, or perhaps because of it, turnout was low. The GIs ended up losing every primary race but one. Sid McMath was nominated for prosecuting attorney over Curtis Ridgeway in a close contest of 3,900 votes to 3,375. The GIs were unable to overcome the McLaughlin machine's ballot box stuffing in Garland County. But since Leo couldn't get a handle on how many votes Ridgeway was down by in Montgomery County, they couldn't cheat well enough to win. The Montgomery County vote put McMath over the top. He was the winner of the Democratic primary, which in Arkansas was as good as winning the general election.

Judge Ledgerwood was eager to show McMath there were no hard feelings. He called a meeting at his house of everyone on the Democratic Party ticket, including McMath. Judge Ledgerwood, Leo McLaughlin, and all the other members of the machine greeted McMath with smiles and handshakes. Judge Ledgerwood knew that McMath could single-handedly gum up the works for everyone as far as gambling was concerned. Their combination worked only if everyone cooperated, and so it made sense for McLaughlin to try to bury the hatchet with Sid McMath. McMath smiled and shook everyone's hands in turn, giving no impression he wasn't open to working together with them. McLaughlin was afraid of McMath, and McMath could tell. And what McMath knew, and McLaughlin didn't, was that the GI Revolt wasn't over quite yet. The GIs didn't intend to surrender.

The general election was three months away, and they would all file to run as independent candidates in a rematch against the machine. Only this time they'd have an ace up their sleeve. They knew they couldn't win if McLaughlin continued to buy up blocks of poll tax receipts. So they came up with a plan to shut the ballot box stuffing down. They were lawyers. They'd do what lawyers do best: file a lawsuit.

Birdie Fulton and Otis Livingstone were former football players at Hot Springs High School. They were big fellows, and not easily intimidated. They were going door-to-door collecting evidence for the GIs' lawsuit, asking voters if they ever paid their poll tax or had ever actually voted. Their canvass had been successful. One person after the next expressed surprise that they were on the record as having cast a vote. Birdie and Otis had collected a briefcase full of sworn statements by the time they knocked on the door at 119 Jefferson Street. As they waited on the porch for someone to answer the door, two men approached them from the sidewalk. One of them was holding a gun. They demanded the briefcase.

Birdie and Otis froze in fear. The men weren't wearing masks, and Birdie and Otis recognized one of them. His name was Ed Spears, a local bookie and a member of a nationwide ring of professional con artists. Birdie and Otis did what they were told and handed over the briefcase. They watched helplessly as Spears walked away, carrying their entire case against the McLaughlin machine.

Later that evening, McMath and some of the other GIs paid a surprise visit to McLaughlin's office. They ignored McLaughlin's secretary's pleas and shouldered their way inside to confront the mayor.

"You want gunplay, Leo?" McMath asked. "Well, we have some people on our side who have some recent experience in that kind of activity."

McLaughlin was flabbergasted. Never in his life had anyone spoken to him this way.

"If anything happens again, we intend to put a stop to it. But we won't waste time with a small fry. We'll start at the top." With that, the GIs left as quickly as they had arrived. By the time they made it back to the campaign headquarters, the briefcase had been returned, all of the affidavits intact.

The GIs presented the court with those statements along with evidence that proved widespread vote rigging using poll tax receipts. They showed that, according to voting records, people were showing up to vote in perfect alphabetical order—a sure sign of fraud. They also showed that multiple poll tax receipts had been signed by the same person. The judge ruled in favor of the GIs and tossed 1,607 voters from the rolls.

OWNEY WATCHED ALL OF this unfold with horror. Things were slipping away from Leo McLaughlin. If there was one thing Owney could spot, it was a sucker bet. He wasted no time in reaching out to the other side. Owney was switching teams.

The 1946 general election was held on a cold, rainy November day. The wind and rain didn't keep many voters home. Sixteen thousand people voted. It was a record turnout, more than double the turnout in the last general election. Twenty members of the state police were dispatched to Hot Springs by the governor out of fear that there could be violence. When all was said and done, nobody was hurt, and the GIs swept every office. Judge Ledgerwood and Mayor McLaughlin weren't on the ballot that day, but neither of them decided to seek reelection the following year. Colonel Earl Ricks was elected the next mayor of Hot Springs in a landslide. Leonard Ellis was the new chancery court clerk for Garland County.

Any hopes that Dane and Bookie had that their friend's election to the court would move them closer to the gambling business were quickly dashed. The GIs who were elected had split on what to do about gambling and turned on each other. Sid McMath, their fearless leader, came out hard against gambling. As prosecutor, McMath was able to file charges and order the casinos shut down. The wisdom of why McMath chose this office over something flashy like mayor became clear. From the prosecutor's desk McMath could enact his reform agenda. He not only closed the clubs down, he sought revenge on his enemies. He tried to bring charges against Leo McLaughlin and Verne Ledgerwood and have them thrown in jail. The pro-gambling members of the GI Revolt who had hoped to become big shot gambling bosses were now forced to settle for becoming simple public servants. For Owney Madden, who had shown political acumen in abandoning McLaughlin to back the GIs, his efforts to buy his way into the gambling combination were now squandered, his bounty worthless. Hot Springs, with all its promise, was turning into a real mess, and Owney had no idea how to fix it.

Owney

They were selling dreams to suckers. And the demand for dreams was insatiable.

About a month after the 1946 election in Hot Springs, Meyer Lansky sent word to all the top hoodlums in America, including Owney, that he wanted to see them in Havana. About two dozen gangsters were called to the meeting at the Hotel Nacional, whose management had closed the hotel to the public to give Lansky and his fellow mobsters privacy. The leaders of organized crime from New York and Chicago were well represented, but their ranks had grown. Over the last decade the syndicate had spread across the South and Midwest. Men arrived from Ohio, Wisconsin, California, Florida. And they were all gathered in Havana that day to discuss what should be done about the crackdown on gambling.

In the forties, Hot Springs wasn't the only gambling town reckoning with political reformers and honest law enforcement. From coast to coast, bookmakers and dice games were being shut down and the mob was sent packing, forcing criminals to set out across America in search of new venues to ply the gambling trade. In 1941, California Attorney General Earl Warren ordered raids on a number of gambling boats floating in the Pacific Ocean that hosted dice games and brothels for the West Coast mob. Unable to open their floating casinos back up again, the proprietors flocked to Las Vegas to try their hand at operating legally. They opened a number of small casinos in roadside hotels along desolate Highway 91. A few months after the arrival of the California mobsters, the Nevada legislature legalized bookmaking by wire, the first state in the United States to do so. Meyer Lansky decided he could no longer ignore Las Vegas. He decided to invest.

For the last decade Lansky had been operating as the moneyman for most of the mobs in the syndicate, controlling where they would invest their resources, and he had managed to keep everyone happy with his returns. Much of his portfolio was in gambling, which he and Lucky Luciano preferred to narcotics. "There's so much dough to be made in everything else we have," Luciano had said. "Why ruin it with the dangers of playing around with junk that would only bring the federal guys down on us?" It was true that the Federal Bureau of Narcotics was staffed by particularly zealous cops. And gambling had proven to be lucrative. The mob was making much more in gambling than it ever had in the bootlegging trade. For one thing, there was no supply to smuggle. There was only probability, odds, chance. They were selling dreams to suckers. And the demand for dreams was insatiable.

Until now Lansky had pinned his hopes for the mob's future right there in Havana, Cuba. He wanted to transform the island into a Monte Carlo, a gambling paradise that would cater to the entire world. The situation was perfect. The government in Cuba, led by Colonel Fulgencio Batista, was for sale. Lansky had already invested hundreds of thousands of dollars in Batista, one suitcase full of money after another. But the American government—the same government trying to throw each and every one of the mobsters at that meeting in Havana into prison—was also backing Batista. In Cuba, the mob could operate casinos and not only would they be welcomed by the Cuban government, but they'd also have the gratitude and support of the American government.

But it soon became clear that most of the American criminal elite, including Owney Madden, weren't interested in leaving the country. For those who insisted on staying stateside, Lansky believed it was better for them to operate legitimately. The mob had managed to run a billion-dollar gambling empire well enough on the sneak, but it required a lot of political wheeling and dealing, and that way of doing business was running its course. What happened in Hot Springs with the young GIs was unthinkable even just five years before. And it was happening in other places, too. Young reformers were betting they could build careers out of throwing gangsters in jail. And even though Owney and Frank Costello were not as violent as some of their contemporaries, they got no special treatment. The newspapers still called Owney "the Killer," even though he hadn't killed anyone in years. The general public was getting soft. The noose was tightening. Nevada, however, offered a chance to build something akin to what they had in Havana, a legitimate operation.

Lansky had dispatched his partner and oldest friend, Ben "Bugsy" Siegel, to head to Las Vegas after the legalization of bookmaking to try to establish the mob's wire service as the main conduit of information for Nevada bookies. Lansky had used this method in other cities, like Chicago and Miami, to maintain control over all of the gambling rackets. The wire service was the direct line of communication between the racetracks around the country and the bookmakers in any city. The wire service paid the racetracks for exclusive access to the results of the races. When the tracks didn't want to sell, the wire service paid people to sit at pay phones near the track and call in the results after the race was run. The results were sent out over telegraph wires through a deal with Western Union. Bookies paid big money, sometimes as much as four or five thousand a week, for access to the results.

The information was so valuable because having the results instantly meant a bookmaker could book more action in a day. Most gamblers waited for the newspaper to arrive the next day to see if they had won their bet. The wire meant gamblers could settle up after each and every race, or every game, and immediately bet the next one. It meant a big increase in action. In a big city you might have a hundred bookies paying for those instant results every week. It was a good business. Good enough that despite its questionable legality, the major wire service in the United States wasn't built by gangsters, but by the newspaper tycoon Walter Annenberg. It didn't stay his. In 1942, one of Owney Madden's closest friends, a former Capone captain named Murray "Curley" Humphreys, got control of the wire service by having the man who ran the wire for Annenberg gunned down on a Chicago street in broad daylight. When the man survived that attack, someone stuffed a fistful of mercury bichloride tablets in his mouth as he slept in the hospital to finish the job.

Even more than Las Vegas, Hot Springs was a horse racing and bookmaking town. It needed access to a wire service, and it was for this reason that the little town in Arkansas caught Meyer Lansky's eye, no matter the legal situation. He and Curley offered Owney something that would put him in the catbird seat with the Hot Springs gamblers—control over the wire.

THE CASINOS AND HANDBOOKS in Hot Springs had always received their race wire information from Continental, the Chicago-based service Curley Humphreys had taken control of, by way of a wire room in New Orleans. That wire room was controlled by Carlos Marcello, who was partners with Frank Costello in running slot machines and gambling across the city and who had become a powerful crime boss in his own right. For more than thirty years the wire service in New Orleans had been run on the square, but Marcello had seized control of the service on behalf of the national syndicate with the help of one of his lieutenants, a round Italian with jet-black, slicked-back hair and a long face with tiny eyes named "Papa Joe" Poretto. Papa Joe had been a member of Marcello's crew for a long time, even before Marcello became a boss, and he had even worked on behalf of the syndicate setting up gambling operations in other southern cities like Houston, Texas.

After the meeting in Havana, Humphreys and Papa Joe came to Hot Springs. They had dinner at the Arlington Hotel. Owney took Papa Joe around town to show him the clubs and introduce him around. Owney would pay Papa Joe's hotel bill and have him over to his house to meet Agnes. Together they hatched a plan. It would be up to Owney to decide who got the wire from then on. If Owney was ever going to run Hot Springs, it would be now or never. He had successfully wiggled his way into the Southern Club, bought a share of the city's slot machines, and bet the right horse in supporting Dane Harris's friends and fellow GIs in the 1946 election. And though McMath had shut down gambling, it was only a temporary setback. McMath had announced that he was running for governor, and his fellow GIs had split on the question of whether to keep the town closed or open it back up. Q. Byrum Hurst encouraged a faction of the GIs to run for office under the umbrella of a new group, the "Progressive Businessmen's Association," which supported gambling. Their hope was that as governor, McMath would have more power but less of an ability to exert it in Hot Springs. Dane even volunteered to fly McMath around the state for his campaign. And with McMath's résumé as a decorated war hero and conqueror of the McLaughlin regime, there was no way he could lose.

Hazel

APRIL 1947

**Surrounded by wilderness, no job to speak of,
her boys running around hell's half acre eating
bugs—it seemed ridiculous.**

Hazel and the boys huddled together in the rickety grandstand outside the sawmill in Mountain Pine, Arkansas, one spring afternoon to watch Hollis play baseball. He was playing outfield for the company team of Dierks Mill, where he had been working for the past several months. The young Hill family had moved out to the mill town of Mountain Pine, which was much smaller than Hot Springs, but the move was worth it if it meant a good job and drying out for Hollis. Mountain Pine was awfully boring, however, compared to Hot Springs. The baseball games between the teams from the various Dierks family mills around western Arkansas and Oklahoma were the only entertainment they had. But Hazel's boys loved watching their father play. And Hazel was relieved that things were getting back on track.

Hollis's brother Edward had been working out at the mill in Mountain Pine since before the end of the war. Mountain Pine was about ten miles outside of Hot Springs. The mill had been there only since 1928, and when the war broke out, a lot of the mills around the country closed down due to a lack of workers. The Dierks family consolidated many of their mill operations to Mountain Pine, putting the workers' shotgun houses on trucks and moving them to Garland County. They laid down a town where there hadn't been much of one before, and built Mountain Pine into the second-largest city in the county.

Edward told Hollis he thought he could get him on at the mill, too. It had a lot of advantages. For one thing, anyone who worked there could live in one of those shotgun houses for just three dollars a month, which was a lot better than any rent you could find in Hot Springs. Mill workers could buy their groceries at the Big Store in Mountain Pine, also owned by the company, on the credit of future wages. It wasn't great money compared to what Hollis had made back at Cook's Ice Cream, but at this point he didn't have a lot of choices. And to make matters worse, he and Hazel had a third child on their hands.

My father, James Allen, was born in August 1946. Hazel had started calling Harold "Larry," and she called baby James "Jimmy." She liked those names. Those were names for boys. She had grown up with her father and brothers on the racetrack, and even now, as an adult, she preferred the company of men to women. She figured she was meant to be a mother to boys, so long as they were good boys.

By the time they moved out to one of the shotgun houses in Mountain Pine, Larry was four and Hollis Jr. was eight. They could have stayed in Hot Springs, but the rent on the company house was too good a deal to pass up. Life out in Mountain Pine was nothing like life back in Hot Springs, however. The town was as country as the day was long. They took baths in washtubs behind the house. They used an outhouse and wiped themselves with corncobs. Larry and Hollis Jr. would dip snuff they found in cans that truckers would throw onto the road. They learned to fish, to build fires. They'd catch grasshoppers and roast them in the fire and eat them.

Hazel hated living in Mountain Pine, but it was practical and they were short on options. Hazel tried to be patient with their new life. But sitting around that rickety old house all day, surrounded by wilderness, no job to speak of, her boys running around hell's half acre eating bugs—it seemed ridiculous. Her party dresses hung on the clothes rack, taunting her. This wasn't the life she'd had in mind when she decided to stay behind in Hot Springs and marry Hollis Hill.

Hazel worked hard in Mountain Pine to make sure that Hollis stayed sober. She told his boss, the clerks down at the Big Store, the boys he played cards with, the bartender down at the little tavern: nobody was to give Hollis a drink, not a single sip. And you better believe they didn't. As Hazel had matured, she had developed a hard edge, and could be downright mean and intimidating when she wanted to be. But despite her best efforts, Hollis found ways to get his hands on liquor.

Mountain Pine had a number of black residents since the mill opened up—the first black residents the town had ever seen. The company recruited black workers for the mills, who brought their families to live with them in mill-owned shotgun houses on the outskirts of town, same as Hollis and Hazel. Some of the black workers were recruited specifically to play on the company baseball team, and Hollis befriended some of them. Those players either didn't know about Hazel's edict or didn't care. Hollis ended up drunk on the black side of town night after night.

Now that Hollis was known to be an alcoholic, he no longer tried to hide it. He could get drunk out in the open without worrying who saw. He could be drunk all night and all day. He could come home drunker than a peach orchard boar, and if Hazel had something to say about it he could give her what for. He would holler at her with a hateful voice. If Hazel hollered back, he would breathe heavy like there was something terrible inside him fighting to come out. He could ball up his fist and show it to her as if to say that when it did come out she'd catch the hard end of it. He could act this way not worrying about the consequences, because everybody already knew what Hollis was: a ruined man. His bosses at the mill might have taken longer than most to figure it out, but eventually they knew it, too. A year after moving to Mountain Pine, they fired Hollis, expelling him and his family from the wilds of Mountain Pine back to Hot Springs. It freed Hazel from the life she despised, but it came at a cost. The Hills were once again without a source of income, once again at the mercy of Hollis's family, their shame deepening drink by drink.

Dane

Dane never ceased to be surprised when, days after he had played a round with some of Owney's less reputable friends, he'd hear about how many men they'd killed or how many years they'd spent behind bars.

Dane Harris loved the sound of a good drive. He could tell if you hit it true just from the thwack of the club hitting the ball. He was that good at golf, the rich man's game. But Dane did not come from a family of rich men. His people hunted ducks and deer with shotguns in the woods. They fished off the sides of bridges. But on the golf course, Dane fit right in among the men of means and influence who made grand plans and conspired to seize power as they teed off. His powerful drives made him anyone's equal on the golf course, even if he himself was not yet rich.

Golf would open doors for Dane. It was out on the golf course that he met Owney Madden, and it was on the very same golf course in 1947 that Dane would meet Frank Niemeyer, whose family owned the Niemeyer Lumber Company. Niemeyer and Dane eventually paired up to play in a few tournaments at the country club, and out on the golf course they forged a friendship and a business partnership.

Frank Niemeyer lived on a large piece of land on the road that connected Hot Springs to Malvern, Arkansas. It was a well-traveled route, but the area was undeveloped. Niemeyer offered Dane the chance to develop the property, to build spec houses and see if he could sell them. He even offered to front some of the money if Dane would act as general contractor.

With the casinos shut down after the GIs' electoral victory, Dane's plan of getting a slice of the gambling business was shot. He still had the Black Cat, which he had been running along with his mother, Hattie, ever since his father skipped town again four years before. Dane knew very little about construction, but he was good with accounting and managing money. He knew he could approach the job like a businessman—hire contractors to do the work, and make sure they got it done cheaply and quickly. He oversaw the construction of four homes on Niemeyer's property, and he and Marcella bought the first of the four houses for themselves. He sold the other three for a profit, which he shared with Frank Niemeyer.

Dane parlayed his success in the houses on the Niemeyer property into another real estate development on some land down the road. He developed a brand-new residential subdivision, named the neighborhood Indiandale, with an Indian chief's head as its logo, and named the streets after various Indian tribes—a subtle nod to Dane's father, who still loomed large in Dane's life despite his frequent absences. Just as he had when he was thirteen years old, Dane continued to assume many of his father's responsibilities, including his mother, Hattie. And Dane used the money from his real estate ventures to expand his father's business and open up a second liquor store.

Though Dane preferred the real estate business to the liquor business, the fact was, the liquor stores gave Dane some measure of power in Hot Springs. While gambling may have been shut down again, liquor was still a big business in the resort. Dane's liquor stores continued to be the suppliers to the bars and restaurants that were illegally serving hard liquor by the glass, and the two stores kept him in business with the powerful liquor magnate Harry Hastings, a partnership that opened more doors for Dane than his golf game, whether he knew it or not.

In 1949 the Arkansas legislature passed a law allowing Arkansas firms to export liquor to Oklahoma and Mississippi, two neighboring states that were also the only two dry states left in America after the repeal of Prohibition. Prior to this law, it was illegal in Arkansas to transport liquor into dry states to sell, which was why Dane had needed to smuggle it over the border for Hastings. The state revenue commissioner for Arkansas, Dan Morley, pushed to pass the new law because he knew that up to a million cases of whiskey were being shipped into Oklahoma, and another million into Mississippi, and that liquor distributors from Louisiana and Texas were transporting the booze across Arkansas highways. The state chose to license three firms to move whiskey into dry states. One of those three was the Harris Export Company, owned by Dane and Marcella Harris, with the financial and political backing of Harry Hastings. Dane wasn't going to repeat the mistake his father made by not partnering with Harry Hastings when he had the chance.

HARRY HASTINGS WASN'T DANE'S only friend in high places. He grew closer to Owney Madden. They would often be seen together out on the golf course, and from time to time they'd be accompanied by whichever famous visitors Owney happened to be entertaining that weekend. The movie star George Raft, one of Owney's oldest friends, was a frequent guest. Wallace Beery would fly his own airplane to Hot Springs to visit Owney. There were prizefighters like Gene Tunney and Rocky Marciano. But mostly Owney hosted gangsters. Dane never ceased to be surprised when, days after he had played a round with some of Owney's less reputable friends, he'd hear about how many men they'd killed or how many years they'd spent behind bars. To Dane they seemed like anyone else he met on the golf course.

The more Dane learned about Owney's friends, the more nervous he grew about associating with them. Especially when that association involved gambling, which it almost always did out on the golf course. Dane and Owney always played for money, and Dane mostly won. But once he was in a foursome with some of Owney's friends and Dane knew they were gangsters. The knowledge must have rattled Dane, because he played terribly, and at the end of the day he owed them much more than he could afford to pay. They told Dane not to worry about it, to come back the next day and they'd play again and give him a chance to win his money back.

That night Dane returned home after Marcella was already asleep. He sat on the edge of the bed and blinked at the darkness of the room, nervous that going to sleep only meant waking up still deep in debt to murderers. Marcella stirred.

"What's wrong?" She reached over and touched his back.

"I lost."

"That's okay. You'll win it back." Marcella had been in that spot before. She was a fine golfer herself, and knew Dane could hold his own with anyone else. And she knew that his bets paid the grocer's bill more often than they didn't.

"If I play again tomorrow, what if I lose even more? I won't be able to pay."

"All you can do is go out there and play your best game. That's all you can do. If you lose, we'll pay it. Just play your best game." Such was gambling. Such too was life. Dane was not someone to shy away from risk. And in these moments of weakness, late at night on the edge of the bed, Dane knew Marcella would remind him of that.

The next morning Dane showed up at the clubhouse early and eager. Out on the links Dane won his money back and then some. Dane must have impressed Owney Madden with his mettle. Just like Frank Niemeyer before him, Owney decided to make his golfing partner a life-changing offer.

———

SID MCMATH HAD SUCCEEDED in his campaign for governor. Candidates affiliated with the Progressive Businessmen's Association won some but not all of their contests, with the remainder going to McMath's anti-gambling allies in the GI League. Hot Springs would remain closed for at least two more years. After a meeting of 250 people at the Willow Room (so named because it boasted an enormous willow tree growing at its center) at the Phillips Drive-In on Park Avenue, Q. Byrum Hurst and the other pro-gambling leaders created a platform that they hoped would return them to power.

The PBA adopted a resolution opposing a return to open gambling save for "a number of high class clubs operating under strict supervision," the presumption being that the leaders of the PBA would get to decide who could and could not operate. Owney didn't need to worry about these new restrictions, for he now controlled the all-powerful race wire. If the major casinos didn't reopen, there would always be a brisk bookmaking business on the sneak in Hot Springs. And if the PBA did manage to get the casinos going again, Owney would be even more powerful, since every club would want the wire.

Dane also had leverage. He could refuse to sell alcohol to any club or bar unless the PBA approved. Owney brought Dane closer to the combination by offering him and his friends the opportunity to run all the bookmaking operations in the reopened clubs. Owney would make sure Dane received the wire service out of New Orleans, and Dane and his friends would kick a percentage of their take to Owney, plus a leasing fee to the clubs they operated out of. Furthermore, the PBA wanted to put Dane's friend Leonard Ellis up as their candidate for sheriff. If Ellis won, Dane and his friends would be permitted to buy into one of the gambling clubs. Another deal had been struck on the Hot Springs Country Club golf course, and Dane began to see a way forward.

Hazel

She'd save their souls by filing for divorce.

It had been rough going for Hazel and her boys since Hollis lost his position at the mill. After moving back to Hot Springs, Hazel took a job as a carhop at Clay's Drive-In to help make ends meet, her first job in thirteen years. Hollis worked odd jobs, but most of the time he was drunk.

The Hills were beside themselves about Hollis's condition. They were proud, strong people who believed in hard work and stiff upper lips. "That boy's gone back on his raisin'," Bessie Mae would complain to her children. The Hills did everything they could to help Hazel out. They would pick up the boys from school when Hazel had to work and Hollis couldn't be found. They'd give Hazel hand-me-down toys and clothes for the children. Occasionally they'd even take Hazel and the boys with them to church.

"You see, back in Matthew, the sixteenth chapter, after Jesus has sent out the disciples and they came back, and there they met him and he said, 'Who do men say that I am?' Now, friend, this is in your Bible . . ."

Millard Shields was a tall, thin preacher in his forties, who preached in the old-time Pentecost style, which is to say he didn't stand behind any pulpit. He stomped back and forth across the stage, up and down the aisles, his shirt collar unbuttoned, his sleeves rolled up at the cuffs, the sweat from his back soaking through his shirt. He was animated, full of the Holy Ghost.

"Some said they thought he was John the Baptist. Some thought he was Jeremiah. Now, what I'm trying to impress upon your mind is that your thoughts don't amount to but a hill of cotton with a boll weevil in it. Your thoughts are not gonna get you by."

Brother Shields preached at Emmanuel Pentecostal Church, the little church that Richard Hill helped build back when Albert Pike Road was barely a road at all. In those early days Albert Pike was mostly populated by small, hand-built homes set on long, flat expanses of land, and there was hardly a store or business to speak of. But by 1949 the Emmanuel Pentecostal Church was squeezed in between a furniture store and a cafeteria. Hot Springs' growth was evident in how busy things were getting this far beyond the hustle and bustle of downtown.

In the early days of Emmanuel, when Brother Shields began preaching to the few Pentecostals, Albert Pike may have been quieter, but there were plenty of sinners in Hot Springs to be prayed over and saved. Josie Hill, Hollis's sister, was out to save them all. She had taken to Brother Shields's wild style of preaching like a fish to water. She was the family's most ardent Pentecostal, never missing a Sunday, and dragging anyone who'd go with her when she could.

Hazel hated going to church with the Hills, but truthfully, not all the Hills enjoyed it much, either. Ressie wasn't even Pentecostal. She married a Nazarene and attended church with him instead. Hollis had never darkened the church's door before he started drinking, and he wasn't about to start now. Josie knew she could usually get Hazel to bring the boys on Sundays, because at the end of the service there was a full spread of biscuits and butter and ham and greens and black-eyed peas. To get the biscuits and ham, however, Hazel and her sons would need to earn them. Brother Shields's sermons were marathons, sometimes lasting for hours. And the service was something to behold. The parishioners would flail their arms, bounce in the aisles, even speak in tongues. Hazel used to say Josie was "full bull Pentecostal." Hazel would keep the boys from squirming and snickering until it was all over, and then they'd feast like hogs.

"You may think because you got the Holy Ghost, spoke in other tongues, that water baptism is not essential. What makes you think that way when the Bible said in John 3, 5, and 6, he said that man is born of water and of the spirit. Why do you think you can leave the water off? That water is not essential? That when Jesus immigrated to Mission, he took the Apostles out to that lake and baptized them."

"Oh, yes, now, preacher, go ahead and tell us how!"

Hazel had not been baptized. Her boys had not been baptized. They were three, six, and ten now. They didn't know Jesus. For them, church was just a place to get something good to eat. Once when Bessie Mae took the boys out to Music Mountain to watch Brother Shields do a baptism in the lake, the boys said it wasn't fair that they couldn't go swimming, too. Their ignorance was fine with Hazel. Whenever Brother Shields would do his altar call and urge any sinners to come forward and be born again, Hazel kept her grip on her sons and her backside in her pew.

"Listen, my friend, there's gonna be more preachers in the lake of fire for telling lies and preaching people into heaven after they die. You can't preach a man into heaven after he died. It's the way he lived here, that's the way he's gonna come up in the day of the resurrection . . ."

A COUPLE OF MONTHS earlier, Hollis had come home drunk in the middle of the day. Hazel was with Larry, who was home sick from school. Hollis burst into the place hollering about how she better never leave him, how she was his woman, how she better not carry on with anyone out at that drive-in where she worked, and did she think she was better than him just because she had a job. The hollering quickly gave way to violence. Hollis whaled away on Hazel. Not like the other times he had hit her—this time it was full-on rage. She shielded herself as best she could, but it was no use. She crumpled to the floor, balled herself up, sucked in her gut, and prepared to take the beating.

"Stop it, Daddy!" Larry pleaded. But Hollis kept on. Larry jumped on Hollis, tried to restrain him, but it was as if he were a gnat on a bull. So Larry bolted out of the house and ran as fast as his little six-year-old legs would go, influenza and all, until he reached the schoolhouse. Larry ran inside, found Hollis Jr.'s classroom, and burst inside right in the middle of the teacher's lesson.

"Come quick, he's hurtin' Mama!"

Hollis Jr. leaped up and ran with Larry back home, where Hollis was still beating Hazel on the floor. Hollis Jr. was all of ten years old, but he was big enough to get his father's attention. He put himself between his parents and wrapped his arms around his father, pulling him with all his might away from his mother. Hollis raised his hand to strike but blinked and saw his oldest son before him, wild-eyed and howling something unintelligible at him.

Hollis stared at his crying sons and his wife on the floor as if he were taking stock of what all he had done. He turned on his heel before he could do any more. When he came back around later that night he didn't speak of it. Hazel fixed him a plate of eggs.

"I can tell you how. In the name of the Father. And the name of the Father is Jesus. Because Jesus said in Hebrew, and the Hebrew, the writer of Hebrew said, in chapter 1 and verse 4, that he inherited a name. Now the inherited name had come from a father. And the father's name has to be the same as my name. If my name is not the same as the father's name, there is something wrong, my friend. Because you inherit your father's name."

Hazel would not baptize her children. Not now, not ever. She'd save their souls by filing for divorce.

Part III

HOLY GHOST

1950–1959

Dane

1950

**Surely nobody would ever drop an
atomic bomb on Hot Springs.**

Dane and Marcella Harris stood at the altar in the First Methodist Church on Central Avenue, beaming down at their writhing baby in Reverend Fred Harrison's hands.

"Will you nurture this child in Christ's holy church, that by your teaching and example they may be guided to accept God's grace for themselves, to profess their faith openly, and to lead a Christian life?"

Reverend Harris sprinkled water on the baby's forehead. Marcia Harris was barely a year old. Her arrival had sparked something in Dane. Being a father meant he had even more at stake. His drive to succeed was motivated by his desire to provide for his family, for the three women in his life: Marcella, Marcia, and his mother, Hattie, who was still an active and perhaps overly involved presence in their lives, at least as far as Marcella was concerned.

Having a child had also sparked something in Marcella, who had never felt closer to her young husband. Prior to Marcia's arrival the two of them had been more than just husband and wife—they had been partners in all things, including business. They even golfed together, and Marcella honed her skills to the point that she and Dane were a feared duo in foursomes with other couples. Marcella's reputation among the female golfers in Hot Springs rivaled her husband's, and the two of them used the golf course to socialize and grow their standing among the monied upper crust. Now, as parents, they would find their bond put to the test even more, and Marcella welcomed the challenge. She would have greater standing in her own home, where Marcella often felt at odds with Dane's mother, who was intensely close to Dane and fiercely protective and jealous.

It mattered that the couple remained close, because things in Hot Springs were changing quickly, and Dane was caught up in the middle of them. He had been swept up into Hot Springs politics, and had become involved in gambling. As he was pulled from one major upheaval to the next, each time seeing his social stock rise higher, Marcella felt him growing more distant, leaning on her wisdom less and less. Marcia, however, brought Dane back to her. They were now parents, a partnership no one could threaten.

DANE HAD ANOTHER CONFIDANT and partner, his old friend Bookie Ebel, who was his coconspirator in cornering the bookmaking market in Hot Springs. The two men had proven themselves skillful bookmakers. Bookie handled the odds and probabilities, and Dane handled politicking and business. They were now leasing space in the Ohio Club and the White Front Cigar Store, which in addition to serving as a handbook was also a popular hangout for the city's political and criminal elite. Dane and Bookie had become important enough players in the combination that when Owney organized a trip to Cuba for a delegation of club owners and political leaders, Dane and Bookie were invited to come along.

Hot Springs, Arkansas, and Havana, Cuba, were worlds apart, both geographically and culturally, but the two places had much in common. Gambling was once against the law in Cuba, but illegal casinos abounded throughout the island. The casinos were run by criminals and were riddled with hustlers and crooks of all types: carnies and gypsies who traveled to Cuba from all over the world to take advantage of sucker tourists and lax law enforcement. The locals would lease space in the casinos to foreign road gamblers, often from America, to run games that were gaffed. The situation was so bad that it became a political liability for the government as tourists returned to their home countries with stories of being fleeced in shady Havana casinos. President Batista ran the worst of the carnies out of the country, even having soldiers arrest them right on the casino floor. But like the PBA in Hot Springs, Batista needed help repairing Cuba's reputation. He asked Meyer Lansky to help him clean up the Cuban gambling business and put Lansky on his payroll as a consultant to the government. Lansky's advice to Batista was similar to what Owney and the PBA were trying to do in Hot Springs: limit the number of casinos by granting licenses, and hold the casinos to a high ethical standard with regard to cheating and rigging the odds. For his services, Lansky collected far more than a government salary. He made sure that bags full of money from each and every gambling club in Havana made it onto a plane each night to Miami, which he distributed to his partners who chose to go in with him on his investment in the island paradise. Some of the money went to Santo Trafficante in Tampa. Some went to Carlos Marcello in New Orleans. Some went to Frank Costello in New York. Some even went to Owney Madden in Arkansas. The government in Cuba didn't care. Lansky could do as he wished. He was more than just a consultant. Lansky was the island's boss gambler.

The delegation from Hot Springs went to Cuba to observe how Lansky was running things. Lansky brought in dealers from the United States—people who had experience running games for him in syndicate clubs in places like New York, Cicero, Palm Springs, and Dallas—to train Cubans as dealers and pit bosses. His men were professional, trustworthy, and smart. They understood the games they dealt, could calculate odds and payouts on the fly, and knew the intricacies of the rules. And they helped Lansky train Cubans to do the same.

Lansky put his Cuban pit bosses up on towers, chairs that were high above the crowd like lifeguard stands, from which they could watch all the action like hawks. More important, however, the players could see them. Their conspicuousness not only deterred cheaters, it made players feel safer. He made the dealers deal out of wooden shoes rather than hold the decks in their hands, which made it harder for card mechanics to second-deal and harder for honest dealers to make mistakes. Lansky also called up the high rollers he knew in the States and invited them to Havana. He offered them everything "on the arm"—compliments of the house—so long as they gave him action at the tables. Eventually the word was out—the bust-out joints were gone. Lansky had transformed the island into a first-rate international tourist destination, and he had a piece of all of the action. He stood to make a killing, and he thought the rest of the national syndicate would be wise to follow his lead and invest in Cuba. Owney and Dane were likely inspired by Lansky's vision for the country, and recognized a similar potential for transformation in Arkansas.

Still, most gangsters remained fixated on the potential of Las Vegas. There, the mobster Moe Sedway had transformed the struggling Flamingo from a playground for the wealthy into a place where anyone could afford to feel wealthy. There were bingo games and cash drawings, as well as a cheap buffet. The appeal to the proletariat worked, and Americans eager for some leisure time in the years after the war started showing up. The new resorts on the Vegas Strip were similar to the rehabilitated Flamingo. They didn't have the same feel as the elegant and intimate nightclubs Lansky was running in Havana, or even the old-school clubs of Hot Springs. And many of the casinos in downtown Las Vegas still had spittoons by the craps tables, and sawdust on the floors in case somebody missed.

Besides, there was no traditional bank in America willing to hand over millions of dollars to these cowboys and ex-cons trying to build casinos in Nevada. To Owney, that hesitancy made sense—why build a resort in the middle of a desert? And not just any desert, the very same desert where they tested the atomic bombs. That's how far away Las Vegas was from anything that mattered. While Lansky hedged his bets by investing in Las Vegas, Owney saw no reason to when he was so close to getting wide-open gambling back to Hot Springs. Though Las Vegas was experiencing a population boom, there were still more people living in Hot Springs than in Las Vegas, and Hot Springs was growing with each passing year. Besides, Vegas had not adjusted well to its sudden growth. There wasn't enough housing for everyone moving there, with many people living in daily-rental auto courts. The streets were in bad shape and the sewers didn't work. There were no playgrounds or parks, no public pools, and the water, power, and phone lines were unreliable. Hot Springs had been a resort for nearly a century, and was surrounded by lakes and mountains. Surely Arkansas had more in common with Havana than Las Vegas. Surely nobody would ever drop an atomic bomb on Hot Springs.

Owney

"We've had our eye on Hot Springs for a good long time now."

Television sets across Hot Springs were tuned in to a shot of nothing but a pair of hands clutching a handkerchief, sometimes a piece of paper, or sometimes just rubbing palm to palm. They were the hands of Frank Costello as he testified before the U.S. Senate Special Committee to Investigate Crime in Interstate Commerce. The committee, led by Tennessee senator Estes Kefauver, had been touring the country, making stops in cities like Miami, New Orleans, Kansas City, Las Vegas, and Chicago, issuing subpoenas and interrogating anyone even remotely connected to the mob. Now the committee was in New York City, and they had reeled in Frank Costello as their big fish. Kefauver called Costello the "Boss of Bosses," and claimed Costello was in charge of illegal gambling throughout America.

At Curley Humphreys's suggestion, most of the syndicate witnesses subpoenaed by the committee pleaded the Fifth and refused to answer any questions. In New Orleans, Carlos Marcello pleaded the Fifth 152 times. Frank Costello saw his compatriots refusing to answer and getting raked over the coals for it. To his mind, he was damned if he did, damned if he didn't, so he decided he wouldn't take Humphreys's advice. Costello decided to go toe-to-toe with the country senator and answer his questions. Costello's only condition, strangely, was that they not show his face on television. So the cameras stayed trained on his fidgeting hands instead.

The gambling combination in Hot Springs had a lot of reasons to be worried about Costello's appearance. Almost everyone else who had come before the committee had been asked at some point or another about Hot Springs. It was clear from the committee's line of questioning that they were probing for details of syndicate involvement in Arkansas. *Have you ever been to Hot Springs? Who did you meet with in Hot Springs? Who were you visiting in the Arlington Hotel? Who owns the Southern Club? Who owns the Belvedere? Who controls the race wire?* So far, all the witnesses had given the committee was "I decline to answer the question on the grounds that my answer may incriminate me." Costello was sure to be asked about Hot Springs, and he wasn't going to plead the Fifth. What would he tell them? The camera may not have been on his face, but everybody would hear his answers clear as day. Those in Hot Springs, gathered around their television sets, braced themselves.

Was he partners in the Beverly Country Club with Carlos Marcello?

"I was just a goodwill man for them. And I would recommend different acts for the club."

"What acts did you recommend?"

"Well, Joe Louis, Sophie Tucker, and a lot of big acts."

"And for that you got eighteen thousand dollars a year?"

"That's right."

What about the fifteen thousand dollars a year he made from a Long Island racetrack? What did he do to earn that money?

"Practically nothing," Costello replied.

Had he visited Hot Springs? Of course he had, he answered. Many times, to take the baths and vacation. Next question.

Did he meet with the sheriff of Orleans Parish in Hot Springs? Did he meet with the California lobbyist Artie Samish in Hot Springs? Longy Zwillman? Nig Rosen? Joe Massei? Tony Accardo? The committee members rattled off the names of prominent syndicate members and corrupt political figures and law enforcement officers on the take, one by one. For Owney or anyone else in Hot Springs watching, it was shocking. The committee seemed to know every criminal who had ever set foot in the spa. Eventually, Costello had answered all the questions he could stand.

"All due respect to the Senate," Costello said as he interrupted one of Senator Kefauver's questions. "I'm not going to answer another question, because I'm not under arrest and I'm going to walk out."

Kefauver warned Costello that he was under subpoena and if he left without being dismissed he'd be charged with contempt.

"Are you refusing to testify?" Kefauver asked.

"Absolutely." And with that Costello got up and walked out.

The gambling combination in Hot Springs was stunned. How long would it be, they wondered, before Kefauver brought his committee to Hot Springs? Several weeks before Costello's appearance before the committee, Kefauver had sent a special investigator named Vivian Lynn to Hot Springs to tail Costello during one of his visits. Thin, with blue eyes, curly hair under a pillbox hat and veil, and a pair of high heels, Lynn cut a striking profile. She had Frank Costello and every other hood in Hot Springs eating out of her palm before they realized what she was up to. It also didn't help that in April 1950, a cabdriver in Kansas City had found the body of Charles "Mad Dog" Gargotta shot to pieces in the local Democratic Club. Mad Dog was a gambling boss in Kansas City, a murderer, and an enforcer for the mob. But he had turned informant, and was cooperating with the government's investigation of the national gambling rackets. The gambling combination would surely wonder what all Gargotta had told the government, given that he was on the payroll at the Southern Club in Hot Springs.

OWNEY HADN'T BEEN CALLED as a witness, but his name was brought up time and again with one witness after the next. *Did you call Owney Madden? Did you see Owney Madden in Hot Springs? What did you talk to him about?* The whole spectacle had the potential to reverse whatever progress Owney was making in Hot Springs. He needed to figure out a way to prevent the hearings from coming to Hot Springs, and to remind the town that, despite Kefauver's comments, taxing crime and immorality was essential to the future prosperity of their city.

Owney went from one club in Hot Springs to the next, to casino owners and gamblers present and past, and collected enough markers and records to compile an entire dossier on Senator Estes Kefauver of Tennessee. As it turned out, Kefauver had lived in Hot Springs in the twenties. He taught math and coached football at Hot Springs High School before enrolling at Yale Law School in 1927. During this time, Kefauver was a regular at the racetrack and the dice tables. His debts, in fact, were considerable.

Lansky met with Kefauver and shared the files with him. Kefauver had plans to run for president, hence the high-profile investigation. Information like this would surely be embarrassing to the senator and throw cold water on his hopes for higher office.

"What's so bad about gambling? You like it yourself. I know you've gambled a lot," Lansky said to Kefauver during their meeting.

"That's right, but I don't want you people to control it," Kefauver replied, enraging Lansky.

Despite Kefauver's posturing, the pressure seemed to work. Prior to his meeting with Lansky, Kefauver had called Hot Springs, Arkansas, the second most important gathering spot for the American criminal underworld and "men of Costello's reputation." "We've had our eye on Hot Springs for a good long time now," he had said. After meeting with Lansky, however, Kefauver announced that "we don't have time to go to Hot Springs." The committee never subpoenaed Owney Madden or any other Hot Springs gamblers.

ONCE HE COULD BREATHE easy, Owney focused his attention on fixing the factional dispute that threatened his efforts to reopen his clubs. In February 1951, a delegation from the PBA had convinced Governor McMath that gambling was crucial to the economic well-being of Hot Springs. He agreed not to send in the state police, telling them, "Gambling is your problem over there . . . until it becomes a statewide problem." That was the green light they wanted, but they had yet to determine who would be permitted to operate.

Owney and his partners summoned Frank Costello to Hot Springs to sort it all out. They reserved three suites at the Jack Tar Hotel, and for three days Costello held court, hearing from every club owner and working stiff in town. He met with the mayor, the aldermen, casino and restaurant owners, cabdrivers, and anyone else who wanted to bend his ear. Frank Costello was one of the most important figures in the American criminal underworld. His gambling empire was worth hundreds of millions of dollars, including considerable investments in Hot Springs. He was in town only to give counsel, and as the "Boss of Bosses" his counsel carried a lot of weight. After hearing everyone make their case, including pleas for him to take over as the new boss gambler of Hot Springs himself, he returned to New York to think it all over before making any commitments or recommendations to Owney.

As soon as Costello made it back to New York, rumors started flying that Costello planned to lam it to Hot Springs to duck his contempt charges from walking out on the Kefauver Committee. A reporter at the *New York Sun* called the *Arkansas Democrat* in Little Rock asking if they could confirm the rumors that Hot Springs was planning to make Costello the new boss gambler. The *Democrat* ran a front-page story with the headline "Costello as Spa Gambling Czar Rumored."

Letters to the editors of newspapers across Arkansas poured in. The public was incensed that this man whose fidgeting hands had captivated the country on national television, this kingpin of violence and vice, could become a resident of their state, and a powerful one at that. It was exactly the kind of publicity that Hot Springs could ill afford. "I can't believe that Costello has any such plans," Governor McMath responded in the *Arkansas Gazette*. "However if he does entertain any such ideas he had best forget them because the people of Arkansas will not tolerate the establishment of an underworld stronghold in this state."

Frank Costello airmailed a letter to the *Sentinel Record* in Hot Springs. They ran it on the front page. It read, in part, "I never had the remotest idea of engaging in or being connected with the gambling business in Hot Springs or any other place in Arkansas—directly or indirectly. For over twenty five years I have been a regular visitor of Hot Springs. Like countless thousands of others, I have found immense enjoyment and pleasure in its wonderful climate, its incomparable mineral baths, and its hospitable people."

DURING ONE OF HIS return visits, Owney invited Frank Costello over to his and Agnes's house to discuss the situation. Owney and Agnes were living on West Grand Avenue in the old Demby family home. It was modest, worth about thirty thousand dollars—a decent sum, but far less than the three hundred thousand dollars in cash Owney kept stashed in his safe. Save for the wooden Chris-Craft ski boat the actor George Raft bought him to tool around Lake Hamilton, Owney wasn't much for showing off. Naturally, Agnes made Frank spaghetti and meatballs.

When Agnes and the maid brought the spaghetti out to serve Frank Costello and Owney, Costello took one bite and remarked, "Hey, what say we all eat out tonight?" Agnes did not hesitate. She picked up the bowl and dumped it right on Costello's head. There was no safe haven for Frank Costello in Hot Springs anymore. Not even in Owney Madden's own kitchen.

Hazel

"Forever held for naught."

Comes the plaintiff Hazel Hill for her cause of action against
the defendant, Hollis Hill, states and alleges:

That he was guilty of such indignities as to render her condition in life intolerable in that he treated her with rudeness,
contempt, unmerited reproach, and studied neglect, habitu-
ally and systematically pursued until it finally became impossible for her to live with him; that defendant has remained in
an advanced state of inebriation for more than one year prior
to the filing of this cause.

Wherefore plaintiff prays that the bonds of matrimony existing between herself and the defendant be canceled, set aside, and
forever held for naught; and that the parties hereto be restored to
all the rights and privileges of single and unmarried persons.

Serving divorce papers wasn't the kind of work Leonard Ellis thought
he'd be doing when he ran for sheriff. He wanted to bust up burglars,

not marriages. Leonard Ellis served Hollis at the cab stand where Hollis had found work driving a taxi, somehow managing to stay sober enough to steer straight and not run anyone over. Hollis had been making an effort since Hazel threw him out—if only he could dry out, put a few dollars together, and show up on her doorstep in a pressed shirt and a straight necktie with some fresh flowers and an invitation to go dancing at the Pines Supper Club, perhaps he could win her back. But now, with this piece of paper in hand, he realized that it was too late.

It had been sixteen years since Hazel's father left her in Hot Springs with Hollis Hill. She was now twice the age she was then, and had lived as long as a married woman as she had with her parents. Every once in a while Clyde Welch would come through Hot Springs with a horse he was training, but he and Hazel were never really close again. But she was now on her own, with nowhere else to turn. And so Hazel took the boys on the train, telling them, "We're going to live with Grandpa and Grandma."

ASHLAND, OHIO, HAD AROUND fourteen thousand residents in 1951, which made it about half the size of Hot Springs. But while Hot Springs hosted hundreds of thousands of visitors each year, nobody ever vacationed in Ashland. The town's biggest draw was the rubber factory, which was where most folks found work.

Clyde and Edna Welch were back together and living in a trailer on the outskirts of Ashland with Lyle, Hazel's oldest brother. Lyle was in his thirties by then, but he had been left developmentally disabled after being kicked in the head by a horse when he was nine years old. All the doctors did was rub some smelling salts under his nose, look at his pupils, and tell Clyde and Edna to put some ice on the welt. Lyle was never the same after that. Now Lyle was a grown man and every day he'd get up and fill a bucket full of water, walk to town, and wash every car he saw until suppertime.

Hazel's other two brothers, Russel and Clarence, had each married and moved in with their wives. They were horse trainers just like Clyde, but they were a mite better at it. Clyde blamed his bad luck at the race-track on his bum foot. Diabetes had caused foot ulcers, and rather than go to a doctor, Clyde just soaked the afflicted foot in lemon juice each night. Only after it got infected and he could hardly walk did he finally get help. The doctor told Clyde he needed to amputate his toes before the infection spread. So Clyde let the doctor cut his toes off, and each night he'd rub lemon juice all over his foot where his toes used to be. The stench would fill the small trailer and torture Hazel's boys. "You stinky old cripple!" they'd taunt him. "Get that rotten stump out of here before you kill us all with that smell!"

Edna would suffer no such talk from the boys. She allowed no loud talking, no running, no horseplay, no climbing on the furniture. She preferred that the children stay out of sight. This was easy for the boys, as there was a swimming pool in the trailer court to keep them busy all summer. But sleeping arrangements were still a problem. The trailer was barely big enough for Edna, Clyde, and Lyle, let alone Hazel and her brood. Hollis Jr. slept on a sofa, and Larry and Jimmy slept on the floor with Hazel. It was not comfortable, but it was, in some sense, normalcy.

It was an idyllic summer despite the cramped conditions. The boys ran wild in the trailer court, splashing and diving in the pool, chasing lizards and kicking cans with the neighborhood kids. There was little to eat, though Clyde would often make potato soup that, to the boys anyway, tasted like something from the finest restaurant. For years, Hazel and the Hill boys had been getting by on nothing more than bread, baloney, and water. Some weeks there wasn't even baloney, and Hazel would mix the bread with sugar and water to fill the boys' bellies.

ONE EVENING LATE IN the summer Clyde came home mad as piss, slamming doors and stomping around the trailer.

"They want to cut my goddamn legs off!"

The image of Clyde Welch's legs being cut off caused Jimmy and Larry to sit straight up. Edna came in from the back room as well.

"Is there any other way?" Hazel asked.

"Well, hell, yes. I can get out of here and go to Tijuana and see a Mexican doctor."

"You just want to go to Tijuana to the races," Edna said. "You don't know no Mexican doctor."

"All I know is I ain't stayin' here to let them cut my damn legs off."

Later that night, after they had finished their potato soup and the boys drifted off to sleep, Hazel and Clyde retired to the patio outside to smoke a cigarette. It was a breezy summer night. Despite the fact that Clyde had abandoned Hazel in Hot Springs so many years before, she still felt something of a bond. She offered to follow him west, to take care of him. He wouldn't hear of it. She had three boys to take care of. She didn't need to worry about her old crippled daddy. He told her to go back to Hot Springs. An old horseman like him could make money only one way, but a young woman like Hazel, someone with a hustler's heart, would have more opportunities in Hot Springs than almost anywhere else in the world.

Hazel had practically forgotten the thrill she first felt when she had been left in Hot Springs sixteen years earlier. The bright lights, the nightlife, the steady flow of visitors from all over the world, and most important, the money. Only a rube could be broke in that town, what with so many rich people intending to practically give their money away, whether to the racetrack or the card table, the barmaid or the auctioneer. Maybe Hazel just needed to hear someone else say it. She was going to go back to Arkansas.

"And you'll come visit?" she asked her father.

"If they don't kill me in Mexico, I'll be there when the races start."

Hazel took her father's advice. She packed up her boys and boarded a train back to Hot Springs, resolved to make the most of what that place had on offer. But her father never came back to visit, and never came back to Ashland, either. After Tijuana he settled in Southern California, started life anew, and never saw Hazel again.

HAZEL AND THE BOYS moved back to Hot Springs after their summer in Ohio. Compared to Ohio, it was a veritable playground for her sons. As a favorite destination for carnies in the off-season, Hot Springs had frequent carnivals for the local kids. Professional wrestlers came to town for exhibitions at the Boys Club. The local movie theaters showed cartoons and gave out prizes during the matinees. There were brand-new fast-food restaurants, the likes of which most Americans had never seen before, with machines that would deliver milkshakes at the press of a button. There were shooting galleries and arcades alongside the casinos and auction houses, giving children the opportunity to lose money just like their parents.

Hazel and the three boys moved into a little house, and she found a job as a barmaid at the Pensioner's Club, a small saloon on top of Mark's Pool Hall. The Pensioner's Club was among the upstart operations that had cropped up around Hot Springs during the last decade. In addition to serving cheap beer, a wire room in the back offered patrons an opportunity to bet on horses and sports.

Hazel was out until late at night, and in bed during most of the day. Her three sons were on the opposite schedule, going to school during the day and then looking after themselves in the evening. Hollis Jr. was now fifteen and able to watch over his two younger brothers. He played football, and his coaches saw promise in him. They kept him on the straight and narrow path by dangling the prospect of the varsity team, and Hollis got himself to school on time and stayed out of trouble to oblige them. His two younger brothers had no such incentives. They ditched school whenever they could and hid from the truancy officer sent to look for them by climbing up on the roof of their house, lying low and giggling under their breath.

Hazel was largely oblivious to what was going on with her sons. Work behind the bar paid decently, but not nearly enough. She had grown used to struggling to stretch every dollar, but those dollars she once stretched came from her husband's odd jobs. Now she had to do it all—the shopping, the cooking, and the cleaning, on top of earning a paycheck. Hazel was grateful for whatever her three sons could do to manage on their own.

HOLLIS HILL HEARD THAT Hazel was back in town. He was two months sober and driving a taxi, one of the better non-casino jobs in Hot Springs. He wanted to win Hazel back and reunite his family, and he worked hard to pull himself together. He was eager to show her that he was back to being his old self, and showed up on her doorstep in his Sunday shirt. Hazel was neither surprised nor happy to see him. They exchanged a few undramatic words, but it was clear to Hollis that Hazel didn't want him. Even sober, he was treated as a drunk.

"You'll take me back, goddamnit!" he yelled. There it was. He lost his temper. Everything that had transpired between Hazel and Hollis was encapsulated in that moment. It didn't matter if he was drunk or sober. He had wounded Hazel, and it was distance from Hollis that had healed her. Distance from his anger, which was clearly still a part of him, drunk or not. Hazel closed the door on him. He walked back to his cab and drove away.

Later that same night Hollis drove by Hazel's house to see if she had left for the Pensioner's Club. Confident that the house was empty, Hollis wiggled through the open window and into Hazel's darkened home, fumbling through the unfamiliar house until he found the boys' bedroom, where Jimmy and Larry lay in the same bed asleep. Larry awoke, startled.

"It's just Daddy," Hollis whispered. "Where's your mama?"

"I don't know," Larry said.

"You mind if I stay here tonight?"

"Naw."

"Go back to sleep, son."

Hollis unlaced his boots and climbed into bed between them. Larry felt himself drifting off, but he fought to stay awake as long as he could. Hollis, too, stayed awake, his wide-open eyes blinking in the darkness. Eventually Larry surrendered and fell asleep. When the sun came up the next morning to wake him, Hollis was gone. Larry wondered if he had dreamed it all.

Owney

The officers let each bookie know that they would keep getting raided and hauled in front of a judge week after week until the wire came back to Hot Springs.

While Hazel struggled to get back on her feet, Owney found himself embroiled in a fiasco of his own making. Five years earlier, he had thrown his weight behind Floyd "Babe" Huff, who wanted to become the new circuit court judge for Hot Springs. Huff had fallen out of favor with many of the GIs who took control of the city, as he was Leo McLaughlin's lawyer when Sid McMath had brought charges against the former mayor. But the GIs changed their minds once they realized that McMath was hell-bent on keeping gambling shut down. Owney went around and collected fifteen thousand dollars to get Babe Huff on the ballot for the 1950 special election, which he went on to win at the age of forty-seven.

It soon became evident that Huff had far more ambitious plans for himself. He began making it clear to anyone involved in the combination that he intended to become the new boss gambler. Huff was vocally opposed to anyone and anything that might threaten his grasp on power—including those who, like Frank Costello and Owney himself, were connected to the national syndicate. Owney had made a mistake, and he moved quickly to organize support behind Municipal Judge Lloyd Darnell to run against Babe in the next election. In doing so, Owney kicked off what would come to be known in Hot Springs as the Gambling Wars, and Babe Huff was ready for the fight.

According to reports in a local gossip rag called *The Hot Springs Rubdown*, Babe paid the Reverend A. R. Puckett, the minister of the influential AME Church in the city's Second Ward, twenty-five hundred dollars in exchange for his support. The Second Ward had time and time again been crucial to political power in Hot Springs. For many years McLaughlin took its support for granted. He bought up the ward's poll tax receipts and voted on its behalf. But since the GI Revolt in 1946 had curtailed some of the worst abuses of the poll tax system, the Second Ward was up for grabs.

African Americans were a formidable political force, not only because they made up nearly a third of the population, but also because the residents of the Second Ward were known to listen to civic and religious leaders in their community and often voted as a bloc. The Negro Civic League, for example, would pay the poll tax for its members and tell them how to vote, which was good for anywhere from three hundred to four hundred votes, more than enough to swing a close election in Hot Springs. Whether or not Huff had bought the support of Puckett, the *Hot Springs Rubdown* stories caused a minor scandal. Huff filed libel charges against the paper's publishers and demanded the grand jury hear them.

Perhaps Huff had overestimated the extent to which he was in the good graces of Hot Springs' sizable black community. He was notorious, after all, for more than just defending the disgraced Mayor McLaughlin. In 1913, when Babe was ten years old, he had found his eleven-year-old sister, Garland, in a closet beaten within an inch of her life. When the girl later died at the hospital, word spread across Hot

Springs that Will Norman, a young black man who had worked for the Huff family, was the one who killed the little girl, despite there being no witnesses to the crime. Lynchings were relatively uncommon in Hot Springs, and there hadn't been one recorded in seven years. But when a crowd of three thousand men turned up to scour the county to look for Norman, there was little doubt he wouldn't make it to a courtroom. When the mob found Norman, they beat him, stripped him, strung him up to an electrical pole, and shot his body full of bullets. They then cut him down, put his dead body on a pile of wood, and set him on fire. Both Babe and his father—also a judge—were there. Young Babe was given a Winchester so that he could join the crowd in shooting at the charred, lifeless body of Will Norman as it burned in Como Square in downtown Hot Springs. For many years, the Huff family would be regarded as martyrs and victims by the white residents of town, perhaps the only justification that could allow the city to live with the most violent lynching in its history.

In addition to buying the support of Reverend Puckett, Huff also issued warrants for raids on a number of clubs whose owners were rumored to support his opponent, including the Southern Club and the Pines Supper Club. More than twenty people arrested in those raids were hauled into Darnell's municipal court, where Darnell summarily dismissed all of their cases. The system as it stood, with the two courts and two judges on opposite sides, meant that neither could effectively stop the other, but each could make life hell for the other side.

In spite of Owney's decision to back Darnell, Babe Huff was reelected to the circuit court in 1954. Huff didn't immediately shut down the clubs that supported Darnell, as many assumed he would. He sent Marion Anderson around to let Darnell's supporters know that they now had to pay 20 percent of their profits to Huff every month. That extended to every bet placed in Hot Springs, from table games to slot machines in the barbecue joints to the bingo games at the American Legion. Not only that, but every club would be hiring someone Huff appointed to keep an eye on business for him. Owney was expected to do the same.

Owney talked it over with Papa Joe Poretto, and they decided they wouldn't abide Huff as boss gambler. A week later they shut down the wire, starving the city's bookmakers and bettors. Nine of the clubs that had supported Huff were visited by the authorities with a court order to remove their phone lines, including the White Front, Blue Ribbon, Pensioner's Club, and the Cameo Club on the east side. Darnell let them know that it was quid pro quo: "It is not right to pick on my friends and let Huff's operate." By shutting down his allies, Owney hoped the pressure would mount on Babe Huff to fold.

Within a month the town grew restless. The bookies and club owners were feeling the pinch. Owney's faction put the word out on the street that as long as Huff was judge, this was how it would be in Hot Springs—the lid would stay on tight.

Babe Huff recruited Dick Galatas, once an intimidating local figure who had been connected to some of the worst criminals in America. When bank robber Frank "Jelly" Nash was arrested in Hot Springs back in 1933, it was Galatas who put the plan together to bust him out of jail, a plan that involved "Pretty Boy" Floyd and a machine gun and ended up with Nash and four cops dead in a car in Kansas City. For his role in the "Kansas City Massacre," Galatas was sent to Alcatraz. When Galatas's sentence ended, he moved to California with his wife and found work as a salesman, trying to lead a life on the straight and narrow path. The straight life must not have suited him, because when Babe Huff asked him to come back to Hot Springs to work for him, Galatas didn't hesitate.

Huff dispatched Galatas down to New Orleans to negotiate directly with Papa Joe. Papa Joe refused to sit with him, but Galatas still knew a few shady characters down in the Big Easy from the old days who still owed him favors, and some of them were even in law enforcement.

Over the next two weeks, police raided every club, barroom, and bookie in New Orleans that paid for Papa Joe Poretto's wire service.

The officers let each bookie know that they would keep getting raided and hauled in front of a judge week after week until the wire came back to Hot Springs. Papa Joe's customers howled. They couldn't believe he'd put them all out of business over some political dispute in Arkansas. The gambit worked. Papa Joe threw in the towel and notified Owney that the wire was coming back on. Owney would need to work something out with Babe Huff.

Owney wasn't content to sit back and let Huff pick his pocket with the race wire. He approached one of his partners in the Southern Club, Jimmy Phillips, and offered him $140,000 to buy out his share in the club. Phillips agreed on the condition that he could continue to run the casino as manager. The sale gave Owney 75 percent ownership of the Southern. To protect his interest, Owney put his shares in Agnes's name. He also brought in a new partner—a rising star in the gambling community named Dane Harris.

BABE HUFF WASN'T THE only important winner in the 1954 election. A country lawyer named Orval Faubus was elected governor of Arkansas, with support from liquor magnate Harry Hastings. Hastings had built his empire, both criminal and legitimate, into a fortune that made him one of the wealthiest men in Arkansas, and Faubus and Hastings were close. They took vacations and hunting trips together. But Faubus's opponents had turned Hastings into a campaign issue, with many of the more pious citizens of the state expressing concern about a liquor boss having so much influence with the new governor.

Hastings was silent partners with Dane Harris, not only in Dane's family liquor business but in his gambling interests, which elevated Dane's standing in Hot Springs. When the gamblers organized to go to Little Rock to kiss the ring of the new governor and make sure they could continue to operate free of harassment from the state police, it was Dane who arranged the visit through Hastings. Now that Owney had brought Dane into the Southern, it was clear that Dane was no longer a bit player in the combination.

Dane had much more to offer Owney than his relationship with Hastings. Dane was methodical, logical, and unemotional. He made smart deals. He wasn't flamboyant or pushy. He didn't care about being a political boss like Leo McLaughlin or holding court on the casino floor in a silk top hat like Jack McJunkins. Dane saw himself as a businessman, plain and simple. He had his fingers in more than just gambling. His real estate projects were blossoming, and he was at the helm of a number of legitimate enterprises, including a service station, a drugstore, and a liquor store. He even joined the chamber of commerce. These qualities impressed Owney. He was plotting to become the top dog, and he intended to take Dane along with him.

Hazel

APRIL 1955

Buster didn't like wearing the suit. A dead man's suit is what he called it.

Josie was tired of Hollis. It was nice that he had come to visit, but he was back to drinking again and could become belligerent. One April day, things got so bad that she called their brother Bob to come and fetch him. By the time Bob got to Josie's house, Josie was really mad. Bob told Josie not to worry about it, that he'd sober Hollis up, and when he did, he'd make sure Hollis apologized for how he was acting toward her.

Bob had done this before. He put Hollis in the truck and just drove. That's how he did it—he just drove and drove until Hollis was all dried out. Bob didn't mind. He liked driving. They'd drive up over West Mountain, through the bright lights of downtown and Bathhouse Row, down Central Avenue, and clear out to Lake Hamilton and back.

Lately, though, it had grown harder to sober Hollis up this way. Hollis was hard up for money, and when that happened he'd opt for less costly means of making himself drunk. He would sometimes drink bay rum aftershave. One time Hollis drank turpentine. Drank it like it was nothing.

That day, Hollis passed out for a bit in the truck. He was just like a baby—the motion lulled him to sleep. When he finally woke up, he told Bob he felt better. It was Hazel's birthday, and Hollis wanted to go see her. Bob didn't think that was such a good idea and said so. Hollis got angry.

"Oh, hell. I'm not gonna do nothin'. I just want to tell her happy birthday. Let her know I was thinkin' about her."

That was enough to placate Bob, so he drove Hollis over to Hazel's house by the racetrack. Bob waited in the truck as Hollis strode up to the front door. When Hazel opened it she wasn't smiling. She looked past Hollis to Bob. She smiled at Bob and waved, probably relieved that Hollis wasn't alone.

Bob could see Hollis and Hazel talking. It was all okay at first, but soon Bob could hear Hollis's voice rising. Hazel was just shaking her head no. Then she closed the door. Hollis banged on it hard with both fists.

"I'll give you a birthday present you'll never forget!" he hollered into the shut door. Bob got out of the truck and went to get Hollis. He had to nearly pick him up off the ground to drag him back to the truck.

Bob figured Hollis wasn't really all that sober yet, so he decided to drive him around some more. They rode along in silence. Hollis rolled down the window. They drove past the country club, where a crowd was watching a big golf tournament. Hollis told Bob how he was supposed to caddy the tournament that day. In recent months, Hollis had started caddying on the golf course for extra money. It was a job for Negroes and children, he'd say derisively. Negroes and children and him. Hollis told Bob he gave up the chance to caddy so he could go see Hazel on her birthday.

"I'll give her a birthday present, all right," he repeated.

"Cut that out," Bob said.

They drove on down Highway 70, out past the airport, past rows and rows of airplanes of rich oilmen lined up on the runway to fly home after a weekend of gambling. They drove all the way to the bridge over the Ouachita River, right where it fed into Lake Hamilton. As they crossed over the bridge, Hollis blurted out, "Stop the car!" Bob pulled over on the other side of the bridge.

"What's the matter?" Bob asked.

"I want to go swimming."

"Are you crazy?" Bob asked. "It's too damn cold!"

"No, it ain't. It will be just fine." Hollis got out of the truck. He stood along the side of the bridge looking down at the lake.

"Remember when we was kids and we used to go swimming out here?"

There used to be a little bank on the side of the lake down by the bridge. When they were boys, they'd walk all the way out there from their house. In those days, back when the government first built the dam and created the lake, the water was so clear you could see all the way down to the bottom. Bob would swim in that water with his brothers and sisters, too afraid to join his siblings when they jumped from the bridge. Bob was twelve years younger than Hollis, and he would tread water down below and watch in awe as his brother spread his arms and leapt, fearless and beautiful.

Hollis dug around in the truck. "You got any trunks I can swim in?"

"I got some, yeah. But just one pair."

"That's okay," Hollis said. "We'll just take turns."

Bob and Hollis stood on the bridge looking at each other. Hollis was supposed to be his older brother. The one who taught Bob everything. But now it seemed like Hollis couldn't figure out how to do a damn thing right.

"You go in first," Hollis said. He handed Bob the swim trunks. Bob carried them down the embankment to the landing below the bridge where he could change into them without anyone seeing. He took off his clothes, slipped on the swim trunks, then dipped his foot into the water. It was cold.

He gave himself a running start and dove headfirst into the freezing water. He came up to the surface with a holler from the violent shock of the cold. He spun around and looked up at the bridge above, where Hollis sat on the guardrail looking down at him.

"Damn, it's cold!" Bob yelled up at Hollis. "I ain't stayin' in here, and I bet you won't neither!" Hollis said nothing. Bob laughed. "Hell with this," he said to himself, and swam for shore.

As Bob reached the bank he looked up once more at Hollis. Hollis was standing now, staring down at the lake. Bob swam under the bridge and climbed up out of the water. He took off his trunks and slid his pants back on, still wet and shivering. He was just lacing his shoes when he saw something hit the water out of the corner of his eye. *That son of a bitch*, Bob thought. Bob kept lacing up his shoes, shaking his head over the fact that his drunk fool brother would jump in the lake with all his clothes on.

After he finished dressing, he stood up on the bank to see where Hollis was. He didn't see him in the water. Maybe Hollis just threw something over the side to mess with him.

"Hollis!" Bob yelled. He climbed up the embankment to the highway to see if Hollis was still standing on the bridge. He wasn't there. Bob peered over the side of the bridge to see if he could see Hollis anywhere in the water. Nothing.

"Hollis!" he yelled again. He ran to a nearby house and banged on the door. An old man answered.

"My brother's out there in the lake but I can't see him. Can I borrow your boat?"

The old man must have seen the worry in Bob's face, because he wasted no time. He tugged Bob's arm to lead him toward the boat, then the two of them put it in the water. The old man handed Bob an oar and Bob rowed out to the middle of the lake, standing up in the boat, hollering *Hollis* over and over.

"Maybe you ought to go under the water and look for him," the old man called out to Bob.

"He's out here somewhere!" Bob yelled to the old man standing on the shore, unwilling to accept that Hollis was still beneath the water. "He's hiding behind these bushes or something."

RICHARD HAD A BURIAL policy on Hollis, which was fortunate, because Hollis didn't have a nickel to his name when he died. Ressie and Bob's wife, Verna, went to Hollis's apartment for clothes to bury him in. He didn't have a suit, didn't even own a necktie. Richard used some of the policy to buy Hollis a brand-new suit to be buried in. Ressie's husband, Buster, was about the same size as Hollis, so he had a suit fitted for himself that they could use. When the tailor remarked what a nice suit it was, Buster told the tailor what the suit was for and the tailor said it was a shame that such a fine suit would be worn only once. Then the tailor reconsidered, and said that it wasn't true he'd only wear it once, but would wear it for all of eternity, and what a blessing that would be.

Buster didn't like wearing the suit. A dead man's suit is what he called it.

"PEOPLE GET SICK AND die like they did when Lazarus died. Oh, yes, they do. People still get sick and die. Hell is still hot. Judgment is still gonna be real. Time hasn't changed that."

Hollis's funeral was held at Brother Shields's church on Albert Pike. Hollis's father might have built Brother Shields's church, but Brother Shields didn't know much of Hollis, so he spoke little of him. He mostly stuck to his usual script, the Pentecost and false preachers and the like. The friends and family who had gathered there didn't mind. Given the turn Hollis's life had taken at the end, they may have even preferred it.

"When you worship God with all of your heart, that Holy Ghost is gonna come in, just like it did in the Upper Room, just like it did in the nineteenth chapter of the book of Acts, just like it did in the tenth chapter

of the book of Acts. Everywhere they got it they spoke in tongues. And when you get it, it will make a change in you! It will turn you around!"

Amen!

"It will clean you out!"

After Bob couldn't find Hollis in Lake Hamilton, he called Edward, who brought the sheriff. They combed the lake until they found Hollis's body in fifteen feet of water not far from the shore. Edward went to tell Hazel about it, and when he did, she actually cried. Hazel may have been the only person alive who knew all of Hollis. She knew the man he had become, the one who was lost and sick and violent and cruel. She also knew the man he once was, the good one who loved her and loved his children, the one who was once young and filled with enthusiasm for his future with her. Hazel was with Hollis before he "took drunk," and though she had no choice but to leave him, she still felt some measure of guilt now that he was dead. At the funeral she confessed this to Ressie. She said that she and Hollis had fallen in with the wrong crowd, that pharmacist and his wife, whom Hazel had so idolized, and now look where they both were—she without a pot to piss in, and he dead and fixing to be buried.

Edward took Larry and Jimmy with him to Richard and Bessie Mae's house to stay until the funeral, or until Hazel was ready for them to come back home. Hollis Jr., who was now in high school, stayed with friends. Edward went to get some nice clothes for the boys to wear to the funeral, but he discovered that just like Hollis, they didn't have anything suitable. They barely had clothes for school. So Edward told Hazel he'd take the boys to buy something to wear to the funeral, but he went ahead and bought them some extra clothes for class, too.

"This here is one of the most changin' times we've ever lived in. You can see it! You can feel it in the air! Hallelujah! One of these days he's gonna step out on that ground and we're gonna ride to meet him and those that haven't accepted the blood and have denied the truth and wouldn't accept it, they're going into that old false church in that time of great tribulation, when the wrath is poured out of God without mercy.

But while all that wrath is being poured out down here, there's gonna be a group up there in that Holy City. Friends, we are goin' someplace."

Hallelujah!

Jimmy was only nine years old, and he didn't really grasp what all was happening. He and Larry never really knew much of Hollis. For most of the years they were old enough to know him, Hollis wasn't around, and if he ever was, he was drunk or mean or both. It was hard for Jimmy to wrap his young mind around all the fuss people were making over Hollis at the funeral. But he came away from it with a feeling that Hollis was important to him, the way everyone kept telling him how sorry they were Jimmy had lost his daddy. Lost this man he never even knew he had.

"There's not gonna be any sin in heaven. It's easy to get rid of sin. All you gotta do is repent of it. Just throw up your hands and say, 'God, I'm sorry I ever sinned.'"

God, I'm sorry!

"I'm sorry I transgressed. Forgive me, God.' And get baptized in his name. Come up out of that water and just get filled up with that Holy Ghost. Just like they did in them early days. He's the same, he hasn't changed. The plan hasn't changed. And he's gonna come back one of these days in that same body that he took with him to heaven."

They buried Hollis out at Rockport, near Malvern, where the rest of Richard Hill's family was buried. The Hills had been burying their folks in that cemetery since the Civil War. Richard had a plot out there, but he hadn't expected he'd need to bury his own child in it. It wasn't unusual in his day to lose a baby to sickness or other complications, but this was different, his forty-year-old son taking his own life. When the newspaper inquired, the family told them he drowned while he was swimming. That became the official story. Hollis Hill could swim from one end of Lake Hamilton to the other and back again, but he drowned treading water.

"Now here's where a lot of people make a mistake. They say, well, we're just gonna be a mist, a ghost floatin' around up there. You know,

just a vapor. Like a vapor. But you know what? You're gonna have a body just like his body when you come up out of the grave. He said that! . . . Don't ask me how it's gonna happen. I don't know. I can't explain it. I can't explain how a black cow gives white milk and eats green grass and makes yellow butter, but she does. I can't explain a lot of things, but I believe it. I don't know how he's gonna do it. Somebody who goes out on that hillside in an old fruit jar or a fancy urn with flowers on the side, I don't want to go up from ashes, I want to go up from here just like this. They're gonna come out of the old tombs, they're gonna come out of those ashes sitting on a shelf somewhere. One day that old boy will be cuttin' the grass outside that mausoleum and then Pop! He's gonna come walkin' out of there with a body. You're all gonna go somewhere. You gotta pick your destination."

An organ started playing at the church where Brother Shields delivered his sermon. Hollis's funeral was held on a Sunday, perhaps to make sure people showed up. In the mainline southern Protestant congregations, funerals were somber affairs. The Pentecostals were more expressive. Their funerals weren't much different from a regular service, with music and swaying and dancing and laying hands and speaking in tongues. Hollis wasn't Pentecostal, but this was Brother Shields's church, and these were his congregants, and so the music started and the folks swayed and clapped and danced in the aisles, same as ever.

The family had told Hazel that she didn't have to come if she didn't feel like it, and nobody expected her to or would have blamed her if she hadn't. They were genuinely surprised when she showed up in her black dress. Nobody knew who had brought her, or if she showed up alone. She just appeared at the church and stood with the rest of the family and cried. She hugged Bessie Mae and Hollis's brothers and sisters and she said she was so sorry to Richard. When she hugged Ressie, she whispered in her ear, "He told me he'd do this. He told me and I didn't believe him."

"I like to get down and pray and pray and all of a sudden that Holy

Ghost takes over. It starts talkin'. Oh, friends, it is an experience. It will give you a greater love. It will give you a greater faithfulness. It will get you ready. And when the trumpet of God sounds, it will make you come out of that ground and meet him in the air."

There were four widows in Brother Shields's congregation. Every Sunday, Bessie Mae would bring them each buttermilk or sweet milk or eggs from her chickens. She brought five buttermilks to her son's funeral, one for each of the four widows and one for Hazel Hill.

And Brother Shields—he had two young twin girls. They were pretty and blond and they had beautiful singing voices. Often during his sermons, when the organ got to cranking and the faithful were worked up into a frenzy with their babbling, Brother Shields would hand it off to his twin girls to start the hymn. Their voices were arresting. Believers, sinners, heathens all—the short hairs would stand up on everyone's neck when those two girls would sing.

Reach out and touch the Lord as He goes by . . .

Dane

JUNE 1956

From here on out, he'd have to deal with Dane Harris, package liquor impresario, slot machine king, and proprietor of the Tower Club.

Early one June morning in 1956, well before the sun had risen and before the streets filled up with tourists, S. V. Shingle heard a loud noise. It was four fifteen, and Shingle, who was a fireman on the railroad, was up getting dressed for work. He couldn't be sure, but he thought it might have been a gunshot. He hurried to tie the laces on his boots so he could go investigate. When he got outside he saw a man facedown on the pavement. Shingle could be sure the man was dead and not just some drunk passed out on the street, because there was a hole in the side of his head and blood and brains all over the sidewalk beneath him.

The dead man's name was Elmer Tackett, and he was the state representative for Garland County. Before Tackett was elected to the statehouse, he had served as the U.S. commissioner of the federal court and had been responsible for putting a number of violent criminals away in jail. Plenty of people had reasons to kill him, but the timing of his death raised eyebrows. Tackett had recently announced that he wouldn't run for reelection as a state representative. Instead, he was running unopposed for the position of prosecuting attorney. The last prosecutor, Hiram A. Tucker, had died unexpectedly of a heart attack a few weeks after his election. Tackett, who was the president of the Garland County Bar Association and an opponent of wide-open gambling, had stepped up to run for the vacant seat.

Police Chief John Ermey ruled Tackett's death a suicide, but locals didn't buy it. If Elmer was so despondent he was willing to shoot himself in the head on a strange street in the middle of the night, then why had he entered the race for prosecuting attorney only weeks before? It didn't seem right that he would leave behind his wife and his five-year-old son, Shelley, whom he adored. Rumors were flying that Tackett was murdered by gamblers.

Owney saw an opportunity in the special election. While Babe Huff held sway over the circuit court, the prosecuting attorney had the power to decide who would be charged. At the very least, the special election could be a proxy battle that could point the way toward eventually defeating Babe Huff. Owney and Q. Byrum Hurst organized behind the scenes to collect money for a campaign. They recruited Walter Hebert, a lawyer who had once been a part of the McLaughlin machine but had been run out of politics by the GI Revolt a decade before.

Hebert won the election, and within weeks he closed down every casino and handbook in Hot Springs. He wasn't opposed to gambling, but he was trying to exert as much leverage as he could on Huff. Huff had become the boss gambler, and in addition to forcing gambling operators to pay him 20 percent of their profits, he had also been keeping the Southern Club shuttered since his election in order to punish Owney.

Hebert's move to shut down the remaining clubs got Huff's attention, and the two sides negotiated a settlement. Owney would divest himself from the Southern for the good of the combination. He sold his and Dane's shares of the Southern Club, but he didn't plan on surrendering. "Huff is out-and-out crooked, but he isn't going to control me,"

Owney remarked one afternoon while kvetching with one of the FBI agents assigned to investigate him. "I feel like going out and shooting him, but he just isn't worth spending time in jail for." Owney wasn't just putting on a display of pacifism for the FBI agent. He had a better plan than killing Babe Huff. The key to beating Huff would be slot machines.

CONGRESS HAD RECENTLY PASSED the Transportation of Gambling Devices Act, which made it a federal offense to ship slot machines and gaming tables across state lines. This meant that whatever slot machines and tables were currently in Arkansas would have to suffice. They had become a nonrenewable resource, which made them worth a lot of money. Whoever controlled access to the gambling equipment would wield just as much, if not more, power than the circuit judge.

Jack McJunkins was more than just a foil for Leo McLaughlin. He had also been a front for Frank Costello's operation, using Costello's money to buy pieces of clubs around town. McJunkins was also partners with Owney in controlling many of the slot machines in Hot Springs, machines that were likely purchased from or owned by Costello, who dominated the slot machine business in neighboring Louisiana. But in January 1957, McJunkins died after a long illness. His slot machines, as well as his ownership of the Tower Club, a modest casino and nightclub on the outskirts of town, needed to be passed on to someone. Owney knew that if he took control of McJunkins's interests, it would invite more of Babe Huff's ire. But if Dane took over the Tower Club and the slot machines, adding these assets to his liquor empire, he would hold more power than Owney had ever held with the wire service or Huff had held as circuit judge. Owney would stay out of gambling in order to let Babe Huff save face, but Huff would soon understand that he couldn't single-handedly extort the gambling establishments of Hot Springs anymore. From here on out, he'd have to deal with Dane

Harris, package liquor impresario, slot machine king, and proprietor of the Tower Club. Hot Springs would have a new boss gambler.

As Dane's business interests and profile grew, so too did his family. Dane and Marcella had another child, a son whom they named Dane Jr. To suit his larger family and his larger role, he moved them into a new home, one befitting someone of his stature. It was located in the center of Trivista Avenue, a circular drive near the racetrack that was home to some of the largest houses in Hot Springs. Trivista was where the town's professional class took root—doctors and lawyers and white-shoe Republicans. Dane's house wasn't a towering Victorian or a plantation home with tall white columns. It was a modern home, long and close to the ground, with a brand-new swimming pool and an ornate fountain on the patio. It was the focal point of the neighborhood, the first thing you would see as you turned on to Trivista. It had been modeled on a home in California, with beamed ceilings and murals painted on the walls. The Harris family purchased the home fully furnished, with each room boasting a different geographic theme—a desert in the sitting room, a jungle in the master bedroom. There were large padded sofas and art deco furnishings.

The house on Trivista had a servant's quarters, a room with its own entrance and bathroom that Dane thought would be perfect for his mother. But Marcella wouldn't have it. Tensions between the two women had grown. Dane and his mother remained close, and Dane still felt a responsibility to take care of her, a feeling he'd never shaken from his younger days. Marcella had grown up the child of strict and religious parents, and though she had strayed far from her life back in Glenwood, she still longed to be the matriarch of her own family. It was hard enough that she was losing Dane's attention to his new business partners. Having to compete every day with Dane's mother was simply too much. Marcella put her foot down, something she too seldom did with Dane in those days. She got her way. The servant's quarters remained empty—though Hattie often showed up at their house, pounding on the door at the crack of dawn, even on Christmas morning.

Though Marcella succeeded at keeping Hattie at arm's length, she was less successful with Dane's business partners. Her relationship with Dane was becoming strained. Early in their relationship, Marcella was a confidante, a coconspirator, a partner. As his profile and his portfolio grew, and many more people entered Dane's life, Marcella felt herself being pushed to the margins. In their new home, her role became clear—she was to entertain. They were socialites now, and she had to learn to act the part. The former country girl from Glenwood, Arkansas, had become a hostess to politicians and celebrities. The first year the Harris family lived in the Trivista house, when Marcella was tasked with planning a party to celebrate Dane's birthday, she roasted an entire pig, from snout to tail, and displayed it on the counter like a trophy. She dressed her children in fine clothing and kept her hair styled in the latest fashion. She received guests and played golf with her husband's partners' wives. At some point Marcella was no longer even on the margins of Dane's business. She was completely on the outside looking in.

Though his work often kept Dane from Marcella, he was cautious not to let it come between him and his children. He would drive Marcia to school in the mornings, singing songs to her along the way. He would play with her and Dane Jr., dragging them through their fancy new house atop a silver tray. He would teach them how the world worked, demonstrating for Marcia the speed of light in the middle of Trivista by shining a flashlight on a stop sign.

AT THE END OF that summer there was a big thunderstorm that blew in after a long, humid day. In Arkansas, the weather could be strange when it got muggy. There would sometimes be storms in which hardly any rain fell, the wind just whipping in every direction. It was almost peaceful, those storms, except they'd have that rolling thunder, rumbling for ten or twenty seconds at a clip.

Marcia woke up from the thunder and wandered into Dane and Marcella's room. Dane took the little girl's hand and led her down the long hallway, past her bedroom and to the front door. He took her outside to the front porch and pointed up at the sky.

"Do you know what causes lightning?" he asked her. She shook her head. Dane told her about the air in the sky rising and falling. He put one palm faceup and the other facedown and moved them up and down to demonstrate how when the two sides met, it caused friction. He met one palm to the other and rubbed his hands together rapidly. Marcia did the same. Their hands got warmer.

Dane explained how an electric charge builds up inside clouds from the friction. But Marcia didn't need to worry, because the lightning was very far away. If she wanted to know how far, all she had to do was start counting as soon as she saw a flash, and stop when she heard the thunder. "Every time you count to five," he explained, "that's a mile."

Dane held his daughter at his side and they waited for lightning to strike. In the distance, just over the mountain, they saw a flash. They counted together.

One.

Two.

Three.

Four.

Five.

Six . . .

Owney

"I believe the cheerful whistling of a true native son could be heard above the din of slot machines."

Frank Costello headed home to his Central Park West penthouse after dinner with friends. As he greeted his doorman in the lobby of the swank building, Vincent "the Chin" Gigante, a former prizefighter turned hit man, rushed in behind Costello and said "This is for you, Frank," as he fired a .38-caliber revolver. The bullet struck Costello in the head above his ear, wounding him but sparing his life.

When police searched Costello's pockets at the scene they found a note that read:

> Gross casino wins as of 4/27/57 $651,284
>
> Casino wins less markers $434,695
>
> Slot wins $62,844
>
> Markers $153,745
>
> Mike $150 a week, totaling $600; Jake $100 a week, totaling
> $400; L.-$30,000; H.-$9,000

Costello denied any knowledge of the slip of paper. He said he had no idea what it meant or how it got there. But investigators didn't have to do too much digging to figure out that the figures perfectly matched the receipts for the first month at the Tropicana Hotel in Las Vegas. The numbers were eye-popping, and it was enough to make Owney blind with jealousy. Here they were in Hot Springs, unsure if they would be open or closed from one day to the next, with a despotic judge who treated Owney like a dog in the street. The Tower Club's casino was bringing in about $150,000 a year in the late 1950s, and the slot machine business even less. Owney's friends were in Las Vegas making truckloads of money, toasting champagne and being celebrated by square businessmen and politicians, all because in Nevada gambling was a legitimate business. In Nevada, they didn't have to get the right person elected or pay off the right judge to operate. They simply made book and got paid. The other side of the coin, however, was that Frank Costello was dodging bullets in his lobby while Owney never needed to look over his shoulder or carry a gun.

COSTELLO WAS SHAKEN BY the close call and decided to retire. He reached out to his rival, Vito Genovese, the man who was likely behind the attack, to let him know he was bowing out. Costello was divesting from his criminal interests and retreating to his home in Staten Island with his family.

With Costello out of the picture, Vito Genovese became the top man in New York City. He sensed an opening to assert himself as the de facto leader of the national criminal underworld. Genovese called for a conference of the national syndicate in November of that year. He summoned nearly every important crime boss in the country to a small town right outside of Binghamton called Apalachin. With a population of roughly three hundred, the town was perhaps too small. When the nearby hotels started booking rooms for the hundred-plus guests coming to the meeting, it didn't take long for word to wind around the Apalachin grapevine and reach the police department. As the phalanx of brand-new Cadillacs paraded down the dead-end road to the country estate where the conference was to be held, the New York state police were waiting for them. The police closed the road behind them, sending the wealthy mob bosses running through the woods.

And so the U.S. Senate Select Committee on Improper Activities in the Labor or Management Field turned its attention from corruption in the Teamsters Union to the leadership of the national crime syndicate. The committee and the FBI were now working together to focus their investigation on the attendees of the Apalachin conference. Conspicuously absent from the doomed Apalachin meeting, however, were some of Frank Costello's closest allies—including Meyer Lansky and Owney Madden. Some gangsters speculated openly that Lansky and Owney were tipped off, that maybe they even dropped the dime on the meeting to put heat on Genovese. In any case, they wouldn't be targeted by the Senate investigation. It couldn't have hurt that the chairman of the committee was none other than Arkansas senator John McClellan, friend to Hot Springs gamblers and endorser of donation checks from Owney and Agnes Madden. Like the Kefauver hearings before them, the McClellan hearings would give the mob fits, but Lansky and Owney, with their Arkansas connections, would somehow get a free pass once again.

Genovese's rise also contributed to an unraveling in Las Vegas. After Frank Costello's note about the Tropicana skim was discovered in his pocket, the Nevada Gaming Control Board decided to deny the New Orleans gangster and former Hot Springs resident "Dandy Phil" Kastel a gaming license. Kastel sold his share of the Tropicana, divesting himself and the syndicate from it entirely. The board refused to issue gaming licenses to anyone with a history working in illegal gambling, which ruled out virtually everyone in America with any experience running a casino.

The other six multimillion-dollar resorts that had opened on the

Las Vegas Strip were all struggling to turn a profit in 1957. After a rollicking start, the customers in Las Vegas thinned out. A cover of *Life* magazine asked, "Las Vegas—Is the Boom Overextended?" Of the seven resorts that had opened in Las Vegas since 1955, none had retained their original owners, and two had shut down completely within a year. The grand experiment in the desert, it seemed, was not working out.

With the national syndicate in disarray and Las Vegas sputtering, the combination in Hot Springs was resolved to seize the opportunity. Q. Byrum Hurst tried to get the state legislature to pass a constitutional amendment to legalize gambling in Garland County. The measure failed by one vote. The close loss stung, and underscored how much Hot Springs was truly an island, surrounded on all sides by an unsympathetic sea of Bible-toting Baptists who detested Arkansas's sin city. "Many, many persons out over the state feel that Hot Springs and Garland County should have the fate of legalized gambling in their own hands," Hurst remarked after the vote. "Property valuations in Hot Springs alone would go up 10 percent with passage of a local option bill. Hot Springs, because of its health and recreational facilities, would become a Mecca overnight." Hot Springs was being held hostage. The combination couldn't legalize gambling as long as the rest of the state's voters opposed them. And as long as gambling remained illegal, the combination couldn't open up without paying Babe Huff whatever he wanted.

After the vote, a local resident named L. K. McClure wrote a letter to the editor of the *Arkansas Gazette*, which had historically opposed gambling in Hot Springs:

> Let's take a look at Reno, Nev. The city of 32,500 population reeks with prosperity as does the state of Nevada . . .
>
> Gambling ceases to be sin when the funds from gambling can build a beautiful city park or a new church . . .

With all the natural resources that Hot Springs has to offer, it could be made into a vacation spot for the world. Why let the dollars go west?

Amid new prosperity, I believe the cheerful whistling of a true native son could be heard above the din of slot machines.

Dane

It got so bad that the cheerleaders at the high school would be sent out on Fridays before football games to roust the players from the rooms so they'd make it to the games on time.

By January the Southern Club was back in action. The current owners, George and Jack Pakis, brought in new partners: Dino Soncini, the owner of a local haberdashery and a fellow prominent member of the Greek community, and a local bookmaker named Gene Stonecipher. They invested a considerable amount of money in the much-anticipated reopening of the Southern. They hired a staff of 110 people. They had lobster flown in to the club's restaurant from Maine every single day. In order to expand the two-story building to make room for more slot machines and dice tables, they had a section of the mountain that abutted the rear of the building carved out and excavated. Once the Southern was back open, the gamblers packed the house, though the vast majority of them preferred the Southern's new bingo parlor to the dice and blackjack games. Owney might not have been a partner in the Southern anymore, but he returned to his seat at his table out front, where he would sit every single day as if he still owned the place. And as far as most visitors to Hot Springs knew or cared, he did.

The next club to reopen was the Tower, now under the management of Dane Harris. Like the Southern, the Tower was reinvented as a more upscale version of its former self. It occupied a white stucco building near the city limits, next to the highway to Little Rock. It sat there all by itself, with a long, tall column on the roof above the front door with the word TOWER spelled out on it. Formerly, it had been something of a roadhouse. When Jack McJunkins inherited control of the Tower, he had tried to reinvent the club as a steak house. He added a fine dining room next to the casino, with white linen tablecloths and steaks trucked in from Kansas City. It was a nice touch, but when Dane took over, most folks said they didn't even realize the place served food at all. Everyone made a beeline for the dice tables when they came in the door.

Dane's innovation was to give people a reason to sit down and stay awhile. He hired a house orchestra, led by Wally Frazee, to play in the dining room, where Dane installed a dance floor. He brought in big-name entertainment to perform with his house band, from singers to comedians to an over-the-top floor show with costumed dancers. Dane was trying to re-create the atmosphere of the Cotton Club in New York or the Sans Souci in Havana there in Hot Springs, and it appeared to be working. Folks started coming to the Tower for dinner and dancing, and sometimes skipped the gambling entirely.

Other club owners thought Dane was off his rocker. Why would you want people to dance all night when they could be pumping money into slot machines? But Dane's Tower Club grew so popular, he had to add a second show every night. While one crowd watched the first show, the crowd waiting for the next one gambled. When the first show let out, the two crowds swapped places at the dice tables and slot machines.

Slot machines were another area where Dane had innovated. In order to get around the Transportation of Gambling Devices Act, he had devised a plan to move new machines from Chicago into Arkansas without being detected: he had the machines disassembled and shipped in different boxes, in different vehicles, at different times. Whenever the boxes were searched by police, they wouldn't identify the pieces and parts as gambling devices. Once the shipments all made their way to Hot Springs, Dane's people would reassemble the machines and put them in play. Little by little he grew his slot machine business into the biggest in town.

DANE AND OWNEY STARTED holding meetings in the back room of the Crawford Pharmacy with the rest of what had become the anti-Huff faction. This included men like Jimmy Phillips and his brother Norwood, who owned the Phillips Drive-In and Willow Room on Park Avenue. Jimmy had been the manager of the Southern Club's casino for thirty years before Huff forced him out for donating to Lloyd Darnell's campaign. They also counted among their allies the mayor, the sheriff, the state senator, the police chief, and the prosecuting attorney. The number of powerful people in that back room was evidence that Babe Huff had worn out his welcome behind the bench. The men who lined up behind Dane and Owney had individual economic interests in gambling, sure, but they also had a civic interest in ending the gambling wars and returning some sense of normalcy to Hot Springs. They missed the tourists from places like New York and Chicago and Paris, the municipal airport filled with private planes. But to keep those visitors coming back, they'd need to prove to the voters of Hot Springs that their side had the best interests of the city at heart.

For years, there had been a connection between gambling and prostitution in Hot Springs, one that sprang from the demands of customers. It was true that for a lot of tourists, the availability of women for hire was a draw, but the prostitution racket in Hot Springs had grown shameless. The top madam in Hot Springs was a tall, stout, and loud blonde named Maxine Gregory. She ran two brothels—one out of her home, which she and everyone in town referred to as "the Mansion," and another on the second story of a saloon on Central Avenue near Bathhouse Row. Maxine drove her women around Hot Springs propped up on the back seat of her pink Cadillac convertible. The women would hang from the windows of the brothel and call out to passersby on the street to come up and see them. And Maxine kept some troubling company. She was married to Worth Gregory, a smack addict and member of a crew of sociopathic tough guys who holed up in Hot Springs between pulling bank jobs around the South.

It would be one thing if Maxine just catered to tourists, but she did a lot of business with locals, which was causing some consternation among the more prim citizenry whose husbands or other family were caught calling on her place. It got so bad that the cheerleaders at the high school would be sent out on Fridays before football games to roust the players from the rooms so they'd make it to the games on time. If Dane could shut Maxine down once and for all, it would go a long way toward showing people that his faction was the one that was going to clean up Hot Springs.

Dane also saw a need to clean up the image inside of their own establishments. He set a dress code, and expected every club to follow his lead. "Persons who bring bottles are excluded," Dane said. "Likewise men must wear coats and ties. There is no room for riffraff in our places."

But if the gambling clubs of Hot Springs had tarnished their image over the last few years, it wasn't only because they let in too much riffraff. In some cases it was because the riffraff were running the casino. Bust-out joints had proliferated, and rumors of gaffed wheels and juiced tables were commonplace. It was one thing for a tourist to get taken by a con artist on the street. That had been part of life in Hot Springs for generations. But to get robbed by crooked dice and bottom-dealing croupiers while sitting at the table—that was unacceptable. If folks didn't think they could get a fair game in Hot Springs they'd stop coming. All it took was one holdout device or razzle-dazzle scam to get

Hot Springs back in the headlines. The city's leaders wanted attention, but not that kind. "We don't want undesirables in the operation of gambling establishments," Dane said.

The cheaters and con artists weren't the only undesirables Dane wanted to push out of the casino business. A growing number of outsiders had investments in Hot Springs, as silent partners with casino operators who had ties to the mob. Hot Springs had long had a more laissez-faire relationship with organized crime than most places, but as the national mood turned against the mob, public opinion in Arkansas was changing, too. Even Las Vegas was experiencing a local backlash as scandals involving organized crime proliferated. The gamblers of Hot Springs and their benefactors, including Governor Faubus, needed to paint a stark contrast between Hot Springs and Las Vegas in order to survive.

If they could do all of this, they'd stand a better chance of winning at the ballot box, and they would need to win from the top of the ticket on down. The men in the back room of Crawford Pharmacy would have to contribute to Governor Faubus. They would make their contributions in cash, and the money would be carried directly to the governor by Harry Hastings. They'd raise fifty to seventy-five grand, and they'd raise that amount every single year. Faubus would eventually use that money to construct himself an outlandish house on a hill, one that the governor's salary of ten thousand dollars a year could never have allowed him to afford. That money would buy the gambling combination assurances that the state police would stay away. But if Faubus lost his election to someone without an unfinished gaudy summer home, the gamblers of Hot Springs would have to start from scratch. So in an election year they'd have to put the political machine to work for the governor, as well as for Sheriff Leonard Ellis, who was being opposed by Clyde Wilson, one of Babe Huff's allies. Between the payoffs to Faubus, the sheriff's election, and a candidate to run against Huff in the following election, Dane put the figure his allies would need to come up with at a quarter of a million dollars. And he'd need the money in cash, and right away.

Owney's days of killing his enemies were long behind him, but it sure must have seemed cheaper than winning a fair election in Hot Springs. "You know, in my day, back in New York, how I'd have handled this . . ." Owney said to the gamblers. "No, no, no!" they quickly cut him off. These were a different breed of gambling bosses, unwilling to follow in the footsteps of the George McLaughlins and Dick Galatases who had come before them. Still, real violence was possible, whether it came from Huff, the mob, Vegas, or all three. If Dane and his allies pulled off their plan, they'd surely make some dangerous enemies. It wasn't clear what, if any, violence they would face, but they chose to be prepared. They muscled up. The Southern, for example, employed nine "heavy men," mainly off-duty police officers and other local head knockers. They watched the club, manned the door, tossed out unruly guests, and kept the peace. At the end of each day the heavy men drove the casino's cash to the bank in a three-car caravan, each of them armed with loaded shotguns.

Hazel

MAY 1958

He was a carny who ran the razzle-dazzle scam on the road for many years until the Pines let him open up his own chuck-a-luck game right on the casino floor.

There had been other men in Hazel's life since Hollis. And not just since he died, either. Working at the Pensioner's put her in the thick of it with all sorts of low-down, desperate men at the end of a long night, men who would make a forty-year-old mother of three working behind a bar feel like the prettiest woman in all of Arkansas if it meant they would not sleep alone. Hazel went home with some of them, and brought the married ones home with her. She was lonely. But she was also alone with three sons and struggling to make ends meet. She didn't mind a man's company, but she also longed for a man's help.

One Sunday morning after coming home from her all-night shift, Hazel was confronted on her front steps by her landlord, who told her he was putting her out. She had been renting a small house on Trivista Avenue, not far from where Dane lived. Hazel's house, however, was nothing like Dane's. It was a simple and squat brick building. Her landlord excoriated her for not keeping her lawn trimmed. She had asked her sons to do it, but she was rarely home to see that they did, and when she was home she was in no shape to cut it herself. The landlord had had enough of the unsightly lawn, and told her she would need to find somewhere else to live. Humiliated and exhausted, Hazel stormed into her house and rose her sons with a roar.

"Why didn't you mow the doggone grass!"

Larry sprang from his bed to his feet. Jimmy moved too slowly. Before he was fully awake, Hazel dragged him from the bed by his ear and had him down over her leg, whupping him with her hand, angry as she'd ever been.

Jimmy would have escaped, too, if only he hadn't been awake the whole night before. Sundays were reserved for sleeping in. As were Mondays, and usually Wednesdays and Fridays, too. Whenever Hazel worked all night, the boys stayed up. The neighbors would gossip about how they'd see the boys sitting out on the steps at all hours, even on school nights. The boys had their routine down cold, and knew how to roam the city alone and avoid the prying eyes of nosy adults, day or night. In fact, Jimmy had missed so much school that year, he was held back to repeat the fifth grade.

"Do you understand what you've done? We have to move! We're out in the street because you didn't mow that damn grass!"

Hazel called up Jack, a man she had met at the Pensioner's Club and had been seeing from time to time. It was Jack who was paying the rent on the little house on Trivista for her every month. She was going to need Jack to find them a new place to live.

Jack Cartwright wasn't the best-looking man Hazel had ever seen. He didn't need to be. He could charm the dew off a honeysuckle. He was forty-four years old, a little round in the middle, and had a full head of hair and a nice-looking square jawline. He had come to Hot Springs from Reno, Nevada, where his family owned a couple of farms. When Jack's father passed away, he left one of the farms to Jack, who sold it and set off on the road, traveling the country in search of ways to blow his father's fortune. Card games, dice games, racetracks, cockfights—wherever there was a man looking for a bet, Jack would find him and fade him. By the time Jack showed up in Hot Springs, his bankroll was running on fumes. But even those fumes were a fortune to Hazel. It wasn't his handsome jaw and his charming wit that first caught Hazel's eye. She'd seen plenty of that across her bar. It was when he'd pull a wad as big as his fist out of his pocket, and peel a hundred-dollar bill off to pay for his tab. That got her attention. She let Jack take her out the first night they met.

Jack liked to take Hazel to the Pines Supper Club, out in the country across from the Belvedere. The Pines was one of the few clubs that was permitted to open back up after the truce between Huff and Owney, and one of the few that wasn't controlled by Owney and Dane's faction. The Pines fancied itself a rival to the Belvedere, a swank supper club for the professional set, but few of the upper crust went there. Instead it functioned more as a place for working stiffs like Hazel and Jack to gussy up and enjoy a nice night out. They'd get their car valet-parked, eat steak on top of linen tablecloths, dance to the orchestra on the dance floor after dinner, then retire to the casino to play roulette and have a few drinks. They did this maybe once a week, but every single time Hazel's head would spin from the excitement of it all. She dusted off her old heels and dresses that she hadn't worn since well before she and Hollis had moved out to the mill.

The Pines was managed by H. P. McDonald, who had once owned the club outright. But McDonald had backed the wrong side in the election, and so he, like Owney, was forced to sell. The men he sold it to were as loose as Babe Huff on the "no outsiders" rule. They gave a percentage of the Pines to Chicago mobsters Les Kruse and John Drew, who would later be denied a Nevada gaming license over their investment in the club. Perhaps hypocritically, it seemed the Nevada Gaming Control Board considered an association with Hot Springs to be as bad as an association with Al Capone.

McDonald was a member of the Showmen's Association, a private social club for carnival workers. He brought a lot of carnival men on to work at the Pines, despite the fact that the carnival community was rife with hustlers and cheats. McDonald hired men like Jimmie Green, who was said to be the best palm man in the whole country, which meant he could palm two regular-sized dice in his hand and swap out one set of dice for another during a game. He also put on Hal Stanger, a carny who ran the razzle-dazzle scam on the road for many years until the Pines let him open up his own chuck-a-luck game right on the casino floor. And then there was James Dolan, an ex-con from Dallas everyone called "Doc." Dolan worked for the American Guild of Variety Artists, which was a union for nightclub acts and dancers. Dolan was no union man, though. He was a grifter who traveled the country running scams on people until he was arrested and locked up in Texas. When Dolan was released, he went to work for the Dallas branch of the AGVA, which was connected to the mob and known to extort nightclub owners in exchange for labor peace.

Hazel would drink with Jack Cartwright and all of his friends and listen to stories from the road—about how they'd play three-card monte, or bust up poker games pretending to be IRS agents. They made a living on their wits, but these men also enjoyed what they did. They knew no other life, nor did they care to. They were just as driven by the satisfaction of outsmarting someone as they were by the money they'd lift in the process. Hazel was drawn into their world. It was mysterious, illicit, exciting.

One thing all the road gamblers and carnival men had in common was that they didn't care for Dane Harris. In Hot Springs, these men played second fiddle to the boss gambler, a local boy who had spent more time on a golf course or behind the counter at a liquor store than he had behind a dice table or the barrel of a .45. These were men who, back in Florida or Mississippi or Texas, had been club owners themselves. They had their own policy wheels, made book on horses, promoted prizefighters, or robbed banks. In their hometowns they were big shots. One by one they had each been run off their home turf, either by the law or by rival big shots. One by one they had made their way to Hot Springs. But in Hot Springs, a guy like Hal Stanger was damn lucky to get to run a chuck-a-luck table in a far-flung casino like the Pines. They were all frozen out of the real action.

FOR HIS PART, DANE wasn't too fond of the Pines, either. He saw it as direct competition for the Belvedere, where Dane was now leasing space from the owners for fifteen hundred dollars a day and running his own casino during the race meet. He didn't figure that there was any need for two clubs across the street from each other out on the highway beyond the city limits. It may have been the connection to the syndicate, or maybe the fact that Owney bought a small piece of the action, but for whatever reason, Dane let the Pines operate. He did, however, make life hard on the owners. He wouldn't let the Pines use his slot machines, and he wouldn't supply them with alcohol, which meant they had to find their own booze from another supplier willing to illegally sell them liquor wholesale. And as soon as the horse races started up, Dane got the Belvedere up and running. Between the Belvedere and the Tower, Dane laid out enough money to attract all the big-name entertainment, which meant he sucked up all the action from clubs like the Pines.

JACK FOLLOWED THE ACTION over to the Tower Club, where he blew through so much of his bankroll, he eventually asked Dane Harris to let him work the other side of the table as a dealer. Jack had been dealing at the Tower for a few months when Hazel informed him she had been put out of the house he was keeping her in. He came up with a deal: he'd move her into his own house, which he was then sharing with his ailing mother. He'd let the woman who had been caring for his mother go, and Hazel could look after his mother in exchange for living there. Jack wouldn't, however, take in her sons. He suggested they could live in a separate house, a small place with cheap rent nearby that he knew about.

By that time, Hollis Jr. had graduated from high school and had enlisted in the air force. Larry and Jimmy were getting older, and had already grown used to looking after themselves. Hazel's own father had left her alone in Hot Springs when she was young, and she'd fared just fine. Blinded by something like desperation, or infatuation, Hazel reckoned it all could work. She agreed to Jack's proposal. It wasn't exactly getting down on one knee, but with all her belongings out on the side of the road, she wasn't in any position to be picky.

Hazel as a young girl, 1929
(Courtesy of Larry Hill)

Hollis poses for a portrait with a
cigarette, 1933 *(Courtesy of Larry Hill)*

Dane as a young man
(Courtesy of Marcia Heien)

Marcella Sellers (later Harris), 1937
(Courtesy of Marcia Heien)

Hollis and Hazel Hill
(Courtesy of Larry Hill)

A damaged photograph of Hollis and Hazel, which Hollis was thought to have carried in his wallet and which was found on his body after his death *(Courtesy of Larry Hill)*

A portrait taken at Hollis's burial *(Courtesy of Larry Hill)*

Black Cat No. 3

The Black Cat liquor store, located across
the street from Oaklawn Park
(Courtesy of Marcia Heien)

A rare portrait of Owney Madden, only
one copy of which is thought to exist
(Courtesy of Wayne Threadgill)

Dane with Marcia Harris and dogs
Buddy and Salty, Father's Day 1949
(Courtesy of Marcia Heien)

Hazel and her
three sons. From
left: Jimmy, Larry,
Hazel, and Hollis Jr.
(Courtesy of Larry Hill)

Hazel Hill and Larry
(Courtesy of Larry Hill)

Jimmy Hill holding
Hollis Jr.'s son, Michael,
Christmas 1963
(Courtesy of Larry Hill)

Dane Harris practices teeing off with Marcia Harris as Dane Jr. and Marcella look on, 1960 *(Francis Miller / The LIFE Picture Collection / Getty Images)*

The author as a child with Hazel in Hot Springs, 1980 *(Courtesy of the author)*

Leo McLaughlin driving his horse and buggy through Hot Springs *(Courtesy of Wayne Threadgill)*

Owney Madden
with his dog
*(Courtesy of Wayne
Threadgill)*

The facade of the Southern Club,
early 1950s *(Courtesy of Wayne Threadgill)*

A roulette table at the Southern
Club, 1960 *(Francis Miller / The LIFE
Picture Collection / Getty Images)*

A typical Hot Springs wire room, 1960
(Francis Miller / The LIFE Picture Collection / Getty Images)

Foibles of Faubus: the governor of Arkansas prepares to bet at Oaklawn Park *(Francis Miller / The LIFE Picture Collection / Getty Images)*

A "vapor cabinet" in one of the many bathhouses in Hot Springs. The comedian Henny Youngman, left, performed at the Vapors. *(Francis Miller / The LIFE Picture Collection / Getty Images)*

The interior of the Vapors after the bombing, January 1963 *(Arkansas Democrat-Gazette)*

Slot machines being burned by the Arkansas state police,
October 1967 *(Arkansas Democrat-Gazette)*

Downtown Hot Springs, 1958 *(Courtesy of Lanny Beavers and Chris Hendrix,
History of Hot Springs Gambling Museum)*

Dane

JUNE 1958

"But, remember this; exploiting the Race Issue to get votes is like playing Russian Roulette, you will never know when the bullet will explode."

The Cameo Club was the busiest spot on the main stem, which is what the hip called Malvern Avenue, and everyone at the Cameo was hip. Danny Boy's Combo was tearing it up late one Saturday night in June, and the Cameo was more packed than usual. There were rumors that B. B. King was going to show up. That's the kind of thing that happened in Hot Springs in those days. Folks like Ray Charles or Ella Fitzgerald would be in town, just hanging out, and might pop in and play a set for the crowd. And when they did, they'd do it at the Cameo.

It wasn't that unusual to see Dane Harris in his long black Lincoln Town Car on Malvern Avenue. He often had business on the black side of town, and this was especially true in election years. In the summer of 1958, Dane was in a tough spot. The Cameo had been aligned with Babe Huff, as had a number of clubs along Malvern Avenue. A. R. Puckett, the minister at the AME Church, had backed Huff in the last two elections, and Puckett was a power broker in the black community. Puckett's son Alroy wasn't a preacher and wasn't involved in gambling, but he was the manager of the National Baptist Hotel, an institution in the black community—not only in Arkansas, but in the eyes of the entire country, which made him one of the most important black leaders in Hot Springs. Dane rolled over to the east side to see if the younger Puckett might be interested in doing a little power brokering of his own.

Dane's vision for Hot Springs likely appealed to Alroy. Dane wanted to get rid of prostitution, run crooked operators out of town, and support the vibrant nightlife on both sides of town, white and black. Dane and Alroy both wanted the same thing in the end: tourists. In Dane's view, the best way to attract tourists from around the country was to present Hot Springs as an upscale, progressive, cosmopolitan resort where people from all over the world of any race could feel comfortable and welcome.

Babe Huff, however, was an obstacle to such progress. In order to beat Huff, Dane would need Alroy Puckett's help winning votes in the Second Ward. And Dane could help Alroy, too. He would eventually set up a separate company, Acme Amusement, that would own the slot machines in the black clubs. Just like the white club owners who used Dane and Owney's machines, the black club owners would keep 40 percent of the take. Alroy's name wouldn't be anywhere on the company, but Dane and Alroy would split the other 60 percent. And Dane would see to it that three of the black clubs in the Second Ward—the Cameo, the Atmosphere, and the Oakland Grill—wouldn't have to pay the city any gambling taxes and fines like the white clubs did. Dane just wanted the Second Ward to back Dane's candidates. The only problem was that the slate included Orval Faubus.

ORVAL FAUBUS HAD BEEN challenged in the 1956 Democratic primary by Jim Johnson, the head of the White Citizens Council of Arkansas, a hellfire Baptist preacher who hated black people worse than he hated the devil himself. Johnson did well in the polls, too. *Brown v. Board of Education* and the federal government's attempts to get southern states to speed up their plans for integration had whipped segregationists in the South into a serious distemper. Wherever Faubus campaigned, segregationists showed up to heckle him. Fistfights between segregationists and more liberal Faubus supporters frequently broke out at campaign events. At a gathering of Arkansas's delegates to the 1956 Democratic National Convention in Chicago, where Faubus and Johnson appeared alongside Estes Kefauver, who was running for the Democratic nomination for president, Johnson accused Kefauver and Faubus of being "traitors to their own race." The delegates must have been moved. Kefauver had expected that the delegates from his onetime home state would back him, especially after cozy conversations with Faubus. After Johnson's intervention, the Arkansas delegates chose not to back Kefauver.

Despite his humble hillbilly upbringing, Orval Faubus was a keen political operator. He could feel the bigoted swell building beneath his feet. Faubus won the election that year, but the state constitutional amendment that Johnson had proposed, one that would give Arkansas the right to ignore federal law on school integration, won as well. Johnson kept the pressure up on Faubus after the election, and Faubus knew he'd need to win over a lot of the white voters who shared Johnson's racism if he wanted to stay governor. Faubus came out hard against integration, and ordered soldiers from the Arkansas Guard to prevent nine black students from attending Little Rock Central High in the fall of 1957. The stunt boiled into a national crisis, with President Eisenhower getting involved and sending the 101st Airborne Division to Arkansas to nationalize the Arkansas Guard and take control of the situation. The students eventually were allowed to attend school that year, but Faubus had no intention of letting the issue die. As the school year drew to a close in early 1958, Faubus was agitating to prevent the integration of the schools, through referenda, through legal challenges, even by closing the public schools and leasing the buildings to segregated private schools. He closed all of Little Rock's schools for the upcoming year. Faubus had originally been elected governor as a populist, taking on the electric utility monopoly and standing up for welfare recipients. Now he had become one of the country's most ardent segregationists, and had put Arkansas in the national spotlight as a hotbed of racial tumult. Charles Mingus, the legendary jazz bassist, heightened the controversy when he recorded "Fables of Faubus" in 1959. Even Faubus's own father, Sam, an open socialist and former supporter of Eugene Debs, was embarrassed, writing letters to the newspaper criticizing his son for opposing integration. "A shame is being brought on us because of all this," he wrote.

The residents of the Second Ward in Hot Springs were equally incensed by Faubus's attack on school integration. For all the poverty that beset the Second Ward, Hot Springs was unique among similarly sized southern cities in that it had a burgeoning black middle class, fueled by the hospitality industry, which employed a good number of the city's nearly eight thousand black residents. There were entertainers, musicians, dancers, and other artists who made a living off the city's tourist trade. It wasn't uncommon in Hot Springs for hotels and gambling clubs to employ black people in both front- and back-of-the-house jobs. Not only were there black dishwashers and cooks, there were black bathhouse attendants, doormen, and bartenders. Hot Springs was also home to a black professional class, with a good number of lawyers and medical professionals alongside small business owners.

While Hot Springs was a segregated city, many white residents held liberal views on civil rights relative to the rest of Arkansas. Some white business owners, for example, would allow the more prominent and wealthy black residents of Hot Springs to enter their stores and shop, though they rarely extended this right to the poorer black residents. In 1953, Hot Springs' minor-league baseball team, the Bathers, was the first team in the league to sign black players, in defiance of league policy. Despite being told that the Bathers would have to forfeit any game in which the black players took part, over seventeen hundred mostly white fans attended their first game in Hot Springs to cheer them on, with another five hundred waiting outside to get in. And while Little Rock was on the verge of civil unrest, with racist white mobs and armed soldiers in the streets fighting over whether or not to permit black students into formerly all-white schools, Hot Springs was one of only six Arkansas school districts to voluntarily draft integration plans in 1957 and start the process without incident.

The anger at Faubus in the Second Ward was twofold. In Faubus's fight against school integration, there was more at stake for the black community in Hot Springs than just access to equal education. The reputation of the state of Arkansas was also on the line. Just as Dane Harris and his allies depended on tourists coming to Hot Springs to make their living, black businesses depended on black tourists. If Faubus continued to stoke racial violence and hostility toward African Americans, fewer would visit and vacation in the state. A boycott was possible.

The Citizen, Hot Springs' black-owned newspaper, ran an editorial on the state of the election that was silent on who to support in the local races. But the editors had this to say about the top of the ticket:

> The only Race issue at present seems to be in the Gubernatorial Campaign. While there are boundaries which even the most radical candidate will not cross, the Governor's race is shaping into a bitter contest with "no holds" barred. But, remember this; exploiting the Race Issue to get votes is like playing Russian Roulette, you will never know when the bullet will explode, and of course when it does explode it means TOTAL ANNIHILATION FOR THE "PLAYER!"

After the Little Rock Central High incident, Faubus's popularity grew across the state among Democrats. In the 1958 primary, Johnson stood down. Instead, Faubus was opposed by Lee Ward, a Calvinist and state judge who left the bench to try to unseat Faubus. Like Faubus, Ward was opposed to integration. But Ward considered Faubus's defiance of the federal government "treason" and believed Arkansas should follow the law, rather than pursue a "bullet and bayonet" approach. Ward was trailing Faubus heavily in the polls, but he was the preferred choice among African American voters.

This dynamic put Owney and Dane's faction in a tight spot. If they stuck with Faubus, they'd lose the Second Ward, which would make it incredibly hard to beat Wilson and Huff in the upcoming election. But if they broke with Faubus, he'd be sure to extract his pound of flesh right out of their asses for not supporting him. It was a bad position to be in. But Dane believed that supporting Faubus was their best bet.

Alroy was a proud man. He despised segregation—so much so, he often said, that if the price of integration was to shut down the National Baptist Hotel, this crown jewel of the black South, then so be it. Supporting a man like Orval Faubus was anathema to him. And who was Dane Harris to make this request? Owney Madden was known around town as being friendly toward black people and liberal on civil rights. He regularly entertained black visitors in his home, dined with them, drove them around town in his car or on the lake in his boat. He was friends with black musicians, singers, prizefighters, and athletes from all over America, and the community appreciated that he brought many of them to town to visit and to perform. Dane Harris, however, wasn't as well known among the residents of the Second Ward. He would have to demonstrate his commitment with more than words, and he knew it.

Dane reached out to Owney and to Jack Pakis at the Southern Club. They had already raised thirty thousand dollars to build a six-thousand-gallon community swimming pool at the Jaycee Center, the biggest swimming pool in the entire state. That swimming pool, like every swimming pool in the South at that time, would be whites-only. Dane and his allies offered to put up thirty-three thousand dollars to build a brand-new swimming pool at the Webb Center, a black community center not far from the Baptist Hotel. Both of the pools would be free, and in a place as humid as Arkansas, the lack of a public pool had always been a source of frustration, especially among young people without any means to get themselves to the lake for a swim. Now, thanks to Dane Harris, there would be two public pools in Hot Springs.

Once the Webb Center pool opened, it was quite a scene, with crowds every day and the swimming classes filling up as soon as they were offered. Dane and Owney put an ad in the newspaper with a photo of the Webb Center pool, giving Leonard Ellis all the credit for it. The Second Ward, it appeared, was suddenly in play.

DANE AND OWNEY WERE finding plenty of allies in the fight against Huff. Ironically, the end of the McLaughlin machine's election rigging didn't end corruption, which was arguably worse that it had ever been. Babe Huff's extortion of 20 percent of profits for himself was as bold and provocative as any political graft that preceded him. And his heavy-handedness was being felt by more than just the gambling combination. Duane Faull, who owned a number of bars and restaurants and operated pinball machines, found that the Huff regime and the gambling war were costing him a fortune. He wrote to Dane, "I am in a position now where I have spent nearly $6,000, including Darnell-Huff election, to help you people get into office besides the years of Huff which cost me, as I say, much more than I have spent on the elections, all this time I had no gambling interests to protect but was merely operating a legitimate business." Dane made the same deal with Faull that he did with Puckett: in exchange for helping Dane topple the Huff regime, Faull could operate slot machines in his businesses and sell liquor over his bar. Once Huff was gone and Dane and Owney were running things, there would be no more payoffs. Instead, they would share the gambling profits within their faction based on how many votes each could deliver. It was an attractive proposition. One small business owner at a time, Dane was raising his army.

The first hurdle to overcome was the sheriff's election, where Babe Huff had put Clyde Wilson up to run against Leonard Ellis. The campaign was a nasty one. Each man accused the other of being a puppet. Ellis ran ads accusing Wilson of doing Babe Huff's bidding. Wilson ran ads claiming that Dane Harris was the real boss gambler and that Ellis was his man, that his campaign was organized in the back of "Dane Harris's gambling casino on the Little Rock Highway."

After his father passed away, Ellis had inherited a large parcel of land on the same road as Dane's first housing development. Ellis partnered with Dane to develop the land, only this time instead of residential homes, Dane oversaw the development of a large commercial shopping center. The project was garnering Ellis lots of attention, and his opponents dubbed him "Shopping Center Ellis." The price tag for what Dane and Ellis were calling the "Indiandale Shopping Center" was rumored to be over a half a million dollars, and one of the silent partners was said to be a "notorious character from Chicago."

Tensions between the two sides were high, and it was clear the vote would come down once again to the Second Ward. Each candidate campaigned hard for those votes, and at one point both candidates held rallies on the very same night on the very same block. There were over a thousand people out on Malvern Avenue to hear the candidates speak, listen to music from the dueling string bands and the Leo Castleberry quartet, and eat free food from the lavish spreads put out by both sides.

Standing on opposite sides of the street, each campaign attacked the other with wild accusations and insults. On one side, Leonard Ellis delivered a rousing speech, accusing Clyde Wilson of being a failed businessman who was being sued by everyone he had ever done business with. "In fact," Ellis said from the stage, "he's being sued for not paying for two head of beef. I guess that makes him a cattle rustler. I'd be careful before you eat that food he's got over there. It might be somebody else's property!"

"Leonard Ellis couldn't sweep my floor," Wilson said in response.

"He is hopelessly beaten and he knows it. He reminds me of a drowning man who will grab any straw."

At the Ellis rally, cash awards were given out every fifteen minutes. The Wilson side tried to keep up. They'd ring a bell every time they were giving away another cash prize, which sped up as the night went on. People ran from one side of the street to the other every time they heard the bell ring. Even though each side tried to get their supporters to wear a hat showing which side they were on (white cowboy hats for Ellis, black cowboy hats for Wilson), there were black and white hats on both sides of the street. It seemed as if the residents of the Second Ward were simply soaking up the attention from both campaigns. It was impossible to predict how it would turn out.

TO FACE OFF WITH Babe Huff himself, the gamblers recruited a thirty-eight-year-old local lawyer named Plummer Dobbs. Dobbs was a criminal defense attorney for some of the roughest characters in town. He even represented the notorious madam Maxine Gregory, who paid him a king's ransom to keep her employees out of jail and fend off independent cops who tried to shake her down for payoffs. Dobbs took on criminal clients like Gregory because he was comfortable with them. He was a fixture at the Southern Club, a gambler and boozehound to rival the wildest cowboys. When Walter Hebert suggested Dobbs for the job, many gamblers weren't immediately convinced. But Owney surely saw a lot to like in Dobbs. He was everything Babe Huff was not—malleable, impressionable, eager. Dobbs wasn't likely to turn on them the way Huff had.

Like the sheriff's race, the circuit judge campaign was bruising. Dobbs came out swinging, calling Babe Huff "little man" and accusing him of being psychologically unfit for the office. Dobbs ran newspaper ads with cartoons depicting Marion Anderson whipping a horse labeled "Huff." He invoked the notorious Dick Galatas in an ad that read,

"Marion says he's sick Dick (Kansas City Massacre) Galatas is gone . . . but if Huff wins they'll both be back riding around town in the pink Cadillac!"

Dane, Owney, and the other members of the gambling combination put their turnout machines to work, this time joined by Alroy Puckett and Duane Faull. Faull hired staff to stuff and mail thousands of envelopes, as well as cars and drivers to fan out on Election Day and drive people to the polls. The drivers carried money so they could pay people's poll taxes, and were reimbursed one dollar per voter they delivered. Dane even reimbursed members of the combination for the cost of beer they may have needed to sway the undecided.

THE FINAL VOTE WAS as close as had ever been seen in Hot Springs. Ellis beat Wilson 6,172 to 5,933. Dobbs beat Huff 6,454 to 6,306. Clyde Wilson asked for a recount, but the result actually added votes to Ellis's total. Then Wilson challenged the whole election on the basis of poll tax fraud and voter intimidation. They claimed that Glenn Buchanan, one of the heavies who guarded the money at the Southern Club, was assigned to the Second Ward as a poll watcher, and that he encouraged people to vote for Ellis using his own special power of persuasion: scaring the life out of them. The vote totals in the Second Ward, however, proved that the voters had exercised their free will. While the Second Ward voted for Ellis and Dobbs by a margin of two to one, they voted more than three to one against Orval Faubus, who won the rest of Hot Springs (and the rest of Arkansas) by a landslide.

Since Huff was still the sitting judge, Ellis requested that another judge hear the case. The circuit judge from the small town of Nashville, Arkansas, Bobby Steel, was given the case. Owney and Dane met with the judge and contributed five thousand dollars to his reelection campaign. He ruled in their favor. Wilson then appealed to the Arkansas Supreme Court, but Dane and Owney had that wired, too. Before the supreme court ruled on the case, a couple of the justices visited Hot Springs. Leonard Ellis called up Gregory and asked her to send some of her best women over to the justices' rooms to entertain them. He even sent a sheriff's deputy over to pick the women up and give them a ride. The supreme court ruled in favor of Dane and Owney's candidates, too.

After the election, Plummer Dobbs boarded an airplane and flew to New York to watch the Yankees play the Milwaukee Braves in Game 3 of the 1958 World Series. His entire trip was paid for by Owney—a small perk of joining the establishment class in Hot Springs for Dobbs, a reasonable investment in his financial future for Owney. One of Plummer Dobbs's first acts as the new circuit judge was to order the sheriff's office to raid and padlock the White Front Club, the Citizens Club, and the Siesta Cafe on the outskirts of town as nuisances to the community. The owners of those clubs filed legal challenges, saying they were being punished in a "gambling war" for supporting the wrong candidates in the election. Dobbs asked the grand jury to conduct their own investigation. The grand jury ruled that yes, the shuttering of the clubs was likely a reprisal for supporting the losing candidates, but that "readjustment" was expected after an election. The grand jury called it "a risk of the trade." There was no mention by the grand jury that the entirety of this "trade" was illegal, as was the use of the courts and law enforcement to extort businesses for political purposes.

None of this mattered to Owney and Dane. Dane was now boss gambler, and his power was absolute.

Hazel

When she came to, she was in handcuffs.

Jack and Hazel were dressed to the nines, strolling arm in arm down Broadway toward Central Avenue. Jack had parked his shiny new Chrysler several blocks from the Esskay Art Gallery, where he and Hazel were headed for a night at the auctions.

Next to the casinos and the bathhouses, the auction houses were the biggest attraction in downtown Hot Springs. There were a number of them along the main drag of Central Avenue, each with its front facade wide open to the street so that passersby could see the action inside. Between auctions, the auctioneers would bark at gawkers on the sidewalk to come inside, lest they miss out on what was up next. They would parade before the crowd all manner of artifice and artifact: oil paintings and African masks, stone carvings and fine crystal. But the real show, what really packed the house, was the jewelry. Costume jewelry, heavy silver and gold accoutrements, rings and bracelets, pins and pendants. And the diamonds. People traveled from all across America to buy diamonds at the auction houses in Hot Springs. It was unbelievable how little these diamonds would go for at auction. It was downright criminal.

One reason may have been that a lot of the diamonds that found their way into Esskay and the other local auction houses were hot. From New York to Miami, the word was out that if you came across a diamond, say in somebody else's hotel room, and you wanted to move it, you needed to see the little man at the Southern. Owney had helped Harry "Dutch" Goldberg in New York move many stolen diamonds over the years with the help of Hot Springs jewelry stores and auction houses. When the diamonds weren't stolen, they were sometimes fake. The less reputable auction houses worked with some of the less reputable jewelers to appraise phony diamonds as real.

Years before, in the late 1940s, the Esskay was robbed and most of the diamonds were taken. When the thieves were caught, Owney drove out to Sid McMath's house late at night to talk him into letting the thieves off the hook. After McMath climbed into Owney's car and sat down between his two bodyguards, Owney told him, "The thieves are friends of mine. If you could dismiss the case against them, I'd sure appreciate it." McMath refused. The prosecutors even put the Esskay's owner, Samuel Kirsch, on the stand, accusing him of arranging the robbery as an inside job. Kirsch pleaded the Fifth.

This was something of an inauspicious start for a future civic leader of one of Hot Springs' diverse religious congregations. Kirsch was Jewish, and the town boasted an exceptionally large and active Jewish community by the standards of the region. Some called it the "Catskills of the South." Many of the town's Jewish residents operated businesses that catered to the many Jewish visitors to the resort. There were a number of kosher eateries, delis that served pastrami and corned beef, a chapter of B'nai B'rith, an Orthodox temple, and even a 125-bed Jewish hospital built to serve the sick who traveled to Hot Springs on doctor's orders to take the baths. By 1959, Samuel Kirsch had become one of the most important people in town. He owned a jewelry store, was in the process of purchasing the Waukesha Hotel, and in addition to the Esskay he owned two other popular auction houses.

The auction houses were still a big draw for tourists, in spite of the scams. Purchasing artifacts and artwork at auction was an experience, and the auction houses were expert at ratcheting up the drama of the whole enterprise. It was, in all actuality, a bit like show business. The auction houses were a facet of the Hot Springs economy that was as old as the casinos themselves, even though many locals were as embarrassed by the auctioneers barking at the passersby as they were by the prostitutes who hung from the windows above doing the same thing.

A few blocks from the Esskay, Jack shook his arm free from Hazel and stopped. Hazel kept walking without him, not missing a beat. She strolled into the gallery and made her way to the front, finding an open seat in the very first row. Several minutes later Jack arrived. He didn't sit by Hazel. He stood at the back of the room. He didn't look for her, and she didn't look for him. They watched intently as the auctioneer brought out the next item. The two of them then set to bidding on the item, bidding against each other and driving the price higher and higher, hoping to trap some poor sucker in the middle and sticking them with an overpriced piece of junk to take home as a souvenir. For their trouble, the auction house paid Hazel and Jack ten dollars each. It wasn't a fortune, but it was easy money. Hell, it was more than that. It was downright fun.

Hazel was good at this type of hustle. So good that Jack convinced Dane Harris to take Hazel on at the Tower Club as a shill player. A shill was someone who gambled with the house's money. There were a number of reasons a club would use shills. They could keep a game from breaking up by livening up the action when players were getting tired. They could keep an eye out for crossroaders and cheaters. They could get new games started at empty tables. The more attractive the shill, the more likely they were to draw other players to join them. Hazel would sit and play blackjack at the Tower Club during the slower periods, like late at night. The manager would give her money to play with, and at the end of her shift she'd surrender her stake back, plus whatever she won, and would be paid five or ten dollars for her time, depending on the shift. Like the gig at the auction houses, it wasn't much money, but

Hazel enjoyed being around the nightlife. She loved being paid to sit and play cards and shoot the breeze with the gamblers and tourists. Mostly she liked getting to spend more time with Jack, who was dealing blackjack at the Tower full-time.

Their relationship had flourished since Hazel had moved in with Jack and his ailing mother. She was so smitten with Jack, this man who had rescued her from the brink, that something went haywire with her motherly instincts. She was awfully quick to agree to let her two younger boys, now in their early teenage years, fend for themselves. When she sat the boys down to explain their new living arrangement, she tried to do it gently, but what came out was "Jack doesn't want you around." She was defensive, declaring she had no choice, that *they* had no choice. Early on she took care to look in on them often, to make sure they had groceries, or to cook them a pot of goulash stew to eat. Once Jack's mother passed away, however, things changed.

Hazel would work all through the night, from behind the bar at the Pensioner's to sitting at the tables at the Tower. She and Jack often slept through the daylight hours. She sometimes had trouble summoning the energy to keep house and work such long, irregular hours. Jack suggested she try some "medicine" that he had, and gave her a sack full of red pills. When Hazel asked him what they were, he told her they were "bennies." Benzedrine had recently been banned by the government. Jack got them from carnies he hung around with from the Pines, who were all hooked on them. It sometimes seemed like half of Hot Springs was hooked on them. The drug contained amphetamines, and had been given to soldiers during the war to keep them awake during battle. After the war they proliferated across America. Housewives used them as appetite suppressants. Factory workers used them to stay alert. But many people were quickly addicted, and by the late fifties they were controlled and required a doctor's prescription. That meant they were illegal. It also meant they were expensive.

Hazel and Jack would take bennies to stay awake. The drug was powerful, however, and difficult to come down from after a binge. Jack told Hazel she could come down by drinking whiskey. The two of them would pop reds until they were sky-high, buzzing and staying up all night long, then return home to drink whiskey until they fell asleep, or passed out, whatever the difference may have been.

Once, while Jack was out of town, Hazel ended her shift at the Tower with a stop at the Frontier, a small tavern across the street from the Oaklawn racetrack with a small casino and a few slot machines on the second story. Hazel wasn't a regular there, but she'd been once or twice. She sat at the bar and ordered a whiskey. A few hours later she figured the buzz had subsided and she was ready for bed. She was drunk, but she figured she could make it home. The Frontier was only a couple of miles from Jack's house, and she had driven after drinking before. That night, however, she found it much more difficult. Hazel ping-ponged her car across every lane on Central Avenue, smashing into one car after another, before finally wrapping it around a utility pole in front of a hotel. The impact smashed Hazel's head into the steering wheel and knocked her out. When she came to, she was in handcuffs.

Hazel spent the night in jail. The police knew all about her and her boys—how they were truants, how they were unsupervised at night. The police picked Jimmy and Larry up and took them to Richard and Bessie Mae's. The police told Hazel she wasn't fit to be a mother. They told her they'd see to it the judge took her sons away from her.

When Hazel was finally brought before the judge, she begged for mercy. She pleaded with him to let her keep her children. Richard and Bessie Mae and Ressie and Almagene and the rest of Hollis's family were in the courtroom. They brought Jimmy and Larry at the court's request. The judge asked Ressie if she'd be willing to take Hazel's boys and care for them.

"If the court says I have to, I'll take 'em and raise them as if they were my own. I love these boys," Ressie began. "But if the court is asking me if I want to, I sure don't. Hazel is a good mother. She works hard. She's all alone. She's been through a lot. She loves her boys and wouldn't do nothing to hurt them, and I think she deserves a second chance."

One by one the judge inquired if any of Hazel's former in-laws would take the children, and they all declined. They weren't rejecting the boys. They were affirming their faith in Hazel. They believed that in spite of her mistakes she was a good mother.

The judge then asked Larry and Jimmy if they wanted to stay with their mother or go live with other relatives. Jimmy and Larry told the judge they wanted to stay with their mama.

The judge sighed. "Mrs. Hill, these boys need to go to school. They need someone to look after them and make sure they do right. They need a mother."

"Please," she sobbed. "I'm their mother."

The judge didn't argue the point with her. He told her that he didn't like splitting up families. He'd give her another shot. "A trial run," he called it. If she slipped up, he'd take them away. She could count on that. Hazel thanked the judge. He told her she'd smashed up a lot of cars. Did she have a job? She told him she did.

That's good, he said. Because you'll pay for the damage you've done.

Owney

"Madam, this has never been a city. It will always be a town."

A pickup truck pulled up alongside the Ritter Hotel on Exchange Street, just behind the jewelry store and the Esskay auction house downtown on Central Avenue. Walter Metzer got out of the truck, walked around back, and hoisted a large coil of wire up on his shoulder from out of the truck bed. He humped the coil up the stairs and into the Ritter Hotel, where he was greeted by a thin old man in a linen suit and driving cap.

Owney led Walter Metzer up to the fifth floor, where he installed two white ceramic insulators to the wall of an office, and then to the roof, where he left the large coil of wire. Before the day was over, Metzer would run the wire from the roof of the hotel to nearly every casino and handbook in Hot Springs, a web of wires as intricate as the Southwestern Bell phone lines themselves.

State Senator Q. Byrum Hurst had put Owney together with Jerry Poe, the traffic manager for Southwestern Bell Telephone, shortly after the election so that Poe could share with Owney some of his ideas about how the wire service could better operate. According to Poe, running the wires directly from the telephone company into the wire room, then out of the wire room across the city on dedicated wires, would not only save whoever was running the wire service a pile of money, it would also be easier to control. But it wouldn't be cheap to operate. Poe wanted one hundred dollars per line per month.

In addition to the extra cost of paying Poe, Owney needed to purchase the Ritter Hotel, which was next door to Southwestern Bell's offices. Owney fronted Hurst the money to purchase the Ritter Hotel to keep it out of his name. Then Owney put the phone lines in the name of Walter Metzer, Poe's best line installation man, who would work on the side for Owney.

After running wires out of the Ritter Hotel, over trees, and across the tops of buildings to bookie joints all over town, Metzer installed a totalizator machine in room 207, the same room where the lines all were connected. The totalizator machine calculated odds based on the money that was taken in on various betting propositions so that the bookmaker could offer accurate lines to customers and avoid getting taken for a ride by sharp players. It was a technological innovation used only by large bookmakers and the racetracks themselves.

Now that Babe Huff was out of the picture, Owney could have gone back to being the broker for the syndicate's wire coming out of New Orleans, and charging the local bookies the regular fee. But he clearly had bigger plans. There in the Ritter Hotel, Owney had built his very own wire service. His service could deliver results instantly, on dedicated wires that ran from room 207 directly into the handbooks, as well as provide bookies with access to his totalizator odds and his syndicate-run layoff rooms. Owney even purchased a printing press so he could make daily wall sheets with betting options for the various clubs and handbooks across town to display. It was one-stop shopping, and it would cost a handbook only $150 a week, or an even hundred for independent operators located in other parts of Arkansas. Owney named his new business the Downtown Printing Company, inspired by Marcello's wire service, the Nola Printing Company—or perhaps as a direct challenge to it.

Owney flew to Chicago and asked Curley Humphreys to bless his new wire operation. Owney was only eight years older than Humphreys, but Owney had been a rackets boss for a lot longer than Humphreys had. When Humphreys was first starting out, kidnapping Chicago union leaders and doing murders for hire for the Capone mob, Owney was already the owner of the Cotton Club and dining with the likes of Jack Johnson and Cary Grant. Owney Madden was an elder statesman of this business, a living legend. Humphreys respected Owney, looked up to him, even. He gave his blessing to the Downtown Printing Company.

OWNEY WALKED THE FEW blocks from the Ritter Hotel to the Southern Club, already filled with customers riding up the escalator to the casino by early afternoon. He sat down at his usual seat. He watched the tourists strolling the avenue outside, the cars lined up bumper to bumper. He listened to the sound of the slot machine gears grinding, the wheels whirring, the boxmen hollering *Eight easy, a no field eight.*

A young couple stopped in their tracks when they noticed him sitting there. They had heard of him, they told him, and hoped they might see him here while they were visiting. Owney smiled and shook their hands.

"Where do you live in Hot Springs, Mr. Madden?" the woman asked.

"Not far from here, on West Grand," he replied.

"West Grand? We passed that. Why, it's right in the heart of the city," she exclaimed.

It wouldn't always be as easy as this. It couldn't be. Owney was inviting trouble from enemies local and from parts unknown. Kefauver and Kennedy had turned an entire generation of local crime figures into wandering nomads in search of a score. Many of them headed to

Nevada, but some could end up in Arkansas to stake their claim to a share of what Owney had helped build. Either way, a fight was brewing. Owney was sixty-seven years old. He had carried nine bullets in his belly for forty years. He sipped his tea and smiled gently at the visitor.

"Madam, this has never been a city. It will always be a town."

Dane

"Mr. Raft, the Revolution is here. Fidel Castro has taken over everything," the operator told him.

The desert between Los Angeles and Las Vegas is hot. Here's how hot: the road that traversed it in 1959 was long and narrow, two lanes of shimmering, buckling blacktop that went on for hundreds of miles through the most desolate stretches of the Mojave Desert. "There were times I thought I would die in that desert," Meyer Lansky said. "Vegas was a horrible place." That year, fewer than half the cars on the road had air-conditioning. Before attempting the journey from Los Angeles to Las Vegas, drivers would buy swamp coolers, contraptions resembling little jet engines that were mounted to the passenger windows of cars. The hot, dry air would be forced into the cooler by the speed of the car flying down the road, where it would come into contact with water. Thanks to evaporative cooling, the car would be filled with cold, humid air, a bit like the vapor that lingered over the hot springs back in Arkansas. But in July 1959, Nevada was in the middle of a heat wave, and the swamp coolers couldn't keep up.

Dane was lucky to have air-conditioning when he drove his entire family through that desert in the middle of the summer. Dane had been invited to Las Vegas to meet with some people about potentially buying a share of the New Frontier casino. Dane, Leonard Ellis, and Q. Byrum Hurst were all going out for the meeting and decided to make a family vacation out of it. They flew out to Los Angeles with their wives and children to visit the new Disneyland theme park. From there they figured they'd just take an easy drive over to Las Vegas. But there was nothing easy about that drive through the desert.

Las Vegas was still struggling, though you wouldn't know it by looking at it. The properties that were being developed on the Strip were eye-popping. The Riviera was nine stories tall. The construction had finished the summer before on the Stardust, the largest casino ever built. The New Frontier was also new, a modern reimagining of the Last Frontier, which was the second hotel built on the Strip, back in 1942. The Last Frontier was an Old West–themed resort, complete with horseback rides, cowboy hats, Native American bric-a-brac, saddles for barstools, and the only dealers in Las Vegas permitted to grow mustaches. The Last Frontier was perhaps best known at the time for a new style of restaurant where you paid one price and could have all the food you could stand to eat.

The New Frontier stood in dramatic contrast to all this. The newer property was designed in the space-age Googie style that Dane's family had seen all over Los Angeles. Sharp edges, sloping sides, glass bricks, block letters, and polka dots. The light fixtures were flying saucers. The floors were marble and the railings were brass. The theater had a revolving stage and a hydraulic lift for the orchestra. The old roadside pool was filled in with concrete and replaced by a heated pool at the rear of the building with a cocktail bar at one end. The visages of cowboys were replaced by murals of spacemen.

Despite the redesign into the sleeker, up-to-date New Frontier, this casino had been passed around like a hot potato from one group of investors to another, bleeding money the entire time. At one point the socialite heiress Vera Krupp even owned it, but she had sold it right back to the people who sold it to her. The issue for everyone buying in and out of the Frontier was that a number of partners were sharing points with mobsters behind the scenes, and the mobsters were skimming all the profits. The various board members were filing lawsuits against one another, with two board members even coming to blows in the middle of a board meeting. The situation was so bad that the Frontier had lost its gaming license and was forced to shut down its casino and theater. When Dane and his family arrived, it was operating only as a hotel.

Back in Chicago they were calling the New Frontier "the mob's amateur operation."

The front men for the Frontier needed investors, people with some experience running successful casinos, and people who weren't tied in to the mob. Dane and his partners fit that description.

Las Vegas, for all of its flaws, boasted one thing that was undeniably attractive to Dane—gambling was legal. But would that be enough? He could at least hear them out. He'd let them wine and dine his family. He'd tour their space-age resort, ride the moving sidewalk, dance with Marcella to Steve Parker's *Holiday in Japan* revue. All in all, Dane liked what he saw. Las Vegas wasn't some hokey country-and-western corral anymore. It felt contemporary, sophisticated, upper-class. The New Frontier's theme was the future. The Stardust towered over the Strip like a moon base. The old roadside signs for the various casinos and hotels were being replaced by massive edifices, each letter as tall as the old buildings themselves, lit up with thousands of blinking bulbs. Here in the middle of this wasteland was a growing garden of concrete and rebar, light and sound. Las Vegas was on the verge of something much bigger and better than it had been, something that looked and felt different than anything Hot Springs or even the rest of America had ever seen. The old-school bathhouses and casinos back in Arkansas, patterned after the likes of Baden-Baden and Marienbad, suddenly began to seem like a relic from a different era that had died with the Second World War.

———

THE SITUATION WAS AIDED by events in Cuba. Las Vegas appeared to have been a bad bet just a few years before, when the well-heeled bosses like Meyer Lansky were investing heavily in the island paradise of Cuba. But in January 1959, a small army of guerrillas led by Fidel Castro came out of the mountains and took control of Havana, and with it the entire island. The revolution happened quickly, catching the Americans off guard. Owney's friend George Raft, who had been working for Santo Trafficante at the Casino de Capri, was asleep in the hotel with Miss Cuba when the guerrillas arrived. They ransacked the casino, shot the place up with machine guns. Raft called the front desk to find out what was going on. "Mr. Raft, the Revolution is here. Fidel Castro has taken over everything," the operator told him. The guerrillas dragged the slot machines into the streets and burned them, chanting, "Death to the American gangsters!"

With Cuba in disarray, the mob's investments in Las Vegas grew. Not all of these investments were in casinos, either. In 1959, the large and much-needed Sunrise Hospital was funded with a million dollars secured through the Teamsters Central States Pension Fund. On the face of it, the Sunrise Hospital deal seemed on the square. The union loaned the money to build the hospital, and in return they'd send their members there for services. In truth, the deal was a trial balloon for using the union fund as the mob's line of credit to develop casinos in Las Vegas. The newly elected president of the Teamsters, Jimmy Hoffa, had a plan to use the fund as a bank for his connections in the syndicate who were in need of financing and couldn't go to legitimate banks. Soon enough, Hoffa would be signing off on loans to build more massive casino resorts where syndicate leaders could skim hundreds of millions of dollars a year right off the top.

Hoffa's relationship with the mob was a two-way street. They had helped Hoffa win union contracts, and even helped him out of some personal jams. At times, Hot Springs played a role in this relationship as well. During a bribery trial, Hoffa retained Hot Springs' state senator, Q. Byrum Hurst, as one of his lawyers, at the suggestion of Chicago mobsters Curley Humphreys and Ralph Pierce. Hoffa already had a battery of high-priced lawyers at his disposal, but Hurst was boyhood friends with A. D. Shelton, city attorney of Hot Springs, who also happened to be the brother of the judge presiding over Hoffa's case. The day before the trial began, Hurst arranged for A. D. Shelton to come to Washington, D.C., to meet with his sister one-on-one. Despite a mountain of evidence against him, including the testimony of the very man he bribed, Hoffa was acquitted of all charges. Hurst didn't charge Hoffa a dime.

HOFFA'S INFLUENCE, ESPECIALLY IN Las Vegas, was only just beginning to blossom that summer. John Drew, on the other hand, was the Chicago Outfit's "inside man," which meant he handled the legitimate side of the business for them, and he was very much an important figure in Vegas at that time. Drew had once owned a stake in the Pines, all the way back in Hot Springs, until the gambling combination ran him out of town. This meant Dane faced some danger in coming to Vegas: it was a place where disputes were settled violently, where "gentleman" gangsters such as Owney seemed as quaint and outmoded as Bathhouse Row and its claims of healing waters.

Marshall Caifano was Chicago's "outside man" in Vegas—he was responsible for the Outfit's less-than-legitimate business. He was one of the most notorious hit men in town, and he had his own unique way of handling business. He was rumored to use a blowtorch on his customers. When the Riviera started losing millions of dollars, the mob suspected their manager, Gus Greenbaum, was to blame. Caifano handled it. He cut Greenbaum's head off, then went into the next room, slit Gus's wife's throat and laid down newspapers so the blood wouldn't stain the carpet.

This was Nevada in 1959, where gambling was supposed to be a legitimate business. Before Dane left his hotel room, he took his pistol out of his suitcase and stuck it in his pocket. Marcella stopped him at the door.

"Where do you think you're going?" she demanded.

"To a meeting," Dane replied.

"What kind of a meeting are you going to that you need to take a gun with you?" Marcella cried, distraught. She put herself between Dane and the hotel room door.

Dane tried to explain that they weren't in Hot Springs anymore. They were on somebody else's turf. Perhaps Dane didn't need to carry a pistol on him wherever he went in Arkansas, but they were a long way from Arkansas. They were in the middle of the desert, and things worked differently out there.

"This isn't what I signed on for," Marcella said.

Dane pushed his way past Marcella and out the door, pistol in his pocket. In the end, Dane turned down the offer to come in on the Frontier. He believed he could do better for himself in Hot Springs. And he wanted better for Hot Springs as well. But if Dane wanted for Hot Springs all that Las Vegas had, then he'd need to get used to looking over his shoulder, to bringing guns with him to meetings. The money was rolling into Las Vegas, but there was a darkness, a heaviness lingering in the hot desert air. It was liable to kill them all.

Owney

Compared to those beatings, these didn't feel like punches at all. He could handle these.

Jimmy Hill was thirteen years old when he laced up his gloves in a dim corner of the Boys Club gymnasium for the first time. He was nervous, but not terribly so. A few butterflies in the belly were natural. This was his debut in the ring, after all. That didn't mean it was his first fight. Down at the newspaper offices, where Jimmy occasionally worked a paper route on his bicycle, the overnight shift workers would pay him to fight bigger kids in the lot in back, then book bets on the fights. Jimmy took a lot of beatings to amuse those guys. He gave a few, too.

Owney Madden missed the fights something fierce. He loved the fights so much, he'd risked getting tossed out of the country once back in 1940 when he violated his parole and snuck off to New York to see Buddy Baer fight Nathan Mann at Madison Square Garden. Less of a risk taker these days, he opted to watch the Sugar Ray Robinson–Carmen Basilio fight in a movie theater in Little Rock, but it wasn't the same. It wasn't like being ringside, like in the old days when he kept company with big-time prizefighters. It wasn't like being within earshot of the trainers pounding the mat and pleading with their fighters to watch for the hook, in the front row of the raucous crowds, the rising and palpable tension all around him, the din of a thousand fans bellowing their appreciation of a knockout nobody saw coming.

In Hot Springs, the closest Owney could get to the feeling of the old days were the Golden Gloves youth fights at the Boys Club. He came to care so much for watching the local youngsters fight that he regularly fronted the money to keep the Boys Club up to snuff with new equipment and suitable facilities. The fights at the Boys Club weren't as spirit-stirring as the professional bouts of his past life, but every now and then they provided a satisfactory dose of violence.

Jimmy stood in his corner across from his opponent and sized him up. The boy looked older than Jimmy, maybe a high schooler, and clearly a practiced boxer, warming up in his corner by throwing combinations at the air. The high schooler was joined by an adult, some kind of coach perhaps, maybe even his father.

Jimmy stood motionless and alone in his corner. Nobody came to see his first fight. Hazel was working. Or maybe she wasn't. Jimmy never knew where she was unless she was passed out at home. For a short spell after Hazel's arrest, things seemed to improve. She'd keep food in the cupboards. She'd give him and Larry money for clothes or whatever else they needed. What she didn't do was leave Jack. It was only a matter of time before she slipped back into their old routine, back into that dark place that had taken her and would never give her back without a fight.

The fights at the citywide Golden Gloves tournament consisted of three one-minute rounds. Most of the kids in the tournament were, like Jimmy, untrained and coaxed by an adult or a friend into entering. The typical fight started with both boys flailing their arms from the opening bell and ended with the judges picking a winner based on who looked less beat-up than the other boy. The goal, Jimmy thought to himself, was to just stay on his feet. If he didn't get knocked down, he might be able to advance.

When the bell sounded for Jimmy's fight, he didn't flail his arms as he had seen the other boys do. He put his fists in front of him, tightened his guts up, and prepared for the older boy's blows to come. The other boy jabbed right through Jimmy's guard, right into his face. The glove connected square with Jimmy's nose and snapped his head back. It stunned Jimmy, but it didn't feel like getting belted in the nose behind the newspaper warehouse, where boys hit him with bare knuckles and split open his lips, opened up his nose like a faucet, knocked him to the pavement unable to catch a breath. Compared to those beatings, these didn't feel like punches at all. He could handle these.

The older boy's hands were loose, and he was landing punches all up and down little Jimmy's body. Jimmy just took it. Then Jimmy finally saw an opening to throw his own blow, a right hook to the older boy's rib cage. The boy went skittering off in the direction of the punch as if Jimmy had shoved him across the ring. He hit the ropes and shot his coach or father or whomever a look that said *What in the devil was that?*

Jimmy chased the boy to the ropes and threw another punch, then another. The boy backed away from Jimmy until his back touched the turnbuckle. He was in the corner. He was in a bad place. The crowd cheered little Jimmy on. *Go get him! Knock him out!* Jimmy obliged the cheers and charged the corner, throwing punches with both hands, moving left and right on his feet to keep the older boy pinned in. The boy put his arms up in front of his face, trying to stay on his feet, to survive the one-minute round. Only that minute never came. The blows became too much for the older boy to bear. He dropped to his knee. The referee started counting. The boy waved him off. No need to count. "I quit."

Jimmy took no great pleasure in his victory. Hazel had raised her youngest son, despite everything, to be a kind, softhearted boy with an acute sense of fair play. He was one of the poorest children in his entire class, wearing the same clothes to school day after day, fueled on a breakfast of bread, sugar, and water. But Jimmy was popular and loved by his classmates, and he came to hold their friendships as sacred. Hazel and Jack didn't pay him and Larry any mind for the most part. Hollis Jr. was away in the service and hadn't looked in on them in some time. He had a family of his own now, too. He had left a girl in New Mexico with child when he went overseas, and now there was a baby boy waiting for him to get back. So Jimmy leaned hard on his school friends to keep him grounded, to have their parents cart him around, to feed him when he was hungry, to keep him company when he felt most alone. In return, Jimmy offered them the one thing he could afford: his unwavering loyalty. He expressed that loyalty the same way he won his first boxing match, by using his body to inflict pain.

Jimmy had a friend in school named Judy Harrod. Her father was the town veterinarian and they lived way out of town on the lake. Jimmy didn't see her much outside of school, but she was always kind to him and he liked her quite a bit. She had a boyfriend, whom Jimmy also knew and played sports with. Whenever it was just the boys, that boy would say all sorts of terrible things about Judy. Things he thought impressed the other boys. Jimmy didn't care for it. He didn't think it was fair to Judy to have some boy who was supposed to be her sweetheart talk about her the way he did. So one day in the schoolyard when the boy went up to talk to Judy, Jimmy stopped him. About a dozen of Jimmy's friends stood around Judy in a circle with their arms crossed so the boy couldn't get to her. Judy had no idea what was going on. Jimmy told the boy he'd better not talk to Judy ever again, or he'd knock him out. After that day Jimmy became Judy's new sweetheart.

But even Judy didn't make it to the Boys Club to cheer Jimmy on in the Golden Gloves. He sat on a chair all by himself and waited for his next bout. When the time came, Jimmy climbed back into the ring and waited some more. The boy who was supposed to fight him didn't show up. The Boys Club director was running around the room trying to hustle up a fighter to take his place. "Do you want to fight this kid?" he asked one older boy. "You're bigger than him."

"Are you kidding me?" the kid replied. They gave Jimmy the trophy after just one fight.

At the end of the night, the fighters and their friends lingered outside of the Boys Club. Owney Madden pulled up in his long Buick. "Does anybody need a lift?" he asked. The boys all piled into the big car.

Owney cared about the young men the Boys Club served, the ones most in need of an outlet, the ones without much else in the community to tether themselves to, the ones like Jimmy Hill. Owney had said before that he didn't see himself as a role model. He complained that newspapers elevated bad men into big shots. When the wife of journalist Leonard Lyons found herself in a golf foursome in Hot Springs with Owney and Chicago mob boss Frank Nitti, she asked Owney what lessons from his life could benefit young boys in America. "The only way I can help boys is financially," he replied. When she argued that we all can learn from the lives of famous people, Owney dismissed her with "From the famous, yes. But not the infamous."

After taking the boys to Cook's for ice cream, Owney headed down West Grand to drop them at their homes. As they passed Owney and Agnes's house, one boy remarked, "That's where that mean man lives."

"Who told you that?" Owney asked, surprised.

"My mama," the boy said. "She told me to stay away from there. Says he's mean."

"Well, maybe he's not as mean as they think he is," Owney said. They drove the rest of the way in silence.

Dane

He'd make a place where everyday, God-fearing, decent people could fraternize with celebrities and senators alike.

The Phillips Drive-In was an all-night diner that sat just under Sugarloaf Mountain on Park Avenue, where Central Avenue met the Little Rock Highway. It was a gathering spot for bleary-eyed gamblers in need of a cup of coffee to rouse themselves from an all-night, card-game-induced haze, or a stiff drink to purge the pain of a crushing run of sevens. It was a late-night hangout for the city's elite, who huddled around the padded circular booths or sat around linen-draped tables under the willow tree that grew in its dining room. They ate Kansas City steaks and gossiped about politics, made deals to move hundreds of thousands of dollars, or hatched plans for the city's future. It was at just such a meal that Dane Harris first suggested to Norwood and Jimmy Phillips that they ought to sell him the place so he could build his own casino.

Dane hadn't been able to get Vegas off his mind. For better or worse, he had seen the future, and it looked nothing like Hot Springs. By 1959, the beginnings of a revolt against the culture of the postwar years were starting to show. Young Americans were idealistic, optimistic, and eager to move America into the future. They embraced civil rights. They experimented with drugs. They broke sexual taboos. Out west, Dane saw a landscape dotted with futuristic architecture. The music, too, was space-age and unbound—Miles Davis and Ornette Coleman and jazz that was nothing like the old big-band sound of the past. In Las Vegas, a city was being built where there had once been nothing, which meant that there were no traditions, no sense of history, that could hold it back. It could be an entirely modern city. It could be whatever America was becoming, without any of the baggage of the past.

And so Dane's new casino would have to be unlike any other club in town. It, too, would owe nothing to tradition, unlike the older, esteemed clubs that anchored the gambling business in Hot Springs. It would defy expectations of what a gambling club should be. It would be modern, futuristic even. It would offer its patrons more than just gambling, though it would offer them that in high style, and with high limits. His club would be a theater, a showroom for talent and celebrity from all over the world. His customers would eat fine food from top chefs by candlelight while they watched revues by comedians, dancers, musicians, and singers. He would take the world that people saw on their brand-new television sets, or listened to each night on their radios, and bring it to life right in front of them on a grand stage. He would create in Hot Springs a palace, as beautiful and impressive as anything in Las Vegas. He'd fill that palace with gamblers, sure, but also with every person of import who hailed from or set foot in Arkansas. He'd make a place where everyday, God-fearing, decent people could fraternize with celebrities and senators alike.

He could do all this, he explained, because Harry Hastings would back him, and together they would spare no cost. The Phillipses should name their price. Their little drive-in was where he wanted to do it. It was on the most-trafficked highway in and out of town, near the largest hotels, and right in the middle of where all of the new development was happening. The Phillips Drive-In was in the prettiest of spots, too, right at the foot of the mountain and atop the spot where the hot water flowed underneath Central Avenue to feed the city's baths. When it would rain or the air would thicken or the wind would turn cold on a warm day, the hot water would steam up the woods above the restaurant on the side of the mountain, and the steam would hover above the treetops like a cloud. Dane knew that he wanted to build his dream in that spot beneath that cloud. And he knew that he wanted to call it the Vapors.

THE GAMBLING BUSINESS HAD been booming since Dane had become boss gambler. Over a hundred million dollars had been bet in Hot Springs since the elections a year before, a staggering amount. The crowds in Hot Springs during the race meet nearly doubled the city's population for four weeks. Complaints abounded about how crowded the casinos had become, and the rest of the city was reaping the benefits of the gambling industry as well. The city's "amusement tax" on casinos, bookies, and card clubs raised hundreds of thousands of dollars for civic improvement projects like a new, state-of-the-art convention center. Bank deposits in the year and a half since gambling had been reinstated were up by more than eight million dollars, the largest increase the city's financial institutions had ever seen.

Despite these successes, a number of factors conspired behind the scenes to threaten Dane's hold on power. Babe Huff and Marion Anderson continued to rally a faction of smaller bookmakers and club owners to help return them to power. Marion's son Sam was a defense attorney who represented many of those club owners, as well as a number of other high-profile clients around town. Verne Ledgerwood worked with them to enlist the services of members of the Democratic Party establishment to try to chip away at the political consensus that the new boss gambler had built. A perception that crime in Hot Springs was on the rise would certainly be used against the sitting judges and law enforcement officials when they stood for reelection. A grand jury investigation into government corruption was likely to bring a few people down for embezzlement, including the police chief. And a wave of burglaries and safecrackings had people speculating that a professional gang was at work in Hot Springs, the result of either police corruption or police ineptitude.

The biggest problem, however, was the perception that the combination was controlled by the mob. The Kefauver and McClellan hearings had brought national attention to the inner workings of organized crime on a national scale. Many of the men seen taking the Fifth Amendment on television were also frequently seen strolling along Bathhouse Row and dining on the verandas of Hot Springs hotels and restaurants. The same men who refused to say whether or not they had thrown people off rooftops were teeing off at the Hot Springs Country Club.

The Baptists in Arkansas stepped up their organizing against gambling, using the issue as a convenient cudgel against Governor Faubus. The governor had held up his end of the deal for the bags of money the gambling combination had delivered him. He had repeatedly said that gambling was a local issue, and that he deferred to local officials as to how it should be handled. "I think the people of Hot Springs know that I have no interest in interfering in their affairs," the governor told a reporter when asked about gambling in the spa. But when pressed about mobsters moving in on the operations, he qualified his position. "I have made it known through public announcements that we don't want gangsters and racketeers in Arkansas. Any time I learn of this type of people moving in to any activity anywhere, I will step in and do so with all the force and authority I can muster."

It was a bold pronouncement, given that Governor Faubus single-handedly held the key to put the padlocks on gambling in Hot Springs permanently. The FBI couldn't stop it unless there was a violation of federal law. The local law enforcement operated at the beck and call of elected officials. The state police was the only arm of law enforcement that could step in and close the casinos right then and there based simply on the violation of state gambling laws. The ministers took notice and, seeing that it was an election year, pressed Faubus to make good on his promise.

There was nothing Dane could do to divest Hot Springs from gangsters. Gangsters ran the wire service that supplied the information to bookmakers. Gangsters owned the factory that made the dice tables and card tables, even the dice and chips. Gangsters owned all the slot machines. Gangsters ran every gambling joint, floating crap game, big-money poker game, and policy wheel in America since who knows how long. If you hired a dealer, they worked for a gangster at some point. If you hired a casino manager, they probably worked for a gangster. If you wanted to extend credit to your customers, you didn't get that credit from the Bank of Arkansas.

But what made someone a gangster? The gambling business was worth billions of dollars in America. Millions of regular folks placed bets on horses from barstools or played cards in the back of an Elks Lodge or played a number on a policy wheel. Was everyone who gambled in America outside of Nevada a hoodlum?

In Las Vegas, they were trying to run a legitimate gambling operation on a scale that nobody in America had ever seen before. There was no way to pull it off without enlisting the help of those who best knew how to run casinos, a list that included a lot of criminals and mob associates. They were able to do their work in relative peace, without Baptist ministers tracking their every move, dropping dimes on them with the governor at every turn. Hell, in Nevada the governor dined openly in the casinos. The senators got credit at the tables. All because in Nevada gambling was legal. Legal gambling was why a murderer in Las Vegas could become an executive. And illegal gambling was why a businessman who'd never seen the inside of a courtroom in his life in Hot Springs was labeled a hoodlum. It was the one advantage that Las Vegas had over Hot Springs when it came to where all of those hundreds of millions of gambling dollars in America would potentially end up.

CASINO BOSSES WERE ALREADY moving their personnel and whatever money they could smuggle out of Havana to Las Vegas. It had been nearly a year since the revolution. Meyer Lansky had escaped, but he left seventeen million dollars in cash behind. His brother Jake and Tampa mob boss Santo Trafficante had stayed in Havana, hoping the Castro government would work with the gamblers. At first it seemed like there was no chance, after the revolutionaries had destroyed the casinos. But Castro's economic advisers suggested he reopen them to help the economy remain stable. Duane Faull, one of the newest members of the Hot Springs combination, owned his own airplane. He flew from Hot Springs to Havana to see it for himself. Faull stayed at the Havana Hilton and was treated as a guest of the revolutionary government. He was impressed by what he saw, not only with the casinos being reopened but also the rebels themselves. He returned to Hot Springs and reported that Havana would soon be back to normal.

Faull's prediction was wrong. In the first four months the rebels operated the casinos, they lost $750,000 at the Riviera alone. By the end of the year, all the major casinos and hotels were in debt. The visitors weren't lining up to visit a country in the throes of a violent revolution, so the tourist trade was dying. The government closed the casinos for good, and a lot of formerly wealthy gambling bosses were on the lookout for a new score. Legalized gambling in Las Vegas seemed like an attractive option.

Q. Byrum Hurst knew that he would have to compete with Vegas, so he paid a public relations firm to poll voters in Arkansas about their attitudes toward gambling. The survey results were discouraging. Fifty-one percent were opposed to legalizing gambling in Hot

Springs. When asked about the state regulating and controlling gambling, however, 59 percent were in favor, including 50 percent of Baptists and 57 percent of rural and small-town residents. The gamblers saw an opening there. Instead of asking for legalization, they would ask for regulation.

Hurst wrote up a bill that he considered even tougher and more restrictive than the Nevada statute. It would put the question up for a local vote in Garland County. It would restrict gambling licenses to those who had resided in Arkansas for at least ten consecutive years. It would allow the government to tax the proceeds and police the financial books through a State Gaming Control Board.

Hurst's bill was controversial, and not just among the teetotaling Baptists. There were those among the gambling establishment in Hot Springs who thought it would be a bad idea to legalize gambling. If it was legal, they reckoned, then it'd be open to anyone with money to invest, rather than being limited to those with the right political connections. Mayor Floyd Housley argued that legalization would make the casinos more susceptible to mob control, rather than less. "As it stands we have control," Housley said. "But if it was legalized the 'hoods' would work in from the state level." That didn't sway Dane. He felt strongly that they needed to get gambling legal in Arkansas by hook or by crook.

Whatever they were going to do, they'd need to do it fast. Their local adversaries had been crowing to Sam Anderson, Marion's son, about helping Babe Huff run another slate of candidates. Governor Faubus, who was their linchpin, had political vulnerabilities. His embrace of segregation had not only enraged his own father, but spurred formerly loyal yellow dog Democrats to openly float the idea of recruiting a pro-civil-rights Republican to challenge Faubus. Dane and Owney were going to need to come up with another quarter of a million dollars for the 1960 campaigns. All of this while Dane invested nearly a million dollars in building a carpet joint for jet-setting, hundred-dollar-a-hand players.

Jimmy and Norwood Phillips weren't completely convinced that Dane's idea would take wing and fly. There were so many obstacles that money alone couldn't fix. Perhaps Hot Springs just wasn't ready for the Vapors.

That didn't matter one bit to Dane. He knew Hot Springs was better than the desert in every conceivable way. Hot Springs deserved a place as good as any they had in Nevada. If Jimmy and Norwood would just shake Dane's hand, he'd give Hot Springs a place like that, whether they were ready for it or not.

They shook on it there beneath the willow tree and it was settled. The Phillips Drive-In would be the rock upon which Dane would build the Vapors. And the gates of hell would not prevail against it.

Part IV
REPENTANCE

1960-1963

Hazel

FEBRUARY 1960

Who in the hell, they must have wondered, gave those heathens a motorbike?

Whenever Larry and Jimmy would show up at Jack's house, Hazel and Jack were already drunk. That wasn't unusual. If they weren't drunk when the boys got home from school, they were already passed out, or just plain gone to who knows where. They'd spend their nights out gambling, drinking, partying, or "working," either at the Tower Club or running any number of scams on the side around town. They'd expanded from bennies to quaaludes, running themselves ragged on the uppers, then coming home in the morning to try to bring themselves back down with the downers. Abuse of amphetamines like bennies was on the rise in the United States, and middle-aged women like Hazel were the major victims, most of them having gotten hooked after taking them to lose weight. But in 1960, there were only about sixty thousand cases of drug addiction nationwide. America was on the verge of an explosion in drug use in the sixties, and that number would balloon to over two hundred thousand before the end of the decade. In 1960, Hazel and Jack's situation seemed ahead of its time.

Eventually, they'd both fall into a deep sleep wherever they happened to be—propped up in a chair, lying on the bed, sitting on the floor, all their clothes still on from however many days since the last time they had bothered to change. Jack splayed across the bed with his boots on. Hazel propped against a wall with a cigarette dangling from her fingers. It was eerie, almost as if they were dead. Jimmy would put his finger beneath Hazel's nose to make sure she was still breathing.

Jack and Hazel were burning through what remained of Jack's money as fast as they could. They spent it on liquor and pills. They lost it playing cards and dice. Jack even bought himself a brand-new car. What they couldn't be bothered to do was spend any on Jimmy and Larry. There weren't groceries in the pantry. No milk in the icebox. When Hazel thought to cook, she'd make soup out of a can. When she didn't, the boys would scavenge. They'd eat hot dog buns. They'd pool their nickels, walk to the store, and buy baloney. Christmas came and went without any gifts, save for whatever toys Hollis Jr. could afford to send them in the mail. Jimmy wasn't even sure what day his birthday was.

All the while, Jack walked around with that big knot of bills wadded up in his pocket. He'd call the cab stand and tell them to send over a couple of bottles of rye, then when the hack showed up at the door he'd flash them a whole stack of hundreds while he peeled off the money to pay them. It was as if he loved showing off how much money he had, even as he pissed it all away.

On the occasions that Jimmy and Larry were over while Jack and Hazel were conscious, Jack would holler at them to do chores. Clean up the yard. Scrub the kitchen floor. Earn your way around here, boys. Make yourselves useful. Jimmy and Larry would pretend to push brooms and rags around the house until Jack and Hazel nodded off.

THE FIRST TIME THEY stole, it was Larry's idea. On the coffee table in front of Jack's lifeless body sat a stack of hundred-dollar bills as tall as two decks of cards. Jack had forgotten to wad it up into his pocket.

Larry didn't hesitate to snatch a bill off the top. He motioned for Jimmy to do the same, but Jimmy seized up with fear. Larry didn't wait around to talk Jimmy into it. He bolted out the front door. Jimmy hightailed it right behind him.

That night the two boys lived it up on Central Avenue. They went to the picture show. They took turns at the shooting gallery. They stopped at every drugstore, lunch counter, and soda fountain downtown to buy a piece of candy or a Coke. They went into a department store and bought themselves brand-new Levi's and white T-shirts. By the time they got home they hadn't even spent a quarter of the hundred dollars. Larry took the change he had left over and squirreled it away in his room. Jimmy tried on his new Levi's and they didn't fit. He was hot about it, too. He'd bought himself an entire wardrobe of Levi's and T-shirts and it was all useless to him now. He stuffed them in his knapsack to take to school the next day so he could give them out to his friends.

The next night when Hazel and Jack passed out, Jack hadn't left the stack of money on the table. Larry peeked in Jack's pockets, but there was no money there, either. The two boys searched the house until they found the jackpot in one of Jack's bureau drawers in the bedroom—stacks of hundred-dollar bills, like a drawer at a bank. Larry snatched a couple of bills. This time Jimmy did not hesitate. He grabbed a hundred dollars and promised himself that this time he'd try everything on before he left the store.

The two brothers split up, each with their own shopping to do. Jimmy bought himself some Levi's that fit, took in another picture show, filled his pockets with candy bars, then went back home and sat on the porch eating candy and waiting for Larry to return. When Larry finally showed up that night, he pulled into the driveway on a brand-new motor scooter, chrome glistening, engine purring like a cat. Jimmy's eyes went big as saucers. He was aiming too low. His older brother had a much better handle on living a life of larceny. Larry gave Jimmy a ride around the block. The boys spun doughnuts in the street outside, laughing as if it were a Saturday afternoon and not the middle of the night on Tuesday. The neighbors peered from their windows at the spectacle. Who in the hell, they must have wondered, gave those heathens a motorbike?

When Larry and Jimmy made it home from school the next day, the motor scooter was gone, and Hazel and Jack were stone-cold sober. Jack took Larry by the arm and dragged him around to the back of the house. He showed him the motor scooter lying on its side, tossed into the back of the garage.

"You want to drive?" Jack asked Larry. "You don't need to drive a motor scooter. You're fixing to turn sixteen, it's time you learn to drive a car." Larry looked at Jack in shock. Jack opened up the driver's-side door of his Plymouth and motioned for Larry to get in.

Larry reluctantly climbed into the driver's seat, unsure of what the play was. Jack gave him the keys and got in the passenger side. Larry started the car and looked at Jack for a clue about what he wanted him to do. Jack just had that same pleased look as when he showed that cab-driver all his money.

Larry had never driven a car before, so they herked and jerked up and down the street for a while before Larry got the hang of it. And even then he struggled as the car just bump-bump-bumped along. Jack didn't seem too upset. In fact, he was downright patient. The whole thing put Larry off, made him nervous as hell.

Jack made Larry drive clear through town, deep into the sticks, all the way to Gar Lewis's general store. This place was out in the middle of nowhere, a bait and tackle outfitter for the serious fishermen, and a place for provisions for the handful of hillbillies who lived around those parts. They parked the car and went inside and Gar acted as if he and Jack were old friends. Larry didn't know why Jack would be a familiar face in such a far-flung stop, especially given that Jack Cartwright was not the outdoorsman type.

Without prompting, Gar told Jack to wait while he went into a back room. He came back with a paper sack and set it on the counter. Jack turned the sack over and out spilled three or four pistols on the counter. He picked each one up and inspected it, spun the cylinders, cocked the hammers. He smiled and took his wad of money out and peeled some off for old Gar Lewis and shook his hand. Gar said, "I'll see you next time," as they walked out the door, a brand-new pistol stuffed in Jack's waistband.

Jack must have wanted Larry to see those guns, but Larry didn't know why. Larry didn't ask about it and Jack didn't tell. They didn't speak about anything. They just herked and jerked and bump-bump-bumped the whole long way back to town.

Owney

It didn't matter that Owney shared his bed with the postmaster's daughter or that he paid for some schoolkids' band uniforms.

"How long will you be staying with us, Mr. Poretto?" the clerk at the Arlington asked Papa Joe as he handed him his room key.

"Indefinitely," he replied.

Joe Poretto wasn't in Hot Springs for a social call. He had business to attend to, and he didn't intend to leave until it was all sorted out. In the previous months, Papa Joe had schemed with Ralph Pierce over how to maneuver his way into Hot Springs now that Owney had his own wire, going from one bookie to the next inquiring how they stood with "the little man at the Southern." Papa Joe had already made Owney sell him his 5 percent of the Pines Supper Club. Owney obliged him, possibly because Dane saw it as competition for the nearby Belvedere and would have wanted Owney free of it anyway. But it wasn't likely to stop there. Papa Joe would keep coming back for more until he had it all.

Owney took Papa Joe to dinner at Coy's Steakhouse and told him that his presence in Hot Springs was causing too much trouble, that the gamblers' political opponents were using it against them. Owney thought Papa Joe should keep a lower profile. When Papa Joe returned to his hotel, the new circuit judge, Plummer Dobbs, was waiting for him; he told Papa Joe to leave town the next day and not return. Papa Joe called Sam Giancana, the boss of the Chicago mob, looking for permission to "take everything."

"It ain't me, Mooney, it's the little man," Poretto said to Giancana, who often went by the name "Momo" or "Mooney." "And that fucker is trying to fight that Baptist judge." When Giancana checked in with Curley Humphreys, Humphreys said, "Owney has a right to go anyplace he wants."

"Joe would fuck his own mother," Humphreys said. "Let's be frank about this."

Papa Joe went straight from the Arlington to the Ritter Hotel, where Owney's wire service operated. Owney had already caught wind of Papa Joe's intentions and had locked himself and "Jimmy the Pro" Vitro, an enforcer from Chicago who had come to Arkansas to look after him, on the other side of the office door, armed and ready for whatever Papa Joe had in mind. Papa Joe banged on the door and demanded to be let in. Owney replied that he wasn't going to let him in, and he wasn't going to let him take over the wire. "I wish you'd stay in New Orleans," Owney pleaded. "When you're in Hot Springs it only causes heat for me." It likely felt like an admission to Papa Joe that Owney had ordered Judge Dobbs to run Papa Joe out of town.

The two continued to argue and hurl violent threats at each other until the police finally arrived, and Papa Joe left without further incident. It must have driven Papa Joe and his fellow gangsters wild to hear Owney talk about himself as a local, to place himself on some different footing in Hot Springs than the rest of the mob. Why should the likes of Joe Poretto have to be run out of town by the law while Owney got to sit in his big office and make book? What made Owney any different?

Owney didn't see himself as an outsider, though. He'd lived in Hot Springs for more than twenty years. He had married into a prominent local family. He spread his money all over town, propped up banks, helped build churches, kept the schoolkids in band uniforms. He showed the small-town hicks how to run a nightclub. He had brought Hot Springs out of the darkness. And while he still thought Hot Springs was more of a town than a true city, he believed Hot Springs was his town.

What Papa Joe likely understood was that to the people of Hot Springs there was no difference between him and Owney. Owney Madden was a gangster, same as him, same as Carlos Marcello, same as Al Capone. It didn't matter that Owney shared his bed with the postmaster's daughter or that he paid for some schoolkids' band uniforms. Owney was a hood. Not only was he a hood, he was one of the biggest hoods in American history, a legendary criminal. The idea that Owney could ever outrun that and leave it behind, that if he surrendered his action to Papa Joe that the good people of Hot Springs would suddenly clutch their pearls and faint upon their couches, was pure delusion.

Then again, it could be that Owney understood all of that just fine. It could be that Owney knew exactly what he was, that he was someone who didn't need to bend the knee to the likes of Papa Joe Poretto or Carlos Marcello. That surely seemed to be the case when Owney boarded a flight to Chicago to talk to Curley Humphreys about Papa Joe. Humphreys told him not to worry about it, that he'd handle it, smooth it over with Papa Joe and let him know that what was Owney's was Owney's. That wasn't good enough. Owney wanted Papa Joe eliminated. And he didn't think Humphreys should stop with Papa Joe. He thought they should get all the Italians out of the wire business. The rackets were under attack across the country, there was a vacuum in leadership, and the Italians would close ranks and snatch up what they could. The days of cooperation were over.

Humphreys respected Owney more than Owney could have known. Owney was a living legend, a direct connection to the old Prohibition days. He was someone who had earned his spot at the top. He had spilled blood, he had done hard time. But that was the distant past.

The criminal underworld had changed. Owney was now in the seventieth year of his life. Once, maybe not even that long ago, Owney could call some shots, but not anymore. Now he relied on old relationships, on his reputation and the respect he believed it commanded. There was a moment, perhaps, when things could have worked out differently for Owney. He could have turned Hot Springs into Havana. They practically gave it to him on a silver platter. He could have brought in the right people and built himself an empire. He chose to put his money in a bank. He chose to play golf. That was fine. That was his privilege. But it meant he wasn't someone who could tell Curley Humphreys to have someone killed. Owney wasn't that kind of crime boss anymore. He wasn't Owney the Killer. He was the little man at the Southern, now and forever.

Dane

"This feller, who was playing with politics before he played with toys, says some betting lettuce is being kept on ice to confound the enemy."

People had been gossiping about the Vapors for the better part of a year. Ever since the construction started on the Phillips Drive-In and people heard what Dane Harris was up to, anticipation had begun to build. The newspaper reported that the cost of the new club was "several hundreds of thousands of dollars." In truth it had eclipsed a million. In addition to the construction costs for the modern, Googie-style building, the Vapors would take hundreds more people to operate year-round, between the theater, restaurant, all-night coffee shop, and casino. It would swell Dane's payroll to over a million dollars per year. He also set aside nearly a half million dollars a year for booking big-name entertainment. And he planned to blast advertising to Louisiana, Oklahoma, Texas, and even as far away as St. Louis with a seventy-five-thousand-dollar advertising budget. He wanted the Vapors to offer visitors to Hot Springs a world-class experience, to rival the best that Las Vegas had to offer. Without Teamster loans, that was an expensive proposition for Dane and his backers. But Dane believed it was worth the risk.

When the Vapors opened its doors to the public in the summer of 1960, it exceeded expectations. There were eighty brand-new slot machines, six dice tables, four roulette wheels, and four blackjack tables. Even with oilmen and heiresses playing with orange one-hundred-dollar chips, there still wasn't enough room in the casino for all the action.

These top-shelf gambling clubs were called "carpet joints," and the Vapors had the plushest carpet of them all. Dane installed shag carpeting throughout his clubs, even in the bar, much to the cleaning staff's frustration. He hung enormous crystal chandeliers in every room. He tiled the walls with mirrors. He had the mahogany bar from the Belvedere moved into the enormous showroom in the Vapors, where diners could sit and eat their expensive steaks while watching entertainers from all over the world. After dinner, when the hydraulic stage retracted and revealed the polished mahogany dance floor, they could get out of their seats and dance to Buddy Kirk and the house orchestra or whoever was in residence that week.

For his opening performance, Dane convinced "Slapsy" Maxie Rosenbloom, the former light heavyweight champion once managed by Owney, to premier his Broadway musical revue in Hot Springs. Rosenbloom had in retirement become a film and television star, and there was a great deal of anticipation for his revue. "This fine club the Vapors compares with any I have seen over the United States—I have traveled extensively—and will attract many celebrities to the city," Rosenbloom told reporters. His opinion was well informed—he owned the popular nightclub Slapsy Maxie's in Los Angeles.

No sooner had Slapsy Maxie's revue called it a wrap than Dane booked Mickey Rooney, who sold out two shows a night. Rooney's first week at the Vapors was one of the biggest weeks of any club in the history of Hot Springs. Unlike some of the more refined acts Dane had booked to perform, like Liberace or the McGuire Sisters, Mickey Rooney brought in customers who liked to gamble. Rooney liked to gamble, too. By the end of his first week, Rooney had essentially worked for free. He had blown his entire guarantee on cards and horses.

The Vapors was off to a good start, and Dane and Owney sought to capitalize on it by putting their plan to legalize gambling into action. Q. Byrum Hurst introduced his gambling bill in the state legislature. Hurst put up a spirited fight for the bill. He pointed to the opinion poll, and stressed that his bill represented the toughest regulations on gambling ever proposed anywhere in the United States. When it was clear that his colleagues were unmoved by his insistence that 59 percent of Arkansans supported him, Hurst resorted to pleading. "If you let us have this, it will mean a lot to Arkansas, and Hot Springs will be a place to be proud of. If we had industry and payrolls like some other places we wouldn't need it," he said. "But Hot Springs has had to accept gambling as an industry." Hurst painted a picture of a community held hostage by its own graft and corruption—corruption that had touched every level of state government. "This is a situation that has been allowed to prostitute every public official from the top to the bottom." The bill was voted down 27–4.

The failure of the bill wasn't the only thing that took the wind out of Dane's sails. Hot Springs was in the midst of yet another heated political battle for the sheriff's and prosecuting attorney's offices. Babe Huff's faction fielded Marion Anderson's son Sam in the prosecutor's race against Walter Hebert. The sheriff's race saw four candidates try to unseat Leonard Ellis, including John Ermey, whom the combination forced to retire as police chief when it was clear he was going to get caught up in the middle of a grand jury corruption investigation. There was also a grocery store manager named Duffie Searcy, who was a bit of a wild-card candidate. Searcy was in his fifties and had never served in law enforcement before. But then again, neither had Ellis when he first stood for sheriff, so that was hardly disqualifying.

All four candidates assailed Ellis for being a do-nothing, a drunk, and in the pocket of the boss gambler, Dane Harris. They said he spent more time in Dane's office at the Black Cat liquor store than he spent at the sheriff's office. They pointed to a spree of safecrackings that had plagued the city in the prior year, which Ellis, Plummer Dobbs, and the mayor went out of their way to blame on "home talent" with "local connections." The rumor, however, was that the robberies were by an out-of-town heist crew who were being protected by someone in office. The forceful denials from Leonard Ellis did little to quell the rumors so long as there hadn't been any arrests.

Sam Anderson's campaign against Walter Hebert focused on poll tax fraud. He insisted that Hebert refused to do anything about rampant abuses of the poll tax system, which he claimed Dane Harris and company had used to keep their allies in power. Sam ran full-page ads with copies of poll tax receipts he claimed were forged by Dane's personal secretary. He took his evidence to the grand jury and asked them to investigate it, but the grand jury refused. The foreman of the grand jury, Joe McRae, wrote a letter signed by every member of the jury but one that said that Sam Anderson was trying to use the grand jury for his own political purposes and was misrepresenting them in his speeches and advertisements. Joe McRae was hardly impartial. His construction company had won the contract to build the Vapors without a bid. That just tore it for Sam. He had a dramatic outburst in front of reporters where he shouted that he didn't trust anyone in government in Hot Springs, effectively ending his campaign.

For their part, the machine candidates ran fairly tame campaigns. Leonard Ellis didn't even look like he was running for sheriff. His advertisements were just more photographs of the swimming pools they had built. He talked about all the money that had been raised for fixing the courthouse roof and building the convention center by taxing the casinos. He made no secret of the fact that he was running as an arm of the gambling establishment. But he reminded voters that if they let any of Huff's men into office, those men would surely shut the casinos down, which would be the ruin of Hot Springs.

There was reason to worry, though. In Hot Springs there was a barometer even more accurate than opinion polls—the bookies in town who took bets on the elections. And the newspaper was reporting that the bookies weren't seeing a lot of action.

One guy who usually has a kroner or so riding on a primary or election says the lack of betting, at least on a couple of specific races, smacks of 'strategy.' This feller, who was playing with politics before he played with toys, says some betting lettuce is being kept on ice to confound the enemy. The same feller says the lettuce will be tossed on the salad before the runoffs—if there are any . . .

The lack of betting could have been strategy or it could have reflected a lack of enthusiasm for either side. One of the non-affiliated candidates in the prosecutor's race, city attorney David Whittington, billed himself as above the fray of the warring gambling factions. His campaign ads depicted a man in a necktie being yanked in two directions, one by a hand that read "Court House Gang" and the other by a hand that read "Old Anderson McLaughlin Gang." It was possible that the fever pitch between the Huff and Harris groups was alienating the voters. To give themselves a little extra insurance, Dane sent his men around the Second Ward offering twenty dollars to anyone who would volunteer their poll tax receipt. It wouldn't be enough. Whittington and Searcy won in landslides.

Whittington on first glance seemed amenable to working with the gamblers. "I am not mad at anybody and I hope no one is mad at me," he said after the election. "I will do what I promised—serve the people." Searcy, on the other hand, wanted to negotiate. There were a lot of folks who were tired of being on the outs and wanted back in. They had spent a lot of money helping the grocer get elected sheriff, and they were ready to make good on their investment. There were just as many bookmakers and club owners who weren't open to negotiating with the new sheriff, or anyone else associated with the old Babe Huff faction. They had thrown their lot in with Dane, and they intended to stick with him. The city braced for another standoff.

DANE BELIEVED THAT THE Vapors and the future of Hot Springs were intertwined. He had already shown in a short period of time how big the Vapors could be for the city, how it could put Hot Springs on the map alongside Las Vegas. But he also knew the failure of Hurst's bill and the election of a new sheriff meant that everything could be lost—the money he had invested, the city's most important industry, and his role at the center of it all. He needed to proceed carefully, to show his worth as the boss gambler by negotiating a deal that would allow things to continue running smoothly. In anticipation of a shutdown, Dane canceled the remainder of Mickey Rooney's dates. He canceled all of his upcoming acts for the start of 1961, including a three-thousand-dollar-a-week appearance by Dorothy Shay. Dane quickly put together a partnership corporation with many of his partners in the Vapors, including Harry Hastings, and bought out all of the shareholders in the Belvedere, who by then numbered over a hundred and were spread out across the country. He wanted to do some renovations and repairs in preparation for the 1961 racing meet, but also sought to limit the ownership to Hot Springs residents, whose loyalty he could count on. The time had come to circle the wagons. He enlisted the help of the chamber of commerce in negotiating a settlement with Duffie Searcy, Sam Anderson, and their allies.

Negotiations went on for weeks, and at times the animosity between the two sides seemed insurmountable. In the end, peace prevailed. In order to keep the Vapors, the Southern, and the Belvedere open, Dane had to agree to sell the Tower. He also agreed that a number of bust-out joints they had closed down, like the Palms, could reopen. A good number of new handbooks were set to open, which angered bookmakers but pleased Owney, who would continue to operate the wire service. In all they agreed to allow some form of gambling, from a single slot machine to full-scale casinos, in over eighty locations in Hot Springs. Each would be expected to pay into the city's amusement fund. Everyone was expected to run a clean operation. No scams, no hookers, no drugs.

Owney continued to be a sore spot for the rival faction. They knew he was still partners with Dane in the slot machine business, and the other side didn't want to give him one red cent. Dane offered a concession: anyone who wanted to could get their slot machines from the Pakises' slot machine company, Southern Amusement, if they didn't want to do business with Dane and Owney. But there wouldn't be another wire service. That was Owney's. That was nonnegotiable. Dane stood behind his old partner.

One thing that came out of the truce was the establishment of a joint fund for advertising in out-of-state newspapers that would feature the clubs and hotels together, in conjunction with the airlines. They would move forward into 1961 a united front, working together for the benefit of the entire industry. The pact worked. A week before the 1961 horse racing season began, hotels across Hot Springs were sold out for the entire meet. Oaklawn extended the meet to forty-three days. The city prepared for what was sure to be the biggest meet on record. There was general consensus that the joint advertising fund was making a difference. If the truce between the factions could hold, Hot Springs could finally compete with Las Vegas.

There was still one major threat to the continued peace among the gamblers. Perhaps the biggest concession Dane and Owney made, even greater than selling the stalwart Tower Club, was allowing the Anderson faction to open up a new club downtown—a brand-new casino all their own, and not in some far-flung location on the outskirts of town but right smack-dab in the middle of downtown. They named it the Bridge Street Club. They said it would be an action spot, with high limits for big-time gamblers. Some worried that Dane had let the snake in the door by giving his enemies a brand-new franchise. It was a small price to pay, however, to keep the Vapors open. One bust-out joint downtown couldn't possibly jeopardize the good the Vapors stood to do for Hot Springs. The Vapors would convince all who entered that gambling was good. One visit and they'd never want to live in a city without it.

Hazel

What they were running toward was unknown, but it was undeniable to those around them that it would be the death of them both.

Jimmy and Larry came by Hazel and Jack's house, which they called "the big house," to pay a visit. When they arrived Hazel was passed out. Jack was not quite there yet. He was still alert and admiring one of his pistols, a .38 revolver. He caressed it in his hands. He spun it around his finger. He leaned back in his easy chair and composed himself, growing serious.

"Somebody's stealin' from me," Jack mumbled. Larry and Jimmy looked at each other, careful not to betray anything to Jack. The motor scooter incident hadn't slowed them down one bit. They were stealing cash from Jack as often as he was blacking out, which was nearly every day. It was only a matter of time before he got wise.

"I tell you what—if whoever's stealin' from me comes in this house, I'll blow 'em away." Jack spun the gun on his finger again, this time fumbling it. He squared the gun up quickly in his hand and aimed it at the front door of the house. "Come in this house and steal from me?"

The boys froze. They'd seen Jack drunk, high, and ornery as all get-out before. But this time he had a gun in his hand.

Jack held the gun up for the boys to look at. "You like this gun? This is my favorite gun." The boys said nothing, just stared at Jack and wondered how it would all end. "This gun will blow someone's fucking head off."

He pointed the gun at the boys and pulled the trigger. Inside the living room, the report sounded like a bomb going off. Hazel woke straight up out of her stupor. The bullet shot between the boys and ricocheted off the wall. They could hear the sound of it whizzing by them as it ping-ponged from wall to wall before it found the window and broke through the glass.

"What in the hell is going on?" Hazel hollered. The boys didn't stick around. They hit the front porch like a bell clapper in a goose's ass and kept right on going into the night.

"That's right!" Jack hollered after them. "You don't come back to this house! You ain't welcome in this house no more!"

Hazel leapt to her feet and stood in the doorway, watching the boys run away. A little more sober, she turned to look at Jack. He stared at the ground, refusing to meet her gaze. He twirled the pistol on his finger.

When Hazel fought in court to keep her sons, she couldn't imagine life without them. They were her children, and her only family. As long as she'd had them, they had been her only reason for living. Her love for her sons carried her through her husband's alcoholism, his abuse, his death. Their impending loss was a consequence of her addictions, which themselves were a consequence of her need to burn the candle at both ends, which at one point she perhaps told herself was a sacrifice she made for her family. How far away she must have felt, only a few years later, from that woman who sobbed before the judge, begging to keep her children. How absurd it all must have felt, the idea that any of this was for her children's benefit. By now, Hazel's addictions were fully in control of her life. She had long given up on mothering her sons. They had been on their own, taking care of themselves, and Hazel had surrendered herself to Jack's lifestyle, living in pursuit of pleasure and escape. Jack had abandoned a family, too. He had a wife and a son, neither of whom were in his life now as he squandered what little fortune his parents had left for him. Jack was running away from his past, and Hazel was accompanying him. What they were running toward was unknown, but it was undeniable to those around them that it would be the death of them both.

HOLLIS JR. SHOWED UP on Jack and Hazel's doorstep one day with his new wife, Martha, and a baby boy named Mike. They had driven down from North Carolina, where they had been living since Hollis Jr. got out of the service. Hollis Jr. had felt guilty that it took him so long to bring the baby to his family in Arkansas, but he was glad he finally had the chance. When they arrived, Hazel was high as a kite on Equanil, a prescription tranquilizer. She was pleased to see them, pleased to meet the baby, but she wasn't all there and Hollis Jr. could tell. She slurred her words and seemed anxious. Hollis Jr. demanded to know where Larry and Jimmy were. Hazel told him that they lived in a different house by themselves.

When Hollis Jr. visited his little brothers, he was shocked at what he found. The boys lived in a small brick house next to the mountain, right behind Jack's place. They had an icebox and a couple of beds. They had their clothes and a few personal things, but for the most part the place didn't feel lived in. There wasn't anything in the icebox but a little bit of milk and baloney.

Jimmy and Larry kept their own schedules now. Larry spent most of his time with his girlfriend. Hazel and Jack would go to work at the Tower Club together at night, riding in Jack's new Chrysler, and Larry would go over to their house, steal the Plymouth, and take it joyriding. He stayed out late. He pressed his luck like that.

Jimmy had a paper route in the mornings still. He had joined the football team and spent a lot of time at practice after school. He spent his weekends and most of his free time out at Judy's house on the lake. Her folks had taken a shine to Jimmy. They liked the way he acted around them. He wasn't afraid of them. He didn't avoid them or act uncomfortable the way most teenagers did. He was polite and confident and conversed with them like equals. They knew about his situation at home. They bought him a winter coat when it turned cold. They invited him to stay during Christmas so he wouldn't be alone.

Other adults felt the same way about him, especially his football coaches. The coaches would lecture the boys about how to act in public, how they should always display good manners and represent the team wherever they went. "Like Jimbo," they'd say. "He knows how to act."

It was a real puzzle that a boy like Jimmy would have any manners at all, let alone be the best behaved of the whole bunch, given his lack of a proper upbringing. But the absence of any parenting meant that he was forced to mature much more quickly than his peers as a matter of survival. His respect for adults likely came from never having any adults in his life to put him in his proper place. Somehow in Jimmy the neglect bred confidence, a feeling of equality with adults.

Even though Jimmy went to great lengths to keep his home life private, everyone seemed to know all about it. Hot Springs wasn't a big town. When Jimmy told people that Jack was his uncle, they'd just go along with it so as not to embarrass him. When he said that his mother was sick with some kind of illness, they would just say, "Bless your heart," and pat him on the hand. When he told people that his mother lived in the little house by the mountain with him and Larry and she just worked over at his uncle Jack's, they wouldn't argue. They'd just smile and say, "Tell your mama I said hello." But whenever his friends came over to visit, they'd have packages of food their parents sent with them.

Jimmy looked up to Hollis Jr. like nobody else in the world. Because Jimmy was too young to remember his father, his oldest brother was as close to a father figure as he'd ever had. He remembered Hollis Jr. playing football for Hot Springs High School. He was a star on the field, a real athlete. He wore a letterman jacket that to little Jimmy Hill looked as distinguished and dapper as army dress blues. He wanted Hollis Jr. to come back and watch him play one day. Hollis Jr. told him he would.

The three brothers, Martha, and the baby all went downtown to stroll the promenade and look at the bright lights together. Jimmy knew that Judy was at the Arlington babysitting for some tourist couple who were in town to gamble at the Southern Club. They dropped in on her and found her alone in a hotel room with an actual baby. Not a little kid like she usually babysat, but an infant, far younger than any fifteen-year-old had any business being alone with. The baby was wailing, face all puffed up and red, tiny arms and legs vibrating with anger.

"I don't know what to do," Judy said, terrified. "Save me."

Martha handed baby Mike to Hollis Jr. and took the infant from Judy to try to get it to shush. Then baby Mike started crying and Hollis passed him back to Martha, who passed the infant to Jimmy, who fared no better at consoling it. They passed the two babies around like a couple of hot potatoes. The babies wailed in perfect harmony, the sound of one's cries egging the other on, growing louder and louder as the room full of children struggled until finally, without rhyme or reason, Martha and Judy somehow managed to settle the babies off to sleep.

Dane

MARCH 1961

They didn't realize it as they passed the dice back and forth, but the cowboys from Dallas owned the Bridge Street Club.

Jack Digby drove Polly Barentine up on Cedar Mountain, right outside of town. At the summit of the mountain there was a small parking area where folks would go to "look at the duck." That's what kids used to say to their parents, that they were going up there so they could look down on Hot Springs and see the way the streetlights formed the shape of a duck. But that wasn't why anyone really went up there. They went up there to neck. Jack Digby, however, was a twenty-nine-year-old man with simple needs and singular focus. He wanted to do much more than neck. He was doing much more than necking when Polly's husband, Everett, showed up.

When Everett got within sight of the car he opened fire. One of the bullets caught Digby in the face. Digby went for his gun in the front seat and managed to get it squared up and aimed toward whoever was firing on him. He returned fire and, being an officer of the law and a practiced marksman, caught Everett several times in the chest and gut. The two men pulled their triggers until both their guns were empty.

Somehow neither man died. Even more remarkably, neither man went to jail over the gunfight. But Jack Digby was kicked out of the Hot Springs Police Department. In a way it was good timing. Digby's lawyer was Sam Anderson. Sam had just cleared the way for the opening of the Bridge Street Club, and he was trying to line up partners. Digby was the perfect fit for the rival gambling faction. In addition to having connections on the police force, Digby was a prolific hustler. He pimped women off barstools. He ran the bingo games at the American Legion. But Digby had never been content with pimping and bingo money. He wanted to be a big shot gambling boss. He was known as a brawler, someone who'd knock someone's lights out for looking at him the wrong way. Just like up on Cedar Mountain, he didn't hesitate to act. Most important, he had a nice chunk of change saved up. He and three other men put up twenty-five thousand dollars apiece to bank the Bridge Street Club's casino, and just like that, Jack Digby went from disgraced patrolman to distinguished gambler.

The 1961 race meet was the biggest race meet Hot Springs had ever seen. Tourists crowded the sidewalks. Automobile traffic clogged the streets. The municipal airport, which usually hosted dozens of private aircraft during the race meet, now regularly packed in over one hundred planes. Much of the renewed interest in Hot Springs around the country was due to the opening of the Vapors.

DANE HARRIS'S STRATEGY OF running his club as an entertainment venue first and a casino second was paying off. His enormous talent budget was bringing in the best acts from around the country—Marie McDonald, Mamie Van Doren, Gary Crosby, Ted Lewis, Pinky Lee, the Andrews Sisters. The popular singer Frankie Laine even hosted an episode of the nationally broadcast *Frankie Laine Show* from the Vapors. Entertainment at the Vapors was such a draw in 1961 that the city's hotels were using the club's upcoming lineups in their advertisements around the country.

At each and every opening night, Dane and Marcella would dress up their children and put in an appearance. It mattered to Dane that his young children be allowed to come and watch these larger-than-life performers. It was a privilege to have them in Hot Springs. Dane was proud of the culture and sophistication of his new club, and he wanted his family to experience it, to be a part of it. There was no point in waiting until his children were older. There was no guarantee any of this would last that long.

Marcella and Dane's relationship was the most strained it had ever been. She spent less and less time with him, and more and more time with her friends on the golf course or at the country club dining room. Marcella was an outgoing woman with a big personality. In the beginning of their relationship, she had helped the more reserved Dane relate to other people, dragging him out to clubs to listen to music or dance, or introducing him to other people and forcing him to socialize. Marcella was the charming one, the one who lured people into their orbit, the one who turned acquaintances into friends. Now Dane was a powerful man, and his reserved and stoic manner was no longer a liability. And while Marcella's intelligence was once a complement to Dane's own intellect, one of the qualities that initially drew him to her, he no longer depended on it. He had surrounded himself with plenty of smart people whom he respected.

Marcella had strong reservations about Dane's role as the boss gambler. The gun in Las Vegas was the tip of the iceberg. In the past year, Dane had started taking a number of alarming precautions. He gave his family a curfew. He hired armed guards for their home. He had the local police check on his family when he wasn't around. Marcella objected to all of this. Dane dismissed her objections, which added to her depression.

Finding no congress with Dane, Marcella withdrew—into their family, into their elegant home, into her own head. She self-medicated with alcohol. She acted out. She argued with Dane, even in public, much to his consternation. On top of all of this, Marcella had heard rumors of another woman, a girlfriend from Dallas whom Dane kept a room for at the Majestic Hotel. Furious, she demanded a divorce. Dane would not grant her one. But his reasons for wanting to stay in the relationship were less love and affection than a practical consideration of his business interests. Splitting up their family wouldn't look right. He was now a public figure, and he wanted to curate his public image as best he could. "If you're going to be in business, you have to be the same all the time," he'd often say. "You can't have a temper." He needed to show that everything was under control.

Things were not, however, under control. In their efforts to command the gambling business in Hot Springs, he and Owney had made as many enemies as they had friends. From jealous mobsters in New Orleans and Las Vegas to locals he had put out of business, the list of people with a grudge against Dane Harris was as nefarious as it was long. And though Dane Harris and Owney Madden had never done anything to wrong Jack Digby, his new role running the casino at the Bridge Street Club put Digby and Dane at cross-purposes.

The Bridge Street Club wasn't anything like the Vapors. It didn't have marble and brass and glistening chandeliers. It wasn't a place at which you'd sport tails and furs while watching a piano player lit by a candelabra. It was, however, an impressive gambling den. It was on the second floor of a building at the intersection of Central Avenue and Bridge Street, which had the unusual designation of being the shortest street in America. The stairs leading up from Bridge Street to the casino were covered in heavy shag carpeting, and inside the shag didn't quit. The floors and ceiling were covered in carpet. The walls were covered with large boards where bookmakers constantly updated the day's odds and results from tracks all over the country. There were betting windows just like the ones at the racetrack. The loudspeakers carried the call of the race from the Ritter Hotel. There were slot machines, blackjack tables, and a craps table in the center of the room.

The first week the Bridge Street Club was open in 1961, there was no shortage of curiosity about the town's newest operation. A lot of the wealthy gamblers who usually got off the airplane in Hot Springs and headed straight for the Vapors or the Belvedere with suitcases full of cash found themselves heading downtown and up the Bridge Street Club's staircase to check out the new addition. One weekend a group from Dallas came in decked out in boots and cowboy hats. But these men weren't yokels. They were pregnant with oil money and looking to gamble sky-high. Jack Digby cleared out the center craps table for them so they could have it to themselves. The cowboys bought racks of hundred-dollar chips and started shooting. Before the end of the night they were up more money than Jack Digby had in the safe. They didn't realize it as they passed the dice back and forth, but the cowboys from Dallas owned the Bridge Street Club.

Digby gave his dealer a signal, and the dealer swapped out the dice for a loaded pair. Jack Digby didn't even stick around to watch it all unfold. A number of the crew from the old Pines Supper Club worked at the Bridge Street Club, including the palm man Jimmie Green, for this very reason. They'd play the string out perfectly. A few more shooters and the cowboys would give Digby all his money back and then some. Loaded dice were supposed to be how crossroaders cheated casinos, not the other way around. The house had a built-in statistical advantage. They just needed to sit back and let the math do the work. But Jack Digby had only a seventy-five-thousand-dollar bankroll. He would need a lot more than math to beat shooters with deep pockets and a lot of luck on their side. And though he'd narrowly avoided disaster that weekend, he was going to need a lot more than a couple of gaffed dice to beat Dane Harris.

Hazel

JUNE 1961

"I'm pressing charges," Jack said. "And if it weren't for your mother you'd go straight to the pen."

Larry met a girl in town whom he couldn't get out of his head, but she lived in Little Rock. He already had a girlfriend, so he resisted the urge to hitch a ride north to see her. But once he and his girlfriend broke up, as high school seniors are wont to do, he couldn't get to Little Rock fast enough. He even put on a bow tie.

Jack's old rebuilt Plymouth wouldn't cut the mustard for a girl like this. This girl called for something more sophisticated. Larry hitched a ride out to the Tower Club and saw Jack's new Chrysler in the parking lot. The car was sparkling because Jack had made Larry and Jimmy wash it earlier that day—just one more reason why Larry felt it was only fair that he should get to take it to Little Rock to see the girl.

Jack was inside gambling and carrying on with his friends, and Hazel was dealing the late shift. It was a bit of a reversal from the usual setup, but Jack had given up on dealing and was back to gambling again. Hazel, on the other hand, was given a chance by the new management to move over to the other side of the table and deal—a job that paid her twenty dollars a shift, which was more than double what she made as a shill. She also earned tips, which made a big difference. Larry supposed Jack would continue to gamble as long as Hazel was working. If Jack went bust, he still had credit at the Tower, and Hazel would deal most of the night. That gave Larry plenty of time to get up to Little Rock, visit the girl, then get the car back to the Tower before sunup. He had an extra key to the car he'd taken from Jack's house. Larry sauntered up to the long shiny Chrysler and got in it as if he owned it. No sooner had Larry left the parking lot than the doorman at the club went over to Jack's table where he was playing blackjack and told him, "Some boy just took off in your car."

Jack knew right away that it was Hazel's son, but he told the doorman to call the police anyway. This would be his last dance with Larry. Jack reported his car stolen.

Later that night, Larry raced against the sun back to Hot Springs. As he weaved the long car through the twists and turns of Gorge Road through the national park, a blue light appeared in his rearview mirror. Larry pulled the car over and rolled down the window. The sheriff's deputy took one look at Larry in his bow tie and grinned.

"License?"

Larry handed over his driver's license. The deputy looked it over.

"This sure is a nice car. This your car, son?"

"No, sir. This is my stepdad's."

"Mmm-hmmm." The deputy looked at the license a bit longer. He flashed his light around in the back seat of the car. "And does your stepdad know you're driving his car?"

"Yessir."

"I tell you what. Why don't you step on out of the vehicle, son?" The deputy led Larry over to the patrol car and put him in the back seat. They drove off and left the Chrysler parked on the side of Gorge Road.

"Where we going, sir?" Larry asked.

"We're going to jail," the deputy said.

When they got to the jailhouse, the deputy put Larry in a cell and left him there until morning, which was only a few hours later. At sunup the deputy opened the cell and brought Larry to the front of the station, where Jack stood waiting on him. Jack didn't look mad. In fact, he looked a little happy, the ends of his mouth ticked up ever so slightly like he was trying to keep from smiling.

"I'm pressing charges," Jack said. "And if it weren't for your mother you'd go straight to the pen. But since she can't handle that I'll give you a choice. You can come with me right now and enlist, or you can go before the judge and get sentenced. That's the deal, and it's the best one you're gonna get."

Jack and Larry rode out to the naval enlistment office straight from the police station. Jack drove. The navy officer asked Larry how soon he'd be available to ship out. Jack said he was available right now.

When Larry left for the navy, Jimmy was preparing to start high school. My father had learned to live without his mother around, and as Larry grew older and spent less time around him, Jimmy had adjusted to life without his older brother as well. But with Larry gone for good, things were different. Jimmy really was all on his own.

Jimmy and Judy were still together. They still spent a lot time with each other, attending dances at the Y, going to the movies, strolling downtown hand in hand. They even told each other that one day they'd get married. It was young love, but Jimmy's situation made it more intense than the usual junior high school coupling. If Jimmy slept in after his paper route and didn't show up for his first class, Judy would call him from the school and chew him out or threaten to come get him. When Jimmy played football on Friday nights, Judy and her parents sat in the stands and watched him, Judy wearing his letterman jacket, Hazel nowhere to be found. Judy's brother took Jimmy hunting and fishing, showed him how to bait his hook and track a deer. Judy's parents always cooked a little extra something for Jimmy, just in case. What Judy and Jimmy had was deeper than just puppy love. It was something more like family.

That summer, Judy's parents didn't like the idea of Jimmy being all alone, so they invited him to come out to their house on the lake to help with a special project that Judy's father had given her. A couple from

Malvern had brought a dog to the veterinary clinic, a boxer that had been hit by a car. The dog's hip and both back legs were broken. Worse than all the broken bones, the dog had lost all motivation to live. It wouldn't even attempt to stand up, let alone try to walk. It wouldn't eat food. It just lay on the floor, waiting to die. Judy's father brought the dog home and introduced him to Judy and Jimmy.

"Y'all's job," her father instructed, "is to give this dog the will to live."

Jimmy and Judy laughed, but her father was serious. He told them that before the summer was over they needed to bring the dog back to life. He left the crumpled and wounded animal on the ground behind the house and told them there was plenty of rabbit meat in the icebox.

Jimmy had never had any pets. He wasn't sure how to act toward the animal. He tried rubbing the dog's head, scratching it on the back. Nothing registered. He took one look at this dog and thought there was no way in hell. "That dog wants to be dead," he said.

"Well," Judy said, "we might as well try."

Almost every day that summer, Jimmy would hitchhike out to Judy's house in the country to work on their special project. Their first task was to get the dog to eat something before he starved to death. Judy would put the rabbit meat in a pot of water and boil up some broth. She put the rabbit broth in a bowl near the dog's mouth, but he wouldn't even blink. She'd spoon the broth into his mouth, and it would dribble to the ground. Finally, she found an eyedropper and used it to squirt the broth into the dog's mouth. Eventually he developed a taste for it and would let her spoon it to him. A week or so later, he was lapping it up. Jimmy watched the dog's progress with awe. Maybe the dog didn't want to be dead after all.

The next step was to get the dog to move. For weeks it had been lying on the ground, covered in bedsores. It didn't even stand to do its business, just urinated and defecated all over itself. Cleaning up the mess day after day was enough motivation for the two kids to get the dog up on its feet. Judy's dad said the dog's bones had healed. It could support itself, if only it would try.

"The only thing that will work is water therapy," he told her. "That dog will move his legs if you put him in the water."

Judy couldn't handle the heavy boxer on her own, so she made Jimmy help her carry the dog to the water. He was sure they would drown the dog. "When you put something in the water," she explained to Jimmy, "it will want to swim. It's instinct."

Skeptical, Jimmy helped Judy lift the dog and carry him into the lake. They each held one side of the dog and waded into the water. As they waded deeper and deeper they sensed the dog's nerves light up, his limbs stiffen a bit.

"Loosen up on him a little bit," Judy instructed. Jimmy let go a little, just enough so that the dog could feel himself floating. Miraculously, the boxer began to paddle his front legs. Jimmy's face stretched, his eyes widened. He couldn't believe it. The two of them beamed at each other across the paddling dog's back.

Day after day, all summer long, Jimmy followed the same routine. Hitchhike to Judy's. Scrub the mess from the dog and the ground. Give the dog some food. Carry the dog out into the water. Each day the dog would get a little more confident, and Judy would say, "Loosen up a little more." After a couple of weeks the dog started to kick its hind legs in the water, and Jimmy let out a whoop that echoed across the lake. *Here he comes! Look out!*

By the end of the summer the dog was fully back to life, as good as the day before the accident. He'd run next to Jimmy, he'd swim with him deep into the center of the bay. He'd leap up into Jimmy's lap, into his arms, press his muzzle into Jimmy's face. The three of them would eat rabbit meat and swim and play until the sun set. At the end of the summer, the couple came back from Malvern to see the miracle that had occurred. When they arrived, the dog ran to them, his tail wagging as if electrified. Whatever love that dog had shown Judy and Jimmy that summer, it had twice as much in reserve for these people. It pained Jimmy some when he realized the dog would go back to be with its owners. But it was their dog, not his. The dog belonged with its family. That was only natural.

Owney

**"Jesus, Mary, and Joseph. I was in partnership with
his father back in the bootlegging days."**

Hot Springs had not yet drawn the attention of the McClellan hearings.
In 1959, when the committee was investigating New Orleans, they questioned a former FBI agent named Aaron Kohn, who had been hired by
local businesses to lead a private effort to investigate Carlos Marcello,
since law enforcement in New Orleans was so corrupt, it couldn't be
trusted to investigate him itself.

"We find their fingers in Texas, and in Mississippi, Alabama, and,
of course, their contacts with fellow mobsters around," Kohn told the
committee.

"Do they reach up in Arkansas anywhere? We are pretty close," asked
the committee's chairman, Senator John McClellan from Arkansas.

"Hot Springs, Arkansas, is rather a popular gathering place for them,
with their friends," Kohn answered.

"Thank you." Senator McClellan smiled. "I didn't want to slight my
own state, if it needs any attention."

But Arkansas was slighted, and continued to be for the next few
years. On wiretaps, mobsters in Chicago were overheard complaining

about how Hot Springs was getting a pass while other cities were getting heat from the FBI. Pittsburgh mob leader John LaRocca, on a visit to Hot Springs, was shocked to find Senator McClellan having dinner in the Arlington Hotel dining room at the same time as thirty or forty mobsters, and so close to the entrance to the Southern Club casino you could hit it with a rock. He called the senator a hypocrite. Washington political columnist Drew Pearson also wondered whether or not McClellan could credibly continue to plead ignorance about the illegal gambling operations in his own state. "The Justice Department will follow up McClellan's closed-door hearings with swift, vigorous prosecutions," Pearson wrote in 1961. "McClellan has overlooked one sin center, however, in his own home state. Gambling and vice are flourishing in Hot Springs, Ark without the slightest interference from McClellan's investigators." McClellan was feeling the heat, but Owney and Dane did all they could to keep the senator happy, from buying Mrs. McClellan a brand-new Buick to ordering fifteen thousand copies of McClellan's book, ironically titled *Crime Without Punishment*.

The FBI had assigned an agent to Hot Springs to keep an eye on things, but most of their resources were focused on places like Chicago and New York. The gangsters, always a few steps ahead of the law, were aware of the discrepancy. Sam Giancana was recorded on FBI wiretaps complaining about the situation. "Look at Hot Springs, it's wide open," Giancana was overheard saying to fellow mob leader Jack Cerone. "They even advertise over the radio and in the papers." Giancana and Cerone worried that the lack of heat from the FBI in Hot Springs was a sign the Chicago Outfit wasn't invested enough in the spa. "A lot of people are freelancing, isn't that right?" Cerone replied to Giancana. "We gotta figure out some way to cough up some money."

On the heels of all of this activity, the FBI's Little Rock office decided to come down to Hot Springs and make a show of force. They kicked in the doors at the Harlem Chicken Shack. They stormed into the Town Talk Barbecue. They rousted the patrons from their barstools at Pat's Lounge. In all they raided three black-owned businesses in Hot Springs, none of which even had a card table to speak of, and seized a total of five slot machines. The residents of Hot Springs assumed the FBI was either out to lunch or on the take, willing only to offer up a few slot machines from the black side of town as a sacrificial lamb.

The FBI stuck around after the raids and kept tabs on the major criminals who were regular guests in Hot Springs, filing reports to J. Edgar Hoover complete with photographs. They sent photos of Ralph Capone, Gus Alex, Sam Giancana, Curley Humphreys, and Tony Accardo—all top echelon members of the Chicago Outfit. While these notorious and violent crime bosses ate, drank, golfed, and gambled, twelve buses carrying seven hundred law enforcement officers arrived downtown at the Arlington Hotel. They weren't there to make any arrests, though. The National Sheriffs' Association Convention was in town, and the attendees lived it up, taking baths during the day and drinking and gambling at night. The sheriffs from around the country took a break from fighting crime to mingle among the sinners in the spa, dining at the Belvedere and taking in a private show arranged for them at the Vapors—compliments of their host, Dane Harris. From the FBI to the sheriffs of America, not even the cops wanted to put the lid all the way back on.

IN JULY OF THAT same year, Paul Kamerick, assistant counsel for the McClellan committee, paid a surprise visit to Owney at the Downtown Printing Company in the Ritter Hotel. Owney and Jimmy the Pro were waiting for the results of the last race of the day when Kamerick arrived. He said he wanted to ask them some questions. Owney told him they were busy and he should come back the next day. Kamerick didn't want to come back the next day. He handed Owney a subpoena to appear before the McClellan committee. It was finally happening.

Owney marched straight down the hall to Q. Byrum Hurst's office and asked him what he thought he should do. Hurst told Owney not to say a word —not to Kamerick, not to the press, and especially not to the McClellan committee. Hurst gave Owney the same advice given by lawyers to each and every mobster subpoenaed by the government over the last eleven years—plead the Fifth.

"Jesus, Mary, and Joseph. I was in partnership with his father back in the bootlegging days," Owney said to Hurst, referring to Robert Kennedy. "How could he do this?"

And yet Owney had likely seen the subpoena coming. Two months before Kamerick knocked on his door, on May 17, Robert Kennedy addressed the House Judiciary Committee in support of proposed legislation to give the government more powers to prosecute organized crime. During his remarks, he brought up Owney and Hot Springs. "Another example of the type of situation which we are trying to curb in proscribing the interstate travel in furtherance of an unlawful activity is the situation which arose in Hot Springs, Arkansas, in 1960. A printing company in Jefferson Parish, Louisiana, receives race wire information from Chicago bookmakers and disseminates the data to gambling establishments in the South and Southwest. The company is owned by a racketeer, since deported, and his race service manager, of New Orleans. The manager, while in Hot Springs in March of 1960, got into a violent argument with the owner of the race wire service there." Kennedy then detailed how Owney traveled to Chicago to secure support from Curley Humphreys in his feud with Carlos Marcello and Joe Poretto, and pointed out that travel across state lines in service of criminal enterprise would be prosecutable under the new laws. "If we could show the existence of race wire services in New Orleans and Hot Springs and the travel on the part of the New Orleans man to expand the New Orleans service and the travel of the Hot Springs man to protect his interest in the Hot Springs service, we could prosecute both of these top racketeers with the enactment of the proposed bill." Kennedy's investigators were clearly building a case against Owney and the wire service.

After Kamerick left the Ritter Hotel, he made stops at clubs all over town. He subpoenaed phone records. He interviewed employees. He questioned gamblers. He met with elected officials. The presence of federal investigators in town had the rumor mill flying and the press in a tizzy. Reporters from Little Rock and Memphis caught wind of it and arrived in town asking questions of their own. Once again, Owney Madden was at the center of the storm, and newspapers were printing stories about "Owney the Killer." Owney couldn't take it anymore. He ignored Hurst's advice to not talk to the press. When a reporter from *Cavalier* magazine came to Hot Springs to write a story about him, Owney confronted him. "If you don't stop asking people around here questions about me, I'll knock your brains out," Owney snarled.

Word had come down from Senator McClellan that there was nothing he could do to protect Owney from Kennedy. McClellan had been embarrassed, repeatedly accused of intentionally ignoring Hot Springs and shielding his home state from investigation. McClellan had perhaps once taken some measure of solace in the public assurances from the Hot Springs gambling combination that they were running a clean operation and keeping the mob out of the state. The appearance, if not the actual fact, was that they were failing on that front. Owney decided he would fall on his sword in order to protect Dane and to salvage whatever they could of the gambling business in Hot Springs. Dane bought out Owney's interest in the clubs and slot machines. Hurst passed Owney on to another lawyer out of Little Rock to represent him at the McClellan hearings. Owney didn't think the investigators were after anything more than the wire service. The Downtown Printing Company would close up shop. It might as well. Once Robert Kennedy got his new law passed, the wire service would be shut down by the FBI anyway. Closing up now, before the McClellan hearing, would give the appearance of Owney's capitulation and McClellan's reforms being put into action.

Owney called a meeting of every bookie in Hot Springs and told them that he was shutting down the wire. The individual bookmakers and handbooks were free to stay in operation and find another source of racing and sports results, but the other wire services around the country were likely going to follow suit, if they hadn't already. Owney's suggestion was that the bookies all close down, at least until the hearings blew over, because the heat was on and Kennedy was looking for convictions. Owney then gave the bookies more bad news. The IRS had hit him with over seven thousand dollars in unpaid taxes on the wire service—money he felt should have been charged to the bookies. He told the bookies he expected them to reimburse him. This was a surprising request. Owney had a reputation for being generous to a fault, but everything Owney had been through had worn away whatever good-natured veneer he once had. He was finished with being a soft touch, just like he was finished being a rackets boss. He insisted that Dane still kick him a piece of the action every month. Owney would step back to save face, as he had before, but he would never relinquish his share of what he had helped build in Hot Springs, of what was rightfully his.

WHEN OWNEY'S DAY BEFORE the McClellan committee finally arrived, the Caucus Room of the Senate Office Building was congested with onlookers, reporters, and television crews all eager to finally hear from the mysterious and legendary Owney Madden. There were all sorts of contraptions set up by the television crews around the table where Owney would be giving his testimony, including can lights aimed right at his face that washed the entire room in hot white light. The hearings had become something of a sideshow. A few days before Owney's testimony, Senator McClellan was filmed trying out the latest in cheating technology, including tinted glasses that could read ink daubs on the backs of cards and electronic message devices that attached to the biceps beneath the shirt. The distinguished senator put on all the ridiculous getup and played some cards for the cameras, then soapboxed about how the gambling business was rife with cheaters and crooks. It made for good television, and so the cameras and lights were all set up and ready for another show.

As Owney settled into his seat next to Jimmy the Pro and his new attorney, Charles Lincoln, television crew members held light meters right up to his face. Owney recoiled from the lights, removing his glasses.

"Does that light bother you?" Senator McClellan asked.

"It bothers the hell out of me," Owney said. "It bothers me a lot."

"All right, turn the lights out. Turn the light out or turn it around so it will not be in his eyes." They turned the lights away from Owney's face. "Is that better?"

"That is fine."

"Mr. Madden," Senator McClellan began. "Did you give us your occupation?"

"I am retired," Owney said.

"Since when?"

"A few years," Owney said. "Quite a few years."

"You have been retired quite a few years from what?"

Owney leaned over to Charles Lincoln and whispered in his ear. Lincoln whispered something back to him. Owney leaned into the microphone and answered. "I refuse to answer on the grounds of . . ."

"I suggest you say 'decline to answer,'" Senator McClellan interrupted him. He knew where this was headed.

"I respectfully decline to answer."

Owney respectfully declined to answer every question put to him that day. As he boarded his flight back to Arkansas, Senator McClellan was already seated on the same plane. Owney stopped in the aisle and looked down at McClellan. McClellan offered his hand. Owney smiled and took it, and the two exchanged pleasantries before Owney went back to his seat. There were no hard feelings. McClellan had helped Owney when he could, and he had tried to avoid this day for as long as possible. If anything, McClellan may have done Owney a favor by forcing him to get out of gambling. The future of rackets around the country was unclear. The future of the rackets in Hot Springs was downright opaque.

Dane

"Of course this town's illegal," Dane told *Sports Illustrated*, "but it's been running open for years."

The year 1961 had been the biggest year for tourism in the history of Hot Springs. According to the National Park Service, 5,130,984 people visited the area. Despite the unwanted attention from Owney's appearance before the McClellan committee, the 1962 horse racing season was even bigger than the year before, and all signs pointed to 1962 eclipsing the record-setting business Hot Springs did in 1961. Over eight hundred new hotel rooms were built or under construction in 1962, with even more in the planning stages. Millions of dollars were being pumped into the city, including by the Teamsters Central States Pension Fund, which had financed so much of the construction on the Las Vegas Strip for the mob. Total receipts across all industries were up by more than ten million dollars since gambling opened back up in 1960. The various clubs in operation in 1962 collectively employed over a thousand people.

As Hot Springs' profile rose, so, too, rose Dane's stature as an important man in the gambling world. When Dane traveled to Las Vegas for the Wine & Spirits Wholesalers of America convention at Harry Hastings's invitation, he was initially nervous about what kind of reception he would receive from the rival gambling bosses. On this trip, however, he was treated like royalty. Wherever he and his guests went, from the Flamingo to the Desert Inn to the Sahara, their bills were inexplicably on the house, they were ushered to the front of long lines at nightclubs and given free tickets to see Louis Prima and Pearl Bailey. The powers that be in Las Vegas had taken notice of Hot Springs, and just like that Dane Harris had become a national crime figure.

In a strange twist of irony, the publicity around the Justice Department's probe of Hot Springs may have, in the end, been good for business. *Sports Illustrated* published a feature on Hot Springs, calling the town "the most unusual spa in the United States" and "pound for pound, the greatest sporting town anywhere." Owney's very public withdrawal from the gambling business gave Hot Springs leaders the opportunity to once and for all declare Hot Springs free of any mob ties—a nice, friendly place to gamble. "The gambling is home-owned and operated," a local lawyer named Nate Schoenfeld told *Sports Illustrated*. "There's no hoodlum element, no oppression, no scum. No one forces himself on anyone else. There is no guy around here with greasy hair and a Mafia smile." Dane bragged to *Sports Illustrated* that the casinos had joined the Chamber of Commerce. "Of course this town's illegal," Dane told *Sports Illustrated*, "but it's been running open for years. People expect it and want it. This is strictly a local operation, has not been anything else and will not be anything else. This is a different type of element. Check the police records for the lack of prostitution and narcotics. Probably our own interest in gambling is more an interest in it as a business than gambling for its own sake. It looked like probably one of the few things that could be big enough to build the town on."

For all Dane's optimism, Hot Springs was not yet in the clear. It was becoming increasingly apparent that David Whittington, who had been elected prosecuting attorney two years earlier, was dead-set on routing the mob. He released a statement to the press, saying: "We are serving notice that any prostitute, hoodlum, or racketeer who attempts to move in here to set up shop during the upcoming race meet will be arrested immediately. I have Federal Bureau of Investigation records on known hoodlums, racketeers, Mafia and other syndicate members and the Police Department and sheriff's office will be instructed to pick them up on sight if they should put in an appearance and book them on vagrancy or whatever charges on which they could be held."

Robert Kennedy, too, was once again training his sights on Hot Springs. He had sent federal agents to observe the casinos in operation and help build a case against them that utilized the gambling laws he had convinced Congress to pass at the end of 1961. One of the two statutes made it a federal crime to transmit illegal gambling information across state lines over telephone wires. Since Owney had shut down the wire service, horse and sports bookmaking had largely dried up around Hot Springs, making it nearly impossible for Kennedy to build a case using the new wire law. When agents checked in on the Vapors in February 1962, they witnessed thousands of patrons wagering many thousands of dollars. They also saw casino employees ferrying checks back and forth from the tables to the cashier's cage night after night. Surely a number of those checks were from out-of-state banks. Kennedy and the FBI decided to find out if the transactions between the Vapors and the bank constituted a violation of the new law.

Many of Dane's customers were gambling thousands of dollars. Few of them traveled with suitcases full of cash. Dane's credit man would approve the customers for whatever amount they needed, and the dealers would fork over the chips. Often the players would write a check for what they had lost before they even left the club. So many players were gambling on credit that the dealers kept check registers from various area banks so customers could fill out checks at the table in the event they didn't have their checkbooks on them.

Using phone records, the FBI built a list of the Vapors' out-of-state customers who had cashed checks larger than three hundred dollars.

They distributed these leads to offices all over the United States, and urged agents in various field offices to conduct interviews. There were well over one hundred leads, many of whom were wealthy and powerful individuals, including the owners of large utilities, manufacturing companies, cotton plantations, and oil interests. The FBI agents showed up at many of their places of business, targeting everyone from a vice president at Goldman Sachs in New York to the CEO of Dr Pepper in Texas. The interviews were causing a stir among Dane's customers, many of whom sought lawyers and refused to answer any questions. Incredibly, a number of the people questioned by the FBI who chose to talk were surprised to learn that gambling was illegal in Arkansas. Who could blame them? They had likely heard about the casinos from colorful advertisements in newspapers or magazines. They probably noticed police officers and politicians hanging around the large, swanky casinos in town. But now that the FBI was questioning them, it was unlikely many of these big-money players would come back. For a gambling boss like Dane, losing his big players could break him.

The Justice Department worked with the U.S. attorney for the Western District of Arkansas, Charles Conway, to build a grand jury case against the casino operators for cashing checks in violation of the new law. Unlike past grand jury investigations into gambling in Hot Springs, this one wouldn't be held in Garland County, where Dane could reward jury foremen with construction contracts. The federal grand jury would be seated in Fort Smith, Arkansas, 130 miles away.

WHEN THE DAY FINALLY arrived for the Hot Springs club owners to appear before the grand jury, Bookie Ebel nearly fainted from nerves. "Y'all go on ahead and I'll ride up in the ambulance with Bookie," Dane joked. But beneath the surface, Dane was as nervous as Bookie or anyone else. This would be the first trial in which the gamblers of Hot Springs didn't have an ace up their sleeves.

Dane and the rest of the combination rode to Fort Smith in a caravan of long Cadillacs and Lincolns, winding their way through the "pig trails," the steep and curvy roads through the Ozark foothills of northwest Arkansas. The crowd of reporters at the courthouse was nearly as large as the crowd of witnesses waiting to testify. After a long day of testimony, the grand jury deliberated for twenty-five minutes before reaching a verdict. On every count, they refused to indict. Despite the quick deliberation, the jury was split. The jurors who wanted to return "no true bills" won by a single vote.

The Hot Springs combination was relieved, but reacted to the verdict with varying degrees of enthusiasm. Dane and the other club owners refused to speak publicly about the decision, and privately resolved to tighten the circle around themselves. By contrast, the political class emerged from Fort Smith publicly triumphant. Q. Byrum Hurst declared to the press that he was "delighted to know that the federal laws were not found to have been violated in the local entertainment industry." Hurst told Dane he thought they should take another stab at trying to legalize gambling in Arkansas. The verdict felt to him like the final hump they needed to get over to convince his colleagues in the state senate to get behind gambling once and for all.

Hazel

The Vapors was real. It was solid brick and mortar, pure crystal and gold.

Hazel had mustered up the courage to walk into the Vapors because she needed to see Dane Harris for a favor. She didn't have any other place to turn. Jack had left her. His wife had tracked him down in Hot Springs and come for him. He didn't even put up a fight, just went back to Reno with her like a beaten dog. There was no fight, no tearful goodbye. He told her she'd need to move out by the end of the month, and then he left. Hazel gave no outward indication that she was heartbroken. She got Jimmy from the little house and the two of them moved into a mobile home. Losing Jack impacted Hazel less emotionally than it did financially. She needed to find a new job, and she hoped Dane could help.

Hazel was finished shilling. She'd been shilling off and on at the Vapors for over a year. The race meet was coming up and the word was it was going to be huge. Hazel had seen firsthand how much money dealers at the Vapors could net during the race meet, and she would do whatever it took to break in. She came to see Mr. Harris about what it would take to get a real job dealing at the Vapors. While Dane and Owney were building this palace, Hazel was trapped in their undertow, drowning in Dane's liquor, casting aside her grocery money at Owney's gambling tables. If Dane could give Hazel a job at the Vapors, she could get out of that undertow. She could ride his wake. From the looks of it, that wake was mighty wide.

ON A TYPICAL NIGHT in 1962, it was difficult to see where the dice tables were through the thick crowds of gamblers that surrounded them. The blackjack tables had three or four customers lined up waiting behind each player. The slot machines, too, had long queues. Meanwhile, the storied Southern Club was losing customers to the Vapors. On a good night the Southern Club may have pulled in a hundred customers, but they almost all came to visit the Southern's new bingo room, which was a hit among the low rollers and old-timers. The Vapors wasn't the largest club in Hot Springs in terms of size, not by a long shot. But most nights it was as if every gambler in the whole town tried to squeeze into the cozy casino to be a part of the action.

The entertainment at the Vapors had only grown more extravagant, too. Dane's show budget had grown to more than ten thousand dollars a week. In the last year he had booked Sophie Tucker, Phyllis Diller, Tony Bennett, Les Paul and Mary Ford, the Smothers Brothers, and Red Skelton. He also lured back repeat performances from acts who had played the year before like Liberace, the Andrews Sisters, and Mickey Rooney, with whom Dane had become close friends—so close that Mickey would stay at Dane's place when he was in town. Dane's goal was to compete with Las Vegas for the same acts. When Mitzi Gaynor, star of *South Pacific*, decided to put together a nightclub act, she chose to premier it at the Vapors rather than on the Vegas Strip. When asked why she'd chosen the South to open her much-anticipated show, she said the audiences in Hot Springs were sophisticated and the surroundings were beautiful.

Those sophisticated audiences were often made up of out-of-town politicians, big-city socialites, and even leaders from the local clergy. Dane made it easy for them. Patrons could see a show without setting foot in the casino. If a guest was offended by the presence of illegal gambling, they needed only to refrain from turning their heads toward the closed casino doors behind them. As a result of Dane's decision to promote the showroom and restaurant over the gambling, the Vapors quickly became one of the most fashionable gathering spots in the entire Mid-South. Dane's commercials for the Vapors played on radio stations as far away as Louisiana, Texas, and Tennessee. And the house orchestra, led by Buddy Kirk, was broadcast nightly over the radio.

It wasn't that people like Hazel weren't welcome there. Plenty of locals dined and gambled at the Vapors, so long as they could afford the prices. Even some who couldn't afford them still indulged themselves. Virginia Clinton, the sister-in-law of local car dealer and GI Revolt supporter Raymond Clinton, moved to Hot Springs in 1953 and had become as much a part of Hot Springs' wild late-night social scene as Hazel. Virginia loved the Vapors and even brought her teenage son Bill, a budding saxophonist, to listen to the jazz trombonist Jack Teagarden there. After a few songs, Bill asked Virginia to take him home. It wasn't the music. Bill Clinton just didn't feel as comfortable as his mother did at the Vapors.

Now that Dane had the money to bring in the really big stars, he was leaving every other club in his dust. Some clubs tried in vain to keep up with him. The Southern booked Brother Dave Gardner, a popular southern comedy act. Gardner drew a dedicated group of local fans, but they didn't diverge too much from the bingo crowd. The Palms booked Sally Rand, the famous burlesque dancer, but at fifty-seven years old she was a little past her prime. Others, like Jack Digby at the Bridge Street Club, made no attempt to follow Dane's example. Instead of investing in world-class chefs or marquee entertainers, Digby chose instead to invest in a juiced craps table—a table with a powerful magnet hidden beneath the felt that could control a pair of loaded dice with a flip of a secret switch.

Digby needed to get his juiced table quickly, because Robert Kennedy convinced Congress to pass a number of anti-gambling laws at the end of 1961, including one that made it a federal crime to transport anything across state lines for the purpose of illegal gambling. Most of the gambling underworld, including the clubs of Hot Springs, purchased their equipment from the same place, Taylor & Company in Cicero, Illinois. Taylor & Co. was once a furniture company that occasionally manufactured gaming tables. After the Capone mob took over the company, it exclusively manufactured gambling equipment, from slot machines to marked cards and loaded dice. The FBI investigated Taylor & Co. and its owner, Joe Aiuppa, for two years to build the case for expanding the 1956 Transportation of Gambling Devices Act, which had been narrowly written and contained enough loopholes to make it ineffective in stopping the supply chain between Taylor & Co. and Hot Springs. The new Interstate Transport in Aid of Racketeering law Congress passed made it illegal not only to transport slot machines over state lines, but even to transport the machines' individual parts, as Dane had been doing.

While other club owners panicked, Dane strategized. He ordered the plans for the slot machines he used in his clubs directly from the manufacturer. He showed the plans to his technicians and asked if they thought they could build a machine from scratch. They thought it was possible. The technicians went to a local manufacturing company that made vending machine coin rejectors to buy fabricating equipment and materials, and within a couple of months had successfully figured out how to clone the slot machines themselves. If Dane Harris couldn't order new slot machines, he'd simply build them in Hot Springs. His technicians built eighty clones of the Bell slot machine, dubbing them Super Bells, and they looked like no other slot machine in America. The Bell machines had been the same shape and design for most of the previous thirty years. But Super Bells were shiny and metallic, like something from the future.

The Interstate Transport in Aid of Racketeering law didn't just stop at chips and dice and nuts and bolts. The new law made it a crime for actual people to travel across state lines to work in gambling clubs. The dealers and pit bosses who worked in the clubs were now considered contraband as well. Any person who crossed a state line in order to work in an illegal gambling club could be prosecuted. This would be a problem for Dane. A sizable percentage of his casino employees came from out of state, many of them from Nevada. Casino work required a very specific set of skills. The most experienced dealers and pit bosses often traveled a circuit around the country—Tahoe, Miami, Saratoga Springs—following the tourist seasons at various locales where gambling was plentiful, because the jobs paid well and there weren't many who possessed the skills to do them. Just like the slot machine problem, this issue would require some ingenuity on the part of Dane.

Dane figured out a workaround to the ITAR restrictions. The casinos would require anyone seeking employment in a casino in Hot Springs, whether they were from Arkansas or anywhere else, to first apply at the Employment Security Division's Hot Springs office. The Employment Security Division would then refer the applicants directly to the casinos, but only after they filled out a form that stated:

> I hereby certify that I was not requested, encouraged, or induced, directly or indirectly, by the above named employer or any officer, director, agent or employee of the employer, to travel from outside of the State of Arkansas into Arkansas for the purpose of applying for or accepting employment or for any other purpose. I was referred to the employer by the Hot Springs, Arkansas office of the Arkansas Employment Security Division.

When Hazel asked Dane if she could come work for him at the Vapors, he was in no position to offer her any favors. If his plan was going to work, he'd need to apply the new rules to everyone equally. Hazel was referred to the state employment office, same as everyone else.

After putting in her application and signing her form, she was told to attend a meeting at the Belvedere. The meeting was attended by a few dozen prospective casino employees, and was conducted by a lawyer Dane and his partners had hired. The lawyer told the prospective employees that there was a new law that might make it a crime for some of them to work there if they had come from another state. He said that anyone who took a job at the Vapors would likely be investigated and possibly contacted by the FBI. He made it clear that the Vapors had not requested any of them to work there or come to Hot Springs, and that they all came of their own volition.

Fewer than a quarter of those prospective employees, however, actually came from out of state. The ITAR law was proving to be the most successful arrow in Robert Kennedy's quiver, not only in Hot Springs but around the country. It seemed as if the circuit was freezing up. Even so, Hazel still didn't make the cut. Dane didn't offer her a dealer position at the Vapors, but he did offer her a job at the Crawford Pharmacy. The drugstore was an important part of Dane's operation. It was a gathering spot for the gambling combination, where Dane often held meetings of his brain trust. And customers could place bets on the day's races and games at the counter while they had their prescriptions filled. Hazel started working the lunch counter, where she served sandwiches, sodas, and pies, and took the occasional horse bet. It wasn't what she'd come looking for, but it was a job. Perhaps if Hazel did a good job at the drugstore, and kept shilling from time to time on the late shift—perhaps then she could make a good impression on Dane. Perhaps her opportunity to get in at the Vapors would come later, if only she patiently bided her time. After a few months at the drugstore, it appeared that the opportunity might come quicker than she had thought.

BY THE END OF 1962, Dane was unhappy with the quality and efficiency of his casino staff. His workaround for the staff problem wasn't nearly as effective as his workaround for the slot machines. If only he could reverse engineer a pit boss. As it turned out, he could.

When Owney brought Dane and the other Hot Springs gambling leaders to Havana after the GIs took control so they could observe Meyer Lansky's training program for the Cubans working in the Montmartre, Lansky was dealing with a similar problem. The locals in Havana were inexperienced and costing the casinos money. Lansky's solution was to bring in American dealers not to work in the casinos, but to train the Cubans who would. Hot Springs was now in the exact same situation. If Dane didn't have enough talented dealers among the locals of Hot Springs, he could train the locals to be talented dealers.

Dane's new dealer training program would launch in January 1963. It would be the first organized school for dealers in the United States. The interest from locals was much higher than Dane had anticipated, and he couldn't take on every applicant. The initial dealer class was limited to forty people, and everyone else was put on a waiting list. Many of the people signing up for the classes were from Dane's current pool of over three hundred employees at the Vapors, but some of them were bona fide civilians, folks with regular day jobs lured by the promise of making as much as a hundred dollars a night. About a dozen of the students in the first class were women, and many more women waited in the wings.

Hazel was among them, having put her name on the list as soon as she heard about the class. For many people, working at the Vapors was about more than just money. Inside the club, it was as though a person had left Hot Springs altogether and entered someplace better, where nobody had any problems, nobody was poor, everyone was happy, and life was good. That happiness, for many, was false. The mood may have been merely a veneer, but the Vapors was still real. It was solid brick and mortar, pure crystal and gold. It was as real as the hot water that pulsed beneath its foundation. The Vapors was no put-on. It was something good, and it belonged to Hot Springs. It made people believe that they all deserved better. If Hazel could get a job dealing for Dane Harris, perhaps she could outrun whatever was hanging on to her. Even if only for a night.

Dane

Casinos in Hot Springs had been fleecing the suckers since the Civil War, and nobody had ever blown anyone up over it.

Early on the morning of January 4, 1963, the first of the dealer training classes was just getting started in the club room of the Vapors. It was a Friday, so they needed to start early in order to be finished and out before the rush of weekend customers hit the door. Some of the students were eager. Others were nervous. The class that day was on craps, which was the game that would either make or break them as potential Vapors or Belvedere employees.

As the students crowded around the craps table to listen to their instructor, a pit boss named W. C. Tucker, go over the day's lesson, another couple dozen people busied themselves throughout the club. W. C. Tucker raised his voice to be heard over the sounds of the staff readying the Vapors for business—dishes clinking in the sink, coffee percolating, chips being stacked, chairs being dragged across the floor, an alarm clock ringing somewhere in the distance.

As the alarm clock rang, students in the dealer class could smell something in the air. Someone said it smelled like firecrackers. Another thought it might be smoke. The smell grew more intense, driving some from the casino into the coffee shop to escape it. Shortly after 11:00 a.m. there was a ferocious boom over the lobby, near the men's restroom. The explosion pulsed through the entire club. The plate glass window in the front of the club shattered. The cocktail glasses at the bar exploded. A roulette wheel splintered into shards. Chunks of concrete and rebar and slivers of glass were sent hurtling through the club in every direction from the center of the blast. A meat salesman from Memphis named William Atkins, who had been in a telephone booth, was cut over his eyes by flying glass. The roof caved in on top of the students from above. One student, a forty-four-year-old woman named Beverly Longinotti, was sliced through the neck and shoulders by glass and steel. The club's popular bartender, Garland Mitchell, was lifted from his feet and thrown through the air by the blast. Thirty-seven-year-old Lila Manuel's eardrum ruptured. In all, the blast injured a dozen people. One of the dealer students, sixty-three-year-old Jack Fry, was crushed by concrete that broke his spine and concussed his brain.

Across the street from the Vapors, Mrs. E. E. Dodd was getting her hair done at the beauty parlor. She had just leaned back in the chair to let the girl give her a shampoo when the windows of the salon shattered from the explosion. Mrs. Dodd didn't scream like the other ladies in the shop. She was a member of the Women's Civil Defense Auxiliary. She had been trained for just such a moment. She ran outside and across Park Avenue, across the shards of shattered glass and twisted copper pipe and rebar, past the survivors fleeing in the other direction. The meat salesman came sprinting out, his hands holding back the blood gushing from the cuts in his head. Mrs. Dodd ran directly into the hole in the side of the Vapors, toward the smoke and flames, wet hair still strung down around her shoulders. Inside the club she found dozens of people burned and bleeding. She dropped to her knees next to the first injured person she saw and began to administer first aid.

The blast could be heard all across town. The explosion lifted the roof from the building and shot debris a hundred feet in the air. It shattered windows in the surrounding hotels. It blew a thirty-foot hole in the roof of the club. Another hole gaped in the front wall near the entrance. A layer of dust settled onto the surrounding cars and businesses. The survivors had glass stuck in their bodies, their skin sliced open. Ambulances rushed victims to nearby St. Joseph's Hospital, where the victims soon filled the emergency room. Ten doctors and nurses tended to the wounded, doing triage right in the emergency room lobby and the corridors of the hospital, victims moaning in pain as they awaited their turn to be seen.

Dane was on his way to the club when it happened. He was greeted by chaos on his arrival, and rushed to a phone. His first call was to Marcella. Dane told her to get the kids and get out of the house.

"Where are we supposed to go, Dane?" Marcella asked.

"To a motel. Just get out. Get the kids and get out."

"I am not leaving my house," she said. "They are not going to run me out of my house." Alice Ebel, Bookie's wife, was there with her. She was incredulous.

"Are you nuts, Marcella?" she asked as she began to gather their things. "You have got to go. We all do."

One of Dane's bodyguards arrived at the house and drove Marcella, Alice, and the kids to a hotel. All over town police officers showed up at various schools to pick up the children of the other gambling combination members and take them somewhere safe. Dane rallied his troops. They gathered a force of over twenty men and armed them with shotguns, rifles, even a machine gun. They had good reason. Phone calls had been made to the FBI claiming this wouldn't be the end of it.

Reports of the bombing went out over the radio. Within an hour, reporters from Little Rock descended on Park Avenue. Police who were busy surveying the crime scene paid them little mind at first. Soon an officer noticed that one of the photographers, the *Arkansas Gazette*'s chief photographer, Larry Obsitnik, wasn't taking pictures of the wreckage. He was taking pictures of the casino, the slot machines, the dice tables—a sight never captured by a newspaper photographer since the club opened, since Dane strictly forbade any photography and confiscated cameras at the door. The officer rushed over to stop the photographer. "We've had enough bad publicity," the officer told him.

The following day those photos ran on the front pages of newspapers all across the region with the headline "The Picture They Didn't Want Taken." The bombing of the Vapors dominated headlines for weeks. In total, fourteen people were injured. Jack Fry would later die from complications caused by his injuries, and Beverly Longinotti was left partially paralyzed. Rumors were flying about who could have done it and why. The list of possible suspects and motives offered by the press and the public was a long one.

Officially, Dane told the press it was the work of a disgruntled customer, the act of a "mentally deranged person" or a "fanatic." He suggested it was perhaps someone who lost some money in the club and was sore about it. Nobody believed this theory. Casinos in Hot Springs had been fleecing the suckers since the Civil War, and nobody had ever blown anyone up over it.

The press speculated that the bomb might have been the work of the mob. Prosecuting Attorney David Whittington had certainly angered enough of them in the past year. Since taking office, he had served over a dozen vagrancy warrants on various well-known gang leaders. He'd even shown up on the runway of the airport to instruct the pilots of a private plane carrying a group of mobsters to turn around and fly back to wherever they had departed from. Perhaps the bombing was a way to get the boss gambler's attention, to force him to get Whittington under control.

Others felt that the message being sent was that the mob was tired of being denied a piece of the action in Hot Springs. The new sheriff in Cook County, Illinois, Richard Ogilvie, believed the bombing was the work of Chicago mobsters whose own illegal gambling operations he had recently shut down. He said he knew for a fact that these mobsters were on the hunt for new territory and were planning on taking over Hot Springs. According to one anonymous source in the *Arkansas*

Gazette, out-of-town syndicate members "saw all that easy money" while the Vapors was crowded during the 1962 race meet, and "just decided they would slice themselves in on some of it."

Or could the bomb have been the work of Las Vegas gambling interests who wanted to put the kibosh on the growing competitive threat Arkansas posed? At its high point in 1962, gambling in Hot Springs was bringing in an estimated $200 million a year. By contrast, the entire state of Nevada reported only $227 million in gaming revenues that year. While the real numbers in Nevada were likely much higher, deflated by the mob's skimming of profits, the fact remained that Hot Springs made a fortune with far fewer hotel rooms and slot machines, not to mention the fact that gambling in Hot Springs was still a crime. The little town in Arkansas was giving Las Vegas some serious competition, and if the state legalized gambling, those who had invested heavily in Vegas stood to lose serious money. By 1963, the Teamsters Central States Pension Fund held over two hundred million dollars in assets, almost all in commercial real estate, and much of it in casino projects in Las Vegas. In 1962, the fund had issued a ten-million-dollar construction loan, one of the biggest loans the fund had ever made, to a massive casino resort called Caesars Palace, the first of what would eventually balloon to over twenty million dollars in Teamster loans to that casino alone. It wouldn't be that far of a stretch to imagine that the people who were the most heavily invested in Las Vegas, men like Teamsters president Jimmy Hoffa and former Dallas boss gambler Benny Binion, would do something to jeopardize the possibility of legalized gambling in Arkansas. These were men who got to where they were by murdering their enemies and blowing people up. More than one of Benny Binion's competitors had been killed by hidden bombs. The Cleveland mob was involved in just such a bombing campaign in a war to control what was left of the gambling business in Newport, Kentucky. Putting a bomb in the Vapors fit their MO.

Plenty of folks in law enforcement and in the gambling community doubted the Las Vegas theory, titillating as it might have been. The FBI believed that Las Vegas was actually rooting for the legalization of gambling in Arkansas, not trying to prevent it. Philadelphia mobster Joseph "Mickey" Tanitsky was overheard on a wiretap discussing a slush fund of millions of dollars that Las Vegas mob connections had established "for just such a jackpot." And if and when Arkansas legalized gambling, the mob planned to move in heavy and hard, even if it meant they'd have to back a local. "They'll spend a half a million dollars on the right guy," Tanitsky said.

THE ACT SCHEDULED FOR the night of the bombing was a children's show. The Ginny Tiu Show, a song-and-dance act of four young Chinese siblings, was coming to the Vapors fresh from a performance for President Kennedy. The Tiu family had been on *The Ed Sullivan Show* five times, and their family-friendly show had been a hot ticket in Hot Springs, sold out well in advance. Dane made arrangements with the local junior high school auditorium to hold two public performances free of charge. "We didn't want our Hot Springs children to be disappointed in not being able to see the show," Dane said. The shows were packed to capacity, with people turned away each night. Parents from all over the state brought their children. It warmed Dane that so many families wanted to come see the performance, and reinforced his opinion that the "high-class entertainment" he brought to Hot Springs was a public good, even after the violence of the bombing.

While the Tiu children performed at the junior high, Dane had the rest of the club's scheduled performances moved over to the Belvedere, which wasn't scheduled to open for the season for another month. The Belvedere would stand in for the Vapors while repairs were made. A sold-out crowd of more than 350 people turned out that Saturday for the "reopening" of the Vapors at the Belvedere, where Gene Barry, who played Bat Masterson on the popular television program of the same name, performed. Dane indicated to the press that the size of the crowd was evidence the bombing hadn't scared people off.

But while Dane presented a calm and steady front to the press, he took no chances. On February 1 he received an anonymous telephone call threatening to set off a new bomb each week until Dane started letting people open up their own "joints." The caller told Dane to take out a pencil and write down what he had to say. He then listed his targets for Dane one by one. The list included Harry Leopoulos and Gerald Vanderslice, both shareholders in the Vapors. Dane upped the security on their homes and at the Belvedere, where each show was patrolled by over a dozen armed guards, including at least one posted at every entrance and a man with a machine gun positioned on the roof. Dane even had guards posted in the ladies' washrooms to check their handbags as they came and went.

The other clubs also added some extra muscle. One operator added four additional men to his security team, bringing his total number of "strong men" to ten. Though he declined to give his name when interviewed by the newspaper, the club owner offered his own theory for who was responsible. He blamed it on "political jealousies." "There are always the ins and the outs," he said.

If indeed the culprits behind the bombing had hoped to deter business from Hot Springs, it didn't work. As the opening day of the 1963 Oaklawn meet quickly approached, one local business leader quoted in the papers stated that the bombing wouldn't have any impact on the busy race meet season at all. "In a matter of days, people will almost forget it happened. It's like a storybook. Things like that just don't happen to them, so they forget about it." The general manager of Oaklawn predicted that crowds in 1963 would break the record set in 1962, and he was right. Tourists returned to Hot Springs for the race meet in droves and set new benchmarks for attendance and money wagered. If visitors were worried about being blown up by bombs, they hid it well.

———

WHILE THE BOMBING DIDN'T sway gamblers to stay home, it did have a significant impact on the rest of the state's opinion of Hot Springs. Since beating the grand jury the year before, Q. Byrum Hurst had been lobbying his colleagues in the state senate to vote for a bill that would legalize gambling in Arkansas. At the start of 1963, Hurst believed he was close to having the votes he needed for the bill to pass. The week after the bombing, Faubus was pressed once again on the question of gambling in Hot Springs. This time, however, Faubus couldn't simply feign opposition to gambling while at the same time declaring it to be a local issue. He was put on the spot about whether or not he would sign Hurst's bill should it get to his desk. The bombing had linked gambling and crime in the public consciousness around the state. Faubus had no choice. He vowed to veto the bill. A day later Hurst announced he was dropping the bill entirely, stating that without the governor's support there was no way to legalize gambling in Arkansas.

Despite the political setbacks, business was back to normal within a few months. The Vapors had been repaired, and business was once again booming as the Arkansas Derby and the end of the race meet neared. Construction was nearly complete on the Teamsters-funded Aristocrat Manor, a modern high-rise hotel next door to the Southern Club, with two glass-bottomed swimming pools above the elegant lobby that visitors could look up into from below. The Majestic Hotel down the street from the Vapors was adding a tower of luxury suites. The state-of-the-art convention center, funded entirely by gambling money, was almost finished, its space-age pyramid roof poking over the tops of the clubs on Central Avenue. Once again, the gamblers of Hot Springs had avoided a major crisis. The roulette wheels spun on.

Then, late on the night of April 22, a call came in to the police department. The man on the line said another bomb would go off at the Vapors that night. The police rushed over to check it out. Another call came in to Dane's house. The person on the other end of the line said someone was on their way to shoot up the house. Dane grabbed his shotgun, gathered up his family, and took them into the closet in his bedroom and waited for Tommy Barker, one of his bodyguards, to arrive. While Dane and his family huddled in the closet waiting for help, across town a bomb went off under the hood of David Whittington's car, parked on the street directly in front of his house. The front end of the car was destroyed, blown up by a small dynamite bomb attached to a twenty-foot fuse.

"I just think somebody doesn't care for me very much," Whittington said when asked about the motive for the bombing. In addition to running mobsters out of Hot Springs, Whittington had been aggressively pursuing cases against local criminals, including members of the rival gambling faction. He had been working to indict Sam Anderson in connection with a major multistate car-theft ring. And about a month before the car bombing, Whittington had announced a campaign to drive out prostitution from Hot Springs. He singled out the Hot Springs Police Department, which was said to be very familiar with pimps who were operating out of local bars, including former police officer turned casino boss Jack Digby.

The FBI turned its attention squarely to Digby, who had conveniently absconded to Atlanta right before the bombing along with his lawyer, Sam Anderson. According to informants, Digby and Anderson were getting out of town to secure their alibis and planned to stay out of town until the heat died down. The FBI's informants pointed the finger at two hoodlums from Chicago, a former prizefighter named King Solomon and his brother Tim, as the actual bombers, hired by Digby and Anderson on behalf of the "outs" faction of would-be casino owners. The brothers Solomon had frequently done these types of jobs in Chicago—bombings and arsons of bars and restaurants on behalf of mobsters looking to extort something from the owners.

But while the FBI searched Chicago for the Solomons and Atlanta for Anderson and Digby, word kept coming in that more violence was on its way. There were rumors that the faction planned to blow up the homes of all of the Vapors shareholders, the Southern Club, and the Belvedere. There was a hit put out on Plummer Dobbs, and someone was said to be planning to shoot him with a high-powered rifle from a long distance. There was even a plan to bomb the Roanoke Baptist Church, the city's oldest African American congregation, because "those in political power have used negro votes to influence elections." The would-be bombers also believed that blowing up a revered black church would hurl the city into racial tumult, which would possibly force the ministers out of their alliances with the gambling combination.

Five weeks later, one of Dane's partners in the Vapors, hotel owner Gerald Vanderslice, found two sticks of dynamite in his front yard with the fuse half-burned. It was near-certain, and near-deadly, proof that the threats were real and that the same people were behind them. Dane knew it would never stop. Not until somebody else ended up dead.

Dane

**"Routine so far, but something still was unnatural.
And then a woman at my elbow burst out laughing
and I knew what it was; these players
were having fun."**

The writer Bern Keating was in Hot Springs on assignment for *Holiday* magazine as part of a trip across the state of Arkansas. After marveling at the abundance of Jewish eateries in the "island of sporty urban life in an ocean of rural austerity and hominy grits," Keating stopped by the repaired and reopened Vapors for a bourbon and some gambling. He found the club still packed at midnight, and was perplexed.

> I have watched other casino crowds, in the Dominican Republic and old-time Havana, in Monte Carlo and Las Vegas; there was something wrong about the crowd in Hot Springs that I could not at first identify.
>
> All the gimmicks are there, the dice tables and the roulette wheels and the blackjack games, which last are dealt incidentally by uncommonly handsome lady bankers. Around the walls were the usual hardfaced idlers built on the lines of a

Rocky Mountain grizzly bear, and one knew well enough who they were.

Routine so far, but something still was unnatural. And then a woman at my elbow burst out laughing and I knew what it was; these players were having fun.

Never before had I seen that in a casino. The Las Vegas gaming rooms have the hush and solemnity of a high-class mortuary chapel, the players move like sleepwalkers, joyless and mesmerized. In Hot Springs, the players laugh and groan, whoop and screech as they win and lose.

Despite the bombing, the 1963 race meet once again broke attendance and wagering records, continuing a five-year upward trend for Hot Springs that had begun with Dane's ascension to boss gambler and the ouster of Babe Huff. Dane was spending six thousand dollars a month on out-of-state advertisements, and as a result Hot Springs had ranked fourth in the country for number of visitors.

Not everyone was happy with the increased fascination with Hot Springs, however. Governor Faubus and Senator McClellan requested that Dane call a meeting of the gambling operators, and sent emissaries from their own offices to attend. They gathered at the Velda Rose Hotel. The governor's man told the gamblers that the media attention was greater than ever, and that the senator and governor were getting too many questions about why they weren't doing more to close gambling down. The government men from Little Rock then laid out new rules they wanted the Hot Springs gambling operators to abide by—rules that had actually been suggested to Faubus by Dane prior to the meeting, but that carried more heft coming from the governor: No new casinos. No enlargements or expansions on the existing casinos. No new bars. All bars close at 3:00 a.m. No visible signs advertising drinking or gambling. Don't display guns when transporting money to and from the casinos. And no "spectaculars" of any kind that will draw attention to Hot Springs. If there were any more hiccups, the governor would shut it all down.

Within days of the meeting, the owners of the Southern Club were on their way to Las Vegas to secure backing for an expansion of the casino. Meanwhile, outside the Southern Club, on one of the busiest intersections in town, George Pakis had hired a barker to stand outside and holler, "Craps and roulette upstairs!" as crowds passed by. Reports streamed into Dane's office of bars staying open all night, or places selling mixed drinks without approval, or bust-out games being run in the backs of restaurants. Dane would send Leonard Ellis to straighten out situations as they arose, but dealing with Hot Springs' misdeeds was frustrating. Dane had it set up so that he alone was in charge of Hot Springs, and no living person except himself knew what all was happening where. He believed this was the right way to operate—the first time in the city's history it had been done like this. The judges, the police and sheriffs, even the governor reported directly to him. When a bill came before Congress to privatize the bathhouses in Hot Springs, and a delegation of the Hot Springs Bath House Association went to Washington to meet with a congressman about the bill, he asked them, "What does Dane Harris think about it?"

But that total control came at a price—a steep one. Dane was spending anywhere from twenty-five to thirty thousand dollars a month, out of his own pocket, to grease the palms that needed greasing to keep Hot Springs open. All day long he wrote checks and stuffed cash in envelopes. Eighteen hundred dollars to the mayor. Five thousand dollars to a former Department of Justice staffer to get the date of a federal grand jury moved to after racing season. An envelope full of money to the state police investigator assigned by Governor Faubus to keep watch over Hot Springs. It added up. And despite his own profits from his clubs (which he split thirteen ways with his partners), Dane didn't feel like the cost should be his to bear alone anymore.

Dane proposed that the city pass a new law to raise the amount of money that the clubs and bars would pay as amusement tax, and this new revenue could offset some of the expenses he was incurring. He lined up aldermen to support him. The FBI, which had been monitoring the developments through informants and electronic surveillance, saw an opportunity to drive a wedge into the situation. It began a disinformation campaign, spreading rumors and sowing discord among the various players. Most of the clubs were unhappy about the new amusement tax. Rumors circulated that George Pakis wanted to replace Dane as boss gambler, and the FBI encouraged informants to make sure that this got back to Dane. Eventually Dane found he had lost support for the bill, which had to be rewritten.

Compared to the bombing, it was a minor setback, and Dane had no idea that the FBI was behind the discord. The race meet had been a major success despite all the internal drama, and Dane and Sheriff Ellis kept folks in line enough to keep the governor and senator at bay. Meanwhile, Dane wasn't going to let the bombing of his club go undealt with. He and Owney had their own ideas about who was responsible. There were plenty of local characters mad enough at Dane and crazy enough to bomb the Vapors. As soon as Dane became boss gambler, every pimp, prostitute, drug pusher, and safecracker in Hot Springs eventually had the book thrown at them, and everyone knew it was because Dane wanted to clean up the city's image. He and his partners had long worried that someone from the rival faction might try to push back in some way.

In the days after the bombing, Dane chased down his own leads. He enlisted Jack Gunter, his accomplice from his whiskey-running days, and the two of them drove down to Fort Worth, Texas, to visit R. D. Matthews, a hit man who sometimes collected debts for Carlos Marcello in New Orleans or Benny Binion out in Las Vegas. Matthews was one of the most feared men in Texas. Matthews was a friend of Jimmie Green and James Dolan and many of the other shady characters who frequented Digby's Bridge Street Club. Dane had heard that Matthews was holding thirty thousand dollars for a job he had recently pulled, and Dane wanted to talk to him about it. When Dane and Jack got to town they tracked down Matthews's daughter, Peggy, and told her they wanted to speak with him right away. When she relayed the message to her father, he told her he didn't want to speak with either of them. Dane and Jack stayed in a hotel for a couple of days to wait him out, but he stayed out of sight. Matthews may have been a Mafia hit man, but he was afraid to sit face-to-face with Jack Gunter and Dane Harris.

As the summer months approached, Dane lined up more top talent for the Vapors. That summer, Virginia Clinton danced to Jerry Lee Lewis during his weeklong run, joined Frankie Laine onstage and sang "Ghost Riders in the Sky," and sat crying in the dark while Patti Page sang "Tennessee Waltz." While Virginia lived it up at the Vapors, Bill Clinton visited the White House as Hot Springs High School's delegate to the American Legion's Boys Nation. Bill Clinton and Jimmy Hill were born on the very same day, and were in the same class at school until fifth grade, when Jimmy was held back. Virginia and Hazel had more in common than their sons' birth dates, too. They both came from poor families, and both were drawn to Hot Springs by the glitz and nightlife. Both enjoyed drinking and gambling and letting loose, and both suffered at the hands of abusive and alcoholic husbands. Yet despite their similarities, they led different lives. Virginia was steadily employed as a nurse anesthetist and dined at the Vapors, while Hazel pieced together hustles and temporary jobs and begged Dane for ten-dollar shifts. And Jimmy ran the streets that summer, backing up his football teammates in fistfights, while Bill shook hands with President Kennedy in the Rose Garden.

Four months after Bill Clinton met Kennedy in Washington, the president was killed while campaigning in Dallas, Texas. Dane ordered the police to shut down every casino and bar in town for three days straight out of respect for the president. Meanwhile, Dane wasted little time in making inquiries to his contacts in Washington, D.C., to find out whether or not Bobby Kennedy would remain on as attorney general now that the president was dead.

Two days after the assassination, the suspected killer, Lee Harvey Oswald, was himself shot and killed while being transported from the Dallas Police Department. The man who killed Oswald was no stranger to the Hot Springs gambling community. He was Jack Ruby, a Dallas nightclub owner who had done deals with and entertained some of Hot Springs' gambling leaders at his Carousel Club.

THE FBI LOOKED AT a number of people in Jack Ruby's orbit in the Dallas area for connections to the assassination, all of whom were tied to Carlos Marcello and Santo Trafficante, and many of whom frequented or worked in the gambling clubs of Hot Springs. Of particular interest to the FBI were James "Doc" Dolan, who dealt with Ruby for Marcello as the AGVA representative in Dallas, and the hit man R. D. Matthews, whose phone number they claimed was in Ruby's pocket when he shot Oswald. After reviewing Matthews's phone records from that summer, the FBI discovered that Dane and Jack Gunter had been looking for him, pulling Dane into the investigation. Investigators came to Hot Springs to question Dane, as well as Jack Pakis, whom Ruby had phoned two months before the assassination.

While nothing ultimately came of the inquiry into Ruby's mob associates or Hot Springs ties, the extra attention from law enforcement was the last thing Dane needed. The FBI joined Dane's own personal bodyguards in keeping watch on his house around the clock. They monitored his phone lines for both admission of crimes and threats to his life. Once, after listening in to one particularly salacious conversation, an alarmed FBI agent dragged Dane out of his house and told him, "You need to know what your daughter and her boyfriend are saying to each other on the phone." Dane thanked the agent and went inside to holler at Marcia, but was still shocked to learn the FBI was tapping his phone. Dane made it a point not to discuss certain things on the telephone, instead conducting his important business in his office in the back of the Vapors. Unbeknownst to him, the FBI had hidden a microphone and was listening to his conversations there as well.

But as the FBI monitored Dane for evidence that he was breaking federal laws, it also kept an ear to the street for threats to Dane's life. Since the two bombings, phone calls threatening more explosions at the Vapors continued. Each time a call would come in, the police would shut the club down to search for bombs. Dane and his fellow operators were in an unusual bind. The FBI was liable to put them out of business, and possibly even in prison, but on the other hand the bureau was protecting their lives. It was a paradox that held the entire town in limbo.

HOT SPRINGS' BLACK RESIDENTS also had mixed feelings about the FBI. Three days before Christmas 1963, James Rice's phone rang at four forty-five in the morning. The caller on the line said, "We have warned you about your troublemaking in this community. We have asked you to stop. You have continued it." Rice was an NAACP leader who had moved to Hot Springs a year earlier in order to lead the Roanoke Baptist Church, one of the oldest African American churches in Hot Springs. Since his arrival, Rice had been active in challenging segregation around the resort, and had received many phone calls throughout the year like this one. The most recent call had come a week before, after it was revealed that Rice had written to President Johnson, the interior secretary, and the head of the National Parks Service calling for an investigation into discrimination in the bathhouses along Bathhouse Row. That time, the caller told Rice, "You'll get the same thing President Kennedy got."

Earlier in the year, civil rights protesters won the right to integrate public places in Arkansas after sit-ins at lunch counters around the state. But Rice and other leaders had been performing "checks" at the federally owned bathhouses and found that they were still discriminating against African Americans, who for many years had patronized segregated bathhouses. While many white citizens of Hot Springs took pride in their town's relatively progressive attitude toward the African

American community, there were limits. Racist southern social norms were reinforced through segregation. Dane could build a pool at the Webb Center that was even bigger and more expensive than the whites-only pool at the Jaycee Center, and he could have the best of intentions, but the message to the black community would still be the same: *Stay out of our pool.*

"Now we want you to look out the door," the caller that early December morning said, "and see what's happening to your church." Rice hung up and went outside into the snowy morning, where a crowd had already formed. The church building was engulfed in flames.

In the coming days, despite the fact that the FBI was warned back in April that the Roanoke Baptist Church was on the list of the aggrieved gambling faction's bombing targets, the local police and fire officials claimed they could find no evidence of arson. Rice was apoplectic. He pleaded with the FBI to get involved. *The Citizen*, Hot Springs' African American newspaper, wrote that they agreed with Rice that the fire was "a simple, unadulterated case of arson." But they cautioned him against calling for the FBI's help, adding that "if it had been declared arson, the FBI would have taken charge of the investigation . . . With our strange set-up here, who wants the FBI looking?"

Part V
PENTECOST

1964–1965

Dane

As they departed the Vapors, they were met by more than a thousand men and women, many in white robes, some playing trumpets.

The crew working on Dane's house were sweating in the midday sun. They were building a stone wall along the perimeter of his home, a tasteful addition with an eye toward his family's safety and security. Dane brought out a wooden crate full of Coke bottles.

"Come over here, I got something for you," Dane called. The masons and laborers gathered around the crate and each took a bottle.

"These are empty, Mr. Harris," one of the workers said, holding up an empty glass bottle.

"I know they're empty," Dane said. "They ain't refreshments."

He took one of the Coke bottles and smashed it against the stone wall, then held the jagged edge toward the assembled crew. "I want you to put one of these every six inches." He stuck the neck of the bottle into the masonry at the top of the wall, the jagged glass edge protruding from the top. "Make sure they're good and sharp."

The months since the bombing of David Whittington's car had been a rough time for Dane. He worried about his business, his city, and especially his family. He took precautions to protect his family, but the city and the gambling business were on thin ice. Dane was so nervous about the feds that when he got an envelope in the mail from Missouri with thirty-four dollars in chips a customer had forgotten to cash out, he immediately called his lawyer, worried that even opening the envelope was violating federal law. The bombings in Hot Springs caught the attention of Robert Kennedy, who was determined to shut Hot Springs down once and for all. Kennedy dispatched two U.S. assistant attorneys general to Hot Springs: William Hundley, chief of the Organized Crime and Racketeering Division of the Justice Department, and Edward Joyce, head of the gambling unit. The FBI agents assigned to Hot Springs took Hundley and Joyce on a tour. They visited the Southern Club, the Vapors, and the Belvedere. At each club the men witnessed packed houses and furious action. The federal agents had no problem getting in. There was no screening, no secret password, no hidden entrance in an alleyway, as was common among illegal gambling clubs in other cities. These clubs had bright, electrified signs, and welcomed all who had money to spend. After Hundley saw the size of the crowd at the Belvedere, where people were lined up at slot machines and roulette tables in the enormous casino, he decided he had seen enough. He asked the FBI agents to set up a press conference the following day.

The next morning, Hundley and Joyce spoke to reporters on the sidewalk outside of the Majestic Hotel. Hundley called Hot Springs the largest illegal gambling operation in any state in the U.S. He expressed skepticism that it was truly homegrown. "It seems awfully hard for me to comprehend that gambling of this scope could be self-contained within the confines of the State of Arkansas." The pronouncement captured the attention of the rest of the country. In the first weeks of March, the New York *Daily News* ran a headline calling Hot Springs the "Biggest Non-Floating Dice Game in the Land," and *The New York Times* called it a "Gambler's Haven."

The anti-gambling clergy across Arkansas smelled the blood in the water. Preachers traveled from all over to stand in the pulpits of Hot Springs and win back the souls of the local faithful. One Sunday in 1964, at the Grand Avenue Methodist Church, just down the road from Owney Madden's house, the pastor turned the sermon over to Dr. William Brown from Little Rock, the director of the Christian Civic Foundation. Dr. Brown had been leading the fight behind the scenes in the legislature to not only defeat legal gambling, but to give the attorney general control over the state police so that gambling could be shut down. His organization was once viewed as a threat to prosperity in Hot Springs, but now there was a willingness to let him take the pulpit.

"On behalf of your children and yourselves, remove this cancer from your county," he preached. "A wave of gambling is sweeping across America with all the fury of a prairie fire and in an infinite number of manifestations. God save us from a Las Vegas in the heart of Arkansas." Ministers took out full-page ads in papers all over the state filled with statistical evidence of Las Vegas's high rates of juvenile delinquency, drugs, prostitution, and suicide.

The pressure mounted on Governor Faubus, who was facing his first significant electoral challenge from a Republican opponent. A Republican hadn't stood a chance at winning statewide office since before the Civil War. This Republican, however, was Winthrop Rockefeller, scion of one of the richest and most powerful families in America. Rockefeller owned a ranch on top of Petit Jean Mountain in Arkansas, where he had moved in 1953 in order to secure a quick divorce from his wife when Arkansas was one of only two states in the country that permitted them. Like his brother Nelson, the governor of New York, Winthrop was supportive of civil rights, which made him an attractive candidate to the liberal Democrats in Arkansas embarrassed by Faubus.

The gamblers in Hot Springs hoped that they could use this building pressure to their advantage. Perhaps the governor would need them now more than ever. Instead, Faubus decided to cut them loose. Gambling alienated Faubus's core supporters, segregationist Baptists. One of the leaders of the anti-gambling movement, State Representative Nap Murphy, had introduced a bill to create a special department of the state police tasked with shutting down illegal gambling. Prior to that bill, the only thing Representative Murphy had ever introduced was a bill requiring that blood for transfusions be labeled with the race of the donor to prevent white people from being given a black person's blood. The enemies of the gamblers were also the enemies of civil rights. Faubus had to choose.

The *Arkansas Gazette*, the state's largest and most liberal newspaper, had long editorialized against gambling. By the end of 1963, most of the other major newspapers in the state were following suit. Faubus found gambling opponents on his right and his left. A group of Baptist ministers organized vigilantes from all over Arkansas to travel to Hot Springs and monitor the clubs themselves. The self-appointed watchdogs would send official reports to the state police and the governor's office whenever they found open gambling, which was every day of the week but Sunday. Unable to ignore gambling any longer, Faubus surprised Hot Springs by announcing on Friday, March 27, that if the clubs didn't close voluntarily, he would order the state police to shut them down. In making the announcement, Faubus couldn't have sounded more like a Baptist preacher himself: "We must be taught the truth—that it is evil," Faubus said about gambling. Never mind that he visited the racetrack every year, money in one hand and betting slips in the other. Never mind that he was a frequent guest at the Vapors. Never mind the satchels of money that were carried out of Hot Springs every year to help build his mountain mansion. "When enough of our people are converted to the truth, organized gambling will no longer be a problem."

DANE WORRIED MOST ABOUT what an end to gambling would do to the state's image. His larger vision, beyond enriching himself and his friends, was to bring his home state into the modern age, away from the old slow-train-through-Arkansas image. "We're forty-ninth and fiftieth in everything," Dane said. "I guess we'll just stay that way. Proud but poor." The Vapors stood in contrast to these stereotypes. Dane would often tell a story about his friends from Little Rock who brought their friends from New York to his club one night. When they left, they told their Little Rock friends, "When you visit us in New York, we're not going to be able to show you anything like this." That was what the Vapors meant to Dane. It was something nobody would expect from a place like Arkansas. Something nobody would expect from somebody like him. "There's nothing like it in any part of the country," he'd say. "Until you get to Nevada."

While Dane believed gambling would advance Arkansas's reputation, the editorial board of the *Arkansas Gazette* took the opposite view. They opined that it was gambling that made Arkansas seem backward, not its prohibition. "The truth is that the flourishing rackets industry at Hot Springs is an anachronism. Only a few of these wide-open sanctuaries for illegal rackets still exist in the country. Hot Springs as it exists today is a hangover from another era and it suggests nothing so much as the illusion that Arkansas is so bankrupt in its economy and principle that it must tolerate a traffic which most other states scorn." In truth, the *Gazette* was right: Hot Springs was a holdout from a different time, one in which entertainment was viewed more holistically— treated as a function of southern hospitality and healing waters instead of neon signs and asphalt strips wider than the entire Valley of the Vapors.

And yet, anachronistic or not, there was no denying that gambling was the bedrock of the economy in Hot Springs. "The way this Federal thing looks, the only thing for me to do is close up," Dane complained one afternoon to Leonard Ellis in his office at the Vapors, "and it doesn't really make a damn to me. The only reason why I'm doing what I am is because I'm dedicated to Hot Springs. The people who will really be hurt are those building the motels." At the start of 1964 there were over a thousand people working in Hot Springs casinos, with more than half of those working for Dane Harris directly, and more than two thousand applicants still hoping to be hired. His payroll was over a million dollars a year. More than eighteen million dollars in new construction loans were written for new hotels and motels in Hot Springs. There were plans to build a new police station with revenue from the casinos, ironic as that might have been. Tourism stood to suffer across the board. The gambling clubs spent more on out-of-state advertising for Hot Springs than the chamber of commerce. According to testimony by Congressman Paul Fino of New York, the amount of money being wagered by gamblers in Arkansas in 1963 was possibly as high as a billion dollars. The actual number was likely closer to a quarter of that—still an incredible sum. The moment that gambling faced its most serious challenge was also the moment it was the most profitable. It had surpassed even Leo McLaughlin's lofty expectations, and Hot Springs stood poised to once again eclipse Las Vegas as America's gambling capital.

None of that mattered, though. Not the money, the numbers, the jobs, the buildings being constructed. In the end, it was clear that even legalized gambling couldn't save Hot Springs. Las Vegas was legal, and it still suffered from internecine violence at the hands of the fractured American mob. Once a proponent of legalization, Owney Madden had even turned against it in his retirement, claiming that it would make the situation much worse because "the big boys" would move in—the same "big boys" he once counted himself among. Despite its frustrations, the current situation had allowed Dane and Owney to hold the mob at arm's length, to maintain some measure of control. Once the bombs started to explode, that control was exposed as illusory. Ordinary Arkansans had tolerated their Sin City when it provided them with a luxurious getaway in their own backyard, but they would not tolerate the bombings. A line had been crossed, and it appeared to Dane there was no going back.

On the morning of Friday, March 27, shortly after Faubus's statement, Dane decided to shut it all down. That Saturday night would be the last Saturday night for gambling in Hot Springs. Dane asked the chief of police to go around that night to every club and spread the word. The next day was Easter Sunday, and the clubs would be closed anyway. But come Monday morning, they'd stay closed. It would all be over in a flash.

AS WORD GOT OUT that Saturday night would be the last hurrah, television crews began to arrive in Hot Springs. Reporters from national networks like CBS and NBC as well as from *The Saturday Evening Post* and *The New York Times* showed up. A UPI wire reporter called it the "last fling night in the most luxurious gambling houses east of Las Vegas." The high rollers showed up, too, and they did not disappoint. It was one of the wildest nights in the history of Hot Springs. As soon as the last race at Oaklawn had concluded, the clubs filled up and stayed full. Most locals never had a shot at getting a spot at a table, where people were betting with hundred-dollar chips into the wee hours.

The Vapors was filled with over a thousand revelers dressed in jewels and mink coats. They lined up at slot machines and crowded around the dice tables. The showroom at the Vapors on the final night belonged to the comedian Jerry Van Dyke. He worked the occasion into his act. "The gambling won't be going quite as fast tonight," he joked at the opening of his set. "It's got a governor on it."

The casinos stayed crowded until four in the morning. A writer from *The Saturday Evening Post* witnessed a man in a cashmere jacket at the blackjack table blow through a stack of twenty-five-dollar chips. When he was down to the felt, he pulled out his wallet and took out five hundred-dollar bills. He lost those in a hurry, too. He followed that up with two fifties and five twenties. The dealer was unkind. The man in the cashmere jacket lost it all. All that was left in his wallet was seventeen dollars. He showed the dealer. She smiled, but wished he'd make room for someone with some cash. Then he took out his checkbook. His wife finally intervened and told him it was time to go.

"Honah," he said to his wife, "weah not goin'. 'Cause after tonight, it's all ovah."

The revelers at the Vapors on the final night came from all over the world. The journalists who had descended on Hot Springs to catch a glimpse of the last gasp of gambling in the spa interviewed guests from as near as Dallas and as far away as France, but few locals turned up. One wire reporter tried to capture the mood of the Hot Springs rabble. He asked his service station attendant what the man thought about the end of gambling in his town, a tradition that had lasted a full century. "Only a few people get the money," the attendant replied. "The rest of us just work 12 hours a day for $50 a week."

But there was one group of locals that was present that final night, as they had been every other night over the last five years. When the festivities at the Vapors finally wound down early the next morning, and the last of the patrons had been rousted out of the casinos, Dane gathered his employees together at the mahogany bar in the back of the theater for a final toast. Buddy Kirk kept the orchestra playing. The bartenders, change girls, croupiers, stickmen, dishwashers, bouncers—the entire staff, one and all—danced and drank, laughed and cried, until the sun came up on Easter morning.

As they departed the Vapors, they were met by more than a thousand men and women, many in white robes, some playing trumpets, following a procession behind an old fifteen-foot-tall wooden cross. For the twenty-ninth year in a row, the churches of Hot Springs were holding a joint Easter morning sunrise service on the top of Hot Springs Mountain, across from the Vapors. As they processed they sang the traditional hymn "The Old Rugged Cross."

> On a hill far away stood an old rugged cross,
> The emblem of suff'ring and shame,
> And I love that old cross where the dearest and best
> For a world of lost sinners was slain.

Hazel

They filled the commode with liquor and drugs and flushed it all away.

Jimmy called them seizures, though he didn't really have any clue what they were. They looked like what he thought seizures might look like. Hazel would be passed out cold, knocked out from whatever combination of booze and pills she had decided to take that day. Then she'd start twitching and jerking until she'd fall off the bed and onto the floor. That was always the scariest part for Jimmy. He'd grown used to her being unconscious, but when she had fits like these, he couldn't take it. He'd break down and call the hospital to come get her. By the end of the year he'd called so many times that the hospital sent them a bill for the ambulance. After she saw that, she told Jimmy he'd better quit calling that damn hospital. So the next time she started twitching and jerking again, he called Judy.

Judy and Jimmy were seniors now, and they were still a couple. Though they had been together for years, Jimmy hid as much of his home life from her and from his friends as he could. It wasn't out of embarrassment or shame. He simply tried to keep these two halves of his life separate. Hazel didn't mix well with Jimmy's contemporaries.

In addition to growing more desperately addicted to drugs and alcohol, Hazel had also grown into an angry person. She had a mean streak and would lash out, particularly with Judy or with Jimmy's friends. It was as if she was jealous of the relationships Jimmy was able to forge apart from her.

Despite her cruelties, Jimmy stayed close to Hazel and did all he could to care for her. He never resented her. He saw it as his duty to keep his mother alive and well. He didn't remember the other Hazel, the doting mother who would dress him up in sharply pressed clothes and cook him meat loaf and give him toys. He only remembered this Hazel. This Hazel was his mother. Perhaps it was because he never knew the other Hazel that he was able to love this one as much as he did.

Judy showed up and found Hazel twitching on the floor and Jimmy running around the house collecting every bottle and pill he could find. He was pouring the whiskey down the drain, flushing the pills down the toilet. He was angry, but he had a calm, easy, almost cold way of handling himself.

"Help me find the rest," he ordered Judy. It was a lot for Judy to take in. In all the years she and Jimmy had been going together, she hadn't even seen the inside of his home.

Judy ran around the little trailer with Jimmy, grabbing anything that looked illicit. Tabs, pills, even cigarettes. They filled the commode with liquor and drugs and flushed it all away.

"Let's get her in the car," Jimmy said. Judy was shocked. She was about to ferry an adult in the throes of a drug overdose in her own mother's automobile.

"Shouldn't we call the ambulance?" she asked.

"No," Jimmy said. "Just get in the car."

Jimmy and Judy lifted Hazel and carried her outside, shuffling along with Hazel's appendages wrapped up in theirs, no different from the sick dog they once carried into the lake. Only this was no dog. This was far more serious. Somehow it was even more hopeless. While the dog was apathetic, Hazel fought as hard as she could. Only she didn't fight to stay alive. She insisted that Jimmy and Judy leave her to die. As they drove to the hospital, Hazel drifted in and out of consciousness. "No!" Hazel would cry out each time she came to. "You don't understand!"

At the hospital, the nurses saw the three of them coming through the door, and Judy could tell this wasn't Jimmy and Hazel's first visit. *You again*, the look on the nurses' faces seemed to say. They took Hazel away down the hall. Jimmy thanked Judy and told her she could head back home. "I'll be fine," he said. "I need to stay here with her." Shell-shocked and drained, Judy was grateful for a reprieve. She marveled at her boyfriend's hidden life, and wondered at how much she might never know.

When Hazel woke up in the hospital, Jimmy was sitting right beside her, just like he always was. He told Hazel he was leaving.

"You're gonna leave me, too, huh?" she said.

"I'm going to college," he said.

"How can you go to college?" she asked. "I ain't got any money to send you to college."

"I got a scholarship for football," he said.

Hazel knew Jimmy played football, but it had been a long time since she had seen a game. Football had become Jimmy's most important outlet. It gave him a reason to show up at school, and people to hit when he felt angry. He was no quarterback. He was built tall and wide, strong and thick. He wasn't a flashy player like his older brother once was. He was tough and mean and could knock guys to the ground. But even though he didn't score touchdowns playing center on the offensive line, his coaches and teammates considered him a leader. They made him a captain that season. And when Henderson State University in Arkadelphia saw him play, they offered him money to attend their school.

Jimmy would be the last of the men in Hazel's life to leave her since the day her father drove away from Hot Springs almost thirty years before. At forty-five years old, Hazel was now facing life all alone. She had no one left to take care of her. In the days since gambling had been shut down, Hazel had lost a sizable portion of her income. More than that, however, she had lost hope. She had once dreamed of working at the Vapors. Now she had to face the reality that she would not spend her evenings pushing hundred-dollar chips toward doctors and lawyers at the craps table. She would not make hundreds of dollars a week and purchase herself a home, or even an automobile. She would not find a place for herself in this town she once loved, the town where she became a woman, the town where she started her family, the town that ruined her and had nearly killed her. And if she didn't sober up and figure out how to take care of herself, Hot Springs would be the death of her.

The doctor came in, clipboard and files in hand, and asked to speak to Jimmy. He took Hazel's teenage son out in the hall to talk about her in private. They were about the same height, Jimmy and that doctor. Side by side, about the same height.

Dane

APRIL 1965

In one eight-block stretch, fourteen stores had gone out of business since gambling stopped.

Dane tried to keep the Vapors open through the end of 1964 as a restaurant and theater. He had a number of entertainment contracts he needed to honor, many of which had been booked months in advance. Those contracts weren't cheap, and without the casino Dane couldn't turn a profit. And he wasn't the only one suffering. The entire city was hit hard by the loss of casino gambling.

Anyone who walked down Central Avenue that winter could see the devastating impact of the shutdown. In one eight-block stretch, fourteen stores had gone out of business since gambling stopped, and a number of others had going-out-of-business signs in the windows. The Esskay auction house, usually a perennial draw, had only six old ladies in the gallery waiting to bid on items. The massive Velda Rose Hotel, a four-million-dollar behemoth built next to the Vapors earlier that year, had only nine occupied rooms. "The period of depression is going to be with us a long time," said Mort Cox, former head of the chamber of commerce.

Next door to the Southern Club, the $2.5 million Aristocrat, with its luxury rooms and glass-bottomed-pool deck, was also struggling. "My friend, this is what you call a plush hotel, and it's starving to death now," Samuel Kirsch told a visiting reporter. "Had I known what was coming, I'd never have done it."

By November, Dane had had all that he could take. He reorganized the Vapors as a membership club, with thirty-two of the hotels and motels in Hot Springs banding together to subsidize the entertainment budget. The participating hotels paid the Vapors three dollars per room per month, giving Dane seventy-five hundred dollars a month to offset his fifteen-thousand-dollar entertainment budget. Guests of the participating hotels were granted free admission to the club. Five hundred locals also bought memberships for five dollars per month.

This time around the card and dice tables were gone. The casino was replaced by a plush cocktail lounge. When the 1965 race meet began, Dane took a chance and wheeled in thirty-six of his Super Bell slot machines, anticipating a crowd. The crowd never arrived.

Owney

1965

They told her the money was tainted.

Robert Kennedy and J. Edgar Hoover kept their attention on Hot Springs, unconvinced that Owney Madden had truly retired. Hoover chastised his agents, who were telling him they were certain that Owney was finished with the rackets. Hoover refused to believe it, and wanted to know if Owney was partners with Dane in the Vapors. He demanded his agents follow Owney and take photos of him. The assignment wasn't difficult. Like many of Hot Springs' senior citizens, Owney maintained the same routine almost every single day. He tended to his flower garden, a hobby he had picked up in Sing Sing while working in the prison greenhouse. He and Agnes raised chickens and pigeons, the former a passion from her youth, the latter a more urban passion from his. Each morning, Owney would visit the barbershop in the Arlington Hotel, take a hot bath in one of the national park bathhouses, then spend the rest of his day at his usual seat in the Southern Club coffee shop. Though he was still sought out by reporters looking to profile him, he was rarely sought out by local leaders looking for his advice. Now in his seventies and divested from the gambling business, he was more of a tourist attraction than a power broker.

After gambling shut down in Hot Springs, Owney found himself with few friends. Some among the gambling establishment believed that Owney's involvement in the wire service was what ultimately did them in. Others simply avoided him because of the constant surveillance and negative attention that he attracted. Dane kept his distance from Owney, but continued to send envelopes of money to him every month through Leonard Ellis. Ellis groused that Owney was "old and senile" and was often confused about the amount of money he was owed. Dane didn't care. He told Ellis to just make sure nobody ever saw him delivering the money. "You know they watch like a hawk," Dane said. "They're still trying to connect him up with us."

Owney grew more despondent. Just over a year after the final night of gambling at the Vapors, on April 22, 1965, Agnes brought Owney to the hospital with chest pains. The doctors diagnosed him with chronic emphysema. Four days later he died. He was seventy-three years old.

ON THE DAY OF Owney's funeral it poured down rain. There were more than 250 people from across the country gathered in Hot Springs to see him off. They huddled beneath the old oak trees in Greenwood Cemetery, waiting for the downpour to subside. When the sun finally broke through the clouds, they lowered Owney's casket into the ground.

Q. Byrum Hurst gave Owney's eulogy at his graveside. "Page after page of sensationalism has been written about him. But when Owney Madden got off that train in Hot Springs, he became a truly different man and a real citizen. He was mild of manner and small of stature. I couldn't name all the people he helped. Every down-and-outer learned that a helping hand for those really in need could be found in Owney Madden . . . We know not or care not what happened before he came to live with us in Hot Springs. We don't care what they say in New York, Chicago, or Washington. We simply know he was a kind, good man.

"It has been said there is much good in the worst of us, and so much bad in the best of us, that it doesn't behoove any of us to criticize the rest of us," Hurst continued. "There is no ball park named after Owen Madden, no silver cup bearing his name. But it is written on the hearts of all the people he helped—with money, by deed, and by words of encouragement in their dark hours."

A few days after the funeral, Agnes offered a ten-thousand-dollar donation to their church for the purchase of a new stained-glass window. The church turned her down. They told her the money was tainted.

Epilogue

The water in Hot Springs is hot. Here's how hot: it rises up from deep inside the earth, some eight thousand feet below the surface, after being heated to about 148 degrees. The water began as rain, collected at the tops of the mountains some four thousand years ago. It takes that long to get down to the bottom. But it shoots back up to the surface so fast, it doesn't have time to cool. The entire process requires perfect harmony between geological actors—the elevation, the folds and cracks of the rock beneath the surface, the water table, the hills around the valley that collect the water, the minerals that join the water during its journey beneath the earth. The combination that causes the hot springs to flow in Arkansas is so unusual that they are the only springs of their kind in the central latitudes of North America.

It was the water that brought people to Hot Springs, long before highways or even the railroad connected the town to the rest of the world. For centuries, people made the trek in covered wagons, in stagecoaches, or on horseback, through dense forests and across rocky mountains, because they believed the water would heal them of what ailed their bodies. It turned out not to be true, and the bathers stopped coming. The water, indifferent, kept flowing.

HAZEL SAT ON THE banks of Lake Hamilton with her former in-laws. She had come at Josie's invitation to see Brother Shields perform a baptism. The pastor was standing in the lake, his arms held aloft over his head as he preached, his congregants lined up waist-deep in the water alongside him. By 1968, a lot of the larger churches had taken to baptizing people in tanks they built right in the nave. These outdoor baptisms were becoming a ritual for old-timers and country preachers. But with all that gorgeous water surrounding Hot Springs, it would be a shame to let it go to waste.

"To everything there is a season. And a time to every purpose under the heaven: a time to be born, and a time to die. A time to plant, and a time to pluck up that which is planted. It goes on and on. Time. Everything, time. And time changes a lot of things . . ."

That's the truth!

The Hills had been doing their best to keep tabs on Hazel. She was struggling to stay sober, a struggle her in-laws were all too familiar with. Hazel found a job working at a rummage store run by the church. It wasn't exciting or glamorous. There were no colorful characters around to tell her stories or to take her home with them. There were no suckers to work. There were no pills to take. There was just a counter, a cash register, and a crossword puzzle each day that needed solving.

For the first time in her entire life, Hazel was truly on her own. The summer after graduation, Jimmy had left Hot Springs with his best friend, Benny Bridwell. Benny's dad was a horse trainer, and their family would leave Hot Springs each summer to work Arapahoe Downs in Denver or Ak-Sar-Ben in Omaha. Jimmy needed to earn money for college, so Benny's family invited Jimmy to come along with them on the horse racing circuit. Jimmy made ten dollars a day hot walking and grooming horses on the track backside. When the summer ended, he started college at Henderson State, playing center for the Reddies on an athletic scholarship. Each summer, instead of returning to Hot Springs, he would hit the road with Benny again to earn some cash for the next school year. Just like his mother and his grandfather before him, Jimmy followed the horses.

When Jimmy left, Hazel had nobody to take care of her. She kept company with a group of women who worked at the rummage store. She fit right in. They weren't church biddies. They were funny and loved to tell jokes and laugh, and they had their vices. Hazel fell in with them, and they tempted and supported one another in equal measure.

"Styles have changed. Everything. Our way of living has changed. But there's some things that time doesn't change. Amen. There's some things time doesn't change."

Praise the Lord!

Not long after Hazel started working at the rummage store, she and her coworkers drove to Las Vegas to visit Caesars Palace, the newest casino on the Strip and the largest ever built anywhere in the world. The owners of the massive resort were already under investigation for mob ties by a federal government task force, and within a year they would be forced to sell. The new owners were in the fast-food business, and had never worked in gambling before. Their squeaky-clean image lit the way for corporations to dip their toes in the water and invest in casino resorts, hopeful that the days of mob rule in Las Vegas were over.

The ladies from Arkansas arrived in Las Vegas for New Year's Eve, just in time to ring in 1968. Caesars Palace was unlike anything that had ever existed in Las Vegas. It didn't aspire to be hip or elegant. It simply aspired to be big, and everything inside was a celebration of excess. The casino was built and furnished in the style of ancient Rome. The waitresses wore togas and fed patrons grapes. The theater, Circus Maximus, was designed after the Colosseum. The operating budget was forty thousand dollars a day. The entire thirty-four-acre property resembled a resort hotel less than it did a temple.

"I'm gonna preach right now, I feel it comin'! In creation he was God the spirit. In redemption he's the Son. In salvation he's the Holy Ghost. These three are one! Time doesn't change him! When he walks up and down the shores healing the sick, opening the blind's eyes, making the lame to leap and to dance and to walk, he was God Almighty. Hallelujah!"

The entrance to Caesars Palace was ringed by eighteen fountains spouting water high into the air, as if to mock the arid desert. Hazel and her friends crowded around with thousands of spectators that New Year's Eve to watch stuntman Evel Knievel attempt to jump the 141 feet of fountains on his motorcycle. He got the motorcycle up over the fountains and cleared them, but lost control on the landing and spilled over the handlebars onto the pavement, tumbling across the parking lot like a sack of potatoes. The crowd screamed in horror. Some people even cried. Knievel crushed his pelvis and his femur, fractured both wrists, and was left in a coma for twenty-nine days.

Hazel and her friends had no problem shaking off the trauma of watching a man nearly die. They walked straight back into Caesars Palace to ring in the new year. The four Arkansas ladies in their early fifties proved to be too much for the Roman Empire to handle. They drank enough liquor and raised enough hell to get themselves kicked out by Caesars Palace security. By the time the clock struck midnight, Hazel had joined up with the drunks and rascals living it up in Glitter Gulch. Downtown Las Vegas was more their speed. It was more like Hot Springs. More like how Hot Springs once was, anyway. The Hot Springs that Hazel had made her life in. The Hot Springs that was now gone forever.

"God hasn't changed. People have changed. Time has changed. But oh, God, he's still the same. And he can be touched right now with the feelings of our infirmities. If he healed back then he can heal now, because he's still the same. And all the Disciples were baptized in Jesus'

name. John the Baptist was baptized. By Jesus. And the work that Jesus did he did in his Father's name."

BACK IN ARKANSAS, GAMBLING was finally gone for good. In 1966, Faubus had decided not to seek reelection. His former foe, the ardent segregationist preacher Jim Johnson, ran on the Democratic ticket instead. Johnson lost to Winthrop Rockefeller in a historic election, and Rockefeller became the first Republican to lead the state since Reconstruction. Rockefeller's election was a rebuke to segregation, but it also spelled doom for the ragtag remains of the illegal gambling industry in Hot Springs.

Q. Byrum Hurst had been able to get his legal gambling bill passed in both houses of the Arkansas legislature. It wasn't that attitudes toward gambling had changed. His opponents claimed Hurst simply bought the votes, and word was that the going rate was one thousand dollars. Hurst had secured a pledge from Rockefeller that if the bill passed, Rockefeller would allow it to become law, not by signing it but by neglecting to act on it for five days after it reached his desk. Instead, Rockefeller shocked Hurst and the people of Hot Springs when he announced in a televised address that he would veto the bill. Rockefeller then sent an armada of state police to Hot Springs to shut down the few rough-and-tumble clubs that had been holding out. The raiding party started at the Bridge Street Club, smashing the glass door open with a sledgehammer and dragging the slot machines and card tables out into the street, just as in Havana a decade earlier. They raided four clubs in all, hauling off three truckloads of gambling equipment. Rockefeller's new state police director, a former FBI agent named Lynn Davis, had the equipment taken to a gravel pit, driven over by a bulldozer, burned to a crisp, and then buried twenty feet underground.

The Vapors wasn't among the clubs raided in 1967. A year after the shutdown in 1964, Dane had tried to reopen the casino in the Vapors once it was designated as a private club. That worked for a while. But then the bombings started up again. Dane's house on Trivista was bombed while he and Marcella and the children slept inside. That same night, Circuit Judge Dobbs had a bomb go off at his house, too. Dane got rid of his slot machines and moved his family out of the house on Trivista to a house on the grounds of the Belvedere. It was safer, but it was also idyllic. Dane and Marcella would play golf until it got dark outside, then they'd park their cars on the fairway and light the way with their headlights to continue their game. Marcia and Dane Jr. would explore the rolling hills. Eventually, Dane decided he didn't want to move back to town. He put their beautiful house on Trivista up for sale. It was eventually purchased by Jack Digby.

SCIENTISTS AREN'T SURE HOW long the hot water will continue to flow from the cracks of the Ouachita foothills. What they are sure of is that the greatest threat to the springs is the people who live among them. If someone digs too deep a well or takes too much rock off the side of a mountain, the intricately choreographed system that produces the springs will stop working. The hot water will turn cold forever. The vapors will dissipate, never to return.

For now, the waters continue to bubble up from the ground, but all the bathhouses save two have been shuttered. The once-busy airport just south of town no longer serves wealthy private planes or commercial airliners, as it did in the 1960s. Today the only flight in and out of Hot Springs is a government-subsidized Cessna flight to Dallas. Central Avenue is quiet, populated by small shops not unlike the rummage store at which Hazel worked (*Faith & Flair Boutique: we love mixed prints, trends & Jesus!*). The Southern Club is now a two-bit wax museum, its inhabitants frozen in time, the younger and elder George Bush leering from the windows of the gift shop. Jimmy Carter, grinning stiffly, rides the broken escalator that used to carry gamblers to the casino floor.

There is, however, a legal casino in operation in Hot Springs today. After trying and failing three more times—in 1985, 1996, and 2000—to legalize gambling by referendum, voters in Arkansas finally approved a measure in 2018 to issue a license for a casino at the Oaklawn racetrack. A new hotel is under construction, its owner betting big that bringing the dice tables out of retirement will mean a return of visitors to the valley.

Many of the once-mighty hotels and casinos downtown have been razed over the years. The Vapors, however, remains intact. The building is now clad in corrugated metal siding. Its retro-futuristic sign still stands. After trying to reinvent itself over the years as a disco and later a honky-tonk, the Vapors was eventually turned into a church.

BROTHER SHIELDS CONTINUED TO preach by the shores of the lake on that summer day in 1968:

"You may see it and think you believe it, but you haven't got the Revelation. I'm gonna give you the Revelation. If you accept him and get the Holy Ghost, you'll get the Revelation! The Holy Ghost is a revealer."

Amen!

"It's a teacher."

Amen!

Ever since her trip to Las Vegas, Hazel had been trying to sober up. She had kicked the pills. She hadn't quit alcohol, but she wasn't drinking every day. When she did drink, she tried to keep it to the soft stuff. It wasn't easy, but she was trying.

Hazel had met a man, a carnival man, and he had invited her to join him on the road. He operated a razzle-dazzle game, a swindle like the one they used to run in the Havana casinos. He needed someone pretty to be his confederate, to pretend to play the game and win, so he could needle the boys into putting down more and more money on the rigged game. "If this pretty little thing can win, you sure can!" he would say.

His offer appealed to Hazel. Hot Springs just wasn't the same. The churches didn't stop with the casinos. In the last year, they had even pressured Rockefeller to enforce the ban on liquor by the glass. The police had started raiding the bars. They were trying to rid Hot Springs of sinfulness. They were squeezing the life right out of it. The crossword puzzles and the rummage store just couldn't compete. She told the carnival man she'd come with him. Maybe she'd end up somewhere else when all was said and done. Maybe even in Las Vegas.

And so perhaps Josie harbored a secret hope that she could get Hazel out into Lake Hamilton that day to let Brother Shields finally baptize her before she left town. Hazel had shown up of her own volition. Perhaps some part of her wanted to be saved. Perhaps deep down, Hazel wanted to have her head submerged beneath the water. Not on that day, but maybe someday.

"Ephesians 3:15. Of whom the whole family in heaven and earth is named. For this cause I bow my knees . . ."

The whole family!

Crown of glory!

"The whole family in heaven and earth!"

Hallelujah!

"The whole family!"

NOTES

PROLOGUE

3 *L. V. Rowe was on one hell of a roll at the dice table*: All of the dialogue and details in this section from the night of April 1, 1961, are taken from depositions given in the case L. V. Rowe v. Dane Harris et al., Civ. A No. 848, United States District Court W.D. Arkansas, filed 4/7/1961 and dismissed 6/29/1961.

4 *Hot Springs was in the middle of a banner season*: "Hot Springs Counts 5 Million Visitors, Prepares for More," *Times* (Shreveport) (October 29, 1961).

4 *"America's first national park"*: "America's First National Park Has 'Gone Reno,'" *Brooklyn Daily Eagle* (March 22, 1931).

4 *first park managed by the federal government*: William Hunt Jr., *More Than Meets the Eye: The Archeology of Bathhouse Row, Hot Springs National Park, Arkansas*, Midwest Archeological Center, National Park Service, U.S. Department of the Interior (2008).

4 *The city's unofficial motto was "We Bathe the World"*: Kent Ruth, "Baths Are Best in Hot Springs," *Daily Oklahoman* (April 8, 1956).

4 *They came to soak in scalding hot baths*: "Hot Springs National Park," circular of general information, U.S. Department of the Interior (1936).

5 *Prizefighters like Jack Dempsey*: Wayne Fields, "The Double Life of Hot Springs," *American Heritage* (April 1991).

5 *Baseball players like Babe Ruth*: Martin Stezano, "Hot Springs, Grapefruits and the Babe: A History of Spring Training," https://www.history

.com/news/hot-springs-grapefruits-and-the-babe-a-history-of-spring -training (March 1, 2017).

5 *The popularity among professional ball players*: Don Duren, "Major League Spring Training in Hot Springs," Encyclopedia of Arkansas, https://encyclopediaofarkansas.net/entries/major-league-spring-training -in-hot-springs-6221/.

5 *As visitors to Hot Springs would disembark from their trains*: J. H. Tilden, *Gonorrhea and Syphilis* (Kessinger, 1912), 177.

5 *Some of the more popular ailments that patients came to treat were venereal diseases*: Elliot Bowen, "Before Tuskegee: Public Health and Venereal Disease in Hot Springs, Arkansas," *Southern Spaces* (October 31, 2017).

5 *Al Capone would "take the waters"*: Orval Allbritton, *The Mob at the Spa* (Garland County Historical Society, 2011), 2.

5 *Despite being deep in the heavily Baptist and segregated south*: Bill Clinton, *My Life* (Vintage, 2005), 27; "Most Businesses, Professions Found Among City's 8,000 Negro Citizens," *Sentinel Record* (Hot Springs) (February 18, 1962).

5 *On the east side of Malvern Avenue were black-owned hotels*: Janis Kearney, ed., *Conversations: William Jefferson Clinton from Hope to Harlem* (Writing Our World Press, 2006), 78–79.

5 *All this in addition to a growing number of Greek, Italian, and other European immigrant families*: Clinton, *My Life*, 27.

6 *In addition to these four main clubs*: "U.S. Sells 1,290 Gaming Devices, 144 Wagering Stamps in State," *Sentinel Record* (Hot Springs) (May 27, 1962).

7 *Despite its physical size, the club employed more than two hundred people*: "Spa Blast Set by 'Fanatic,'" Associated Press (January 5, 1963).

7 *The payroll at the Vapors*: Theodore Link, "Gamblers Edgy in Hot Springs Over US Inquiry," *St. Louis Post-Dispatch* (December 2, 1962).

8 *The entertainment budget was over ten thousand dollars a week*: Wallace Turner, "Hot Springs: Gamblers' Haven," *New York Times* (March 8, 1964).

8 *"The Vapors is like a miniature Las Vegas Strip"*: Theodore Link, "Election Time Fails to Halt Illegal Gaming in Hot Springs," *St. Louis Post-Dispatch* (July 1, 1962).

8 *hundreds of millions of dollars in revenue*: Jerry Greene, "Biggest Non-Floating Dice Game in the Land," *Daily News* (New York) (March 9, 1964).

8 *construction had begun on over a dozen new luxury hotels*: "Hot Springs Counts 5 Million Visitors."

10 *a job that could pay as much as fifty dollars a night plus tips*: Edna Lee Howe, "'School' Trains Residents for Casino Jobs to Meet Need, Avoid

Clash with U.S. Laws," *Sentinel Record* (Hot Springs) (November 25, 1962).

10 *The city government levied fines on the clubs*: Theodore Link, "Hot Springs Got $300,000 in Tax from Illegal Game Operation," *St. Louis Post-Dispatch* (July 2, 1962).

13 *nine-billion-dollar illegal gambling industry*: Daniel Moynihan, "Can It Be Controlled? The Private Government of Crime," *The Reporter* (July 6, 1961).

13 *single biggest source of revenue*: Ibid.

14 *He had launched the careers*: Graham Nown, *Arkansas Godfather* (Butler Center, 2013), 12.

15 *"the largest illegal gambling operation in the United States"*: Turner, "Hot Springs: Gamblers' Haven."

Part I: Water

HAZEL, APRIL 4, 1935

21 *Hazel wasn't sure where she was headed*: The scenes at the Hill family house between Hazel, Clyde, and Richard come from an interview with Ressie Parker (July 20, 2015).

22 *Horse racing was experiencing a surge in popularity across America*: Dorothy Ours, *Man o' War: A Legend Like Lightning* (St. Martin's, 2007), 164.

22 *chose to keep the track closed rather than operate in defiance of the law*: Orval Allbritton, *Leo and Verne* (Garland County Historical Society, 2003), 401–402.

22 *It was the casino operators*: Ibid.

23 *back in 1907 the original owners of Oaklawn*: Ibid.

23 *a gregarious man who paraded around town*: Patty Hawthorne Ramsey, "A Place at the Table: Hot Springs and the GI Revolt," *Arkansas Historical Quarterly* 59 (Winter 2000).

23 *He taxed the craps games and the brothels*: Allbritton, *Leo and Verne*, 262–64.

23 *"the sin city of the whole world"*: Frank Deford, "Once a Valley of Vapors and Vice," *Sports Illustrated* (April 16, 1973).

24 *"little white church in the valley"*: Luther Summers, "Select Poems and Park Place Baptist Church," church publication (1933).

24 *"Your church will burn and you will be among the missing"*: Allbritton, *Leo and Verne*, 404.

24 *tens of thousands of visitors did*: Ibid., 407.

24 *She worked on the backstretch, scurrying*: Interview with Larry Hill (July 2015).

25 *On April 4, the final day of the race meet*: Allbritton, *Leo and Verne*, 407.

25 *the dances at Fountain Lake*: Ibid., 344.

26 *"I'm goin' to Tijuana"*: Interview with Larry Hill (July 2015).

OWNEY, FEBRUARY 13, 1931

28 *a long Duesenberg convertible pulled up*: Graham Nown, *Arkansas Godfather* (Butler Center, 2013), 203.

28 *That day in 1931 was Owney's first visit*: Ibid.

29 *lit up the dance floor at the Belvedere Club*: Ibid., 200–201.

29 *no shortage of potential suitors*: Ibid.

29 *The total came to over a thousand dollars*: Ibid., 203.

29 *When Owney invited her to dinner, Agnes turned him down*: Ibid.

29 *The rest of the day Agnes fretted*: Ibid., 204.

29 *followed wherever he went by magazine photographers*: Ibid., 271.

29 *"When you wanted anything in New York, you saw Owney Madden"*: Charles Samuels, "Owney Madden: Only Gangster Exiled in America," *Cavalier* (November 1961).

30 *killed six, maybe seven people*: Ibid.

30 *When he was eleven he approached the Gophers*: Dave Anthony and Gareth Reynolds, "The Gopher Gang," *The Dollop*, podcast (January 29, 2017).

30 *The Gophers were known for muggings*: Ibid.

30 *"bomb insurance"*: Orval Allbritton, *The Mob at the Spa* (Garland County Historical Society, 2011), 190.

30 *including rival Gophers when it suited him*: Samuels, "Owney Madden."

30 *In 1912 Owney was shot eleven times*: Nown, *Arkansas Godfather*, 66–68.

30 *"Nothing doing," he said. "The boys'll get 'em"*: "The New York Gangster—from Leeds," *Yorkshire Evening Post* (April 21, 2010).

30 *Within a week of Owney's release*: Nown, *Arkansas Godfather*, 69.

30 *ten-to-twenty-year sentence*: Ibid., 84.

30 *He quickly organized a gang to rob and hijack bootleggers*: Samuels, "Owney Madden."

31 *Dwyer, Owney, and Costello operated their own private armada*: Nown, *Arkansas Godfather*, 135.

31 *"Madden's Number 1"*: Ibid., 257.

31 *He made everyone he worked with sign contracts*: Ibid., 143.

31 *Dwyer bought a professional hockey team*: Jeff Klein, "85 Years Ago, Pro Hockey Roared into the Garden," *New York Times* (December 14, 2010).

31 *Costello invested in slot machines*: Nown, *Arkansas Godfather*, 318.

31 *Madden was a boxing fan, so he backed a number of professional boxers*: Ibid., 156.

32 *whom he would ask to take a dive*: Samuels, "Owney Madden."

32 *His men walked into the Plantation*: Nown, *Arkansas Godfather*, 114.

32 *Owney sent a few emissaries to Philadelphia*: A. H. Lawrence, *Duke Ellington and His World* (Routledge, 2004), 111.

33 *"Do you still want to go to dinner?"*: Nown, *Arkansas Godfather*, 204.

33 *in the company of America's most notorious criminals*: Ibid., 209.

33 *My dearest darling*: Ibid., 207.

33 *"Life is very uninteresting"*: Ibid., 212.

34 *killing dozens of people, including a five-year-old boy*: Peter Levins, "Killer Coll and the Embarrassing Case of Mr. Brecht, Star Witness," *Daily News* (New York) (July 2, 1933).

34 *"That was very unwise, Vincent"*: Nown, *Arkansas Godfather*, 187.

34 *"baby murder"*: "$5,000 Reward, Dead or Alive, for the Capture of the Murderer of This Boy," *Daily News* (New York) (August 3, 1931).

34 *"damnable outrage"*: "NY Police Comb Little Italy for Slayers of Child," Associated Press (July 30, 1931).

34 *Thousands of people attended Vengalli's funeral*: "Gang Gun Nest Is Raided in Little Italy," Associated Press (August 2, 1931).

34 *He asked Coll to wait by a pay phone*: Details of the Coll shooting, including quotations, are from Nown, *Arkansas Godfather*, 195–97.

35 *The parole board worried Owney might try to flee*: Ibid., 243.

35 *went to work for Owney behind the scenes*: Ibid., 278.

35 *sentenced Owney to a single year in prison*: Ibid., 251.

35 *"I've got a fine day"*: "Owney the Hermit Quits Prison in Style," *Brooklyn Daily Eagle* (July 2, 1933).

36 *He summoned Owney along with all of the top criminal figures in America to the Waldorf-Astoria Hotel*: Hank Messick, *Lansky* (Putnam, 1971), 72.

36 *the population of Las Vegas from five thousand to over twenty-five thousand*: James Roman, *Chronicles of Old Las Vegas* (Museyon, October 1, 2011), 47.

36 *before Las Vegas even had a post office or a paved road*: The first casino license was issued in 1931 to the Northern Club. The first paved road, Fremont Street, had a few blocks partially paved in 1925 but wasn't completed

until the mid-1930s. Lynn M. Zook, Allen Sandquist, and Carey Burke, *Las Vegas 1905–1965* (Arcadia, 2009). The post office opened in 1933. "Historic U.S. Post Offices in Nevada 1891–1941," National Register of Historic Places Multiple Property Documentation Form, U.S. Department of the Interior (February 1990).

37 *His son Buddy had been born with spina bifida*: Sandra Lansky, *Daughter of the King: Growing Up in Gangland* (Hachette, 2014), 22.

37 *parole board transfer his care to her family home*: Nown, *Arkansas Godfather*, 267.

HAZEL, AUGUST 1935

38 *Hazel Welch didn't take to life on the Hill family farm*: Quotes and details of Hazel's life at the Hill home are taken from an interview with Ressie Parker (July 20, 2015) unless otherwise noted.

39 *"smells of the brimstone of Hades"*: Orval Allbritton, *Leo and Verne* (Garland County Historical Society, 2003), 410.

39 *sparked celebrations in the streets*: Ibid., 411.

39 *four of the six local banks to fail and close their doors*: Ibid., 394.

39 *Unemployment stood at 37 percent, and the state's finances were at a "low ebb"*: Maurice Moore, "Futrell Was Advocate of Legalized Gambling," Palmer News Bureau (March 17, 1967).

39 *advocated legalizing the sale of liquor*: Ibid.

39 *ten cents per admission and four cents per dollar bet*: Ibid.

39 *More than twelve thousand people attended the track's opening day*: Henry Dorris, "12,000 Turn Out for Opening of Horse Race Track in Hot Springs," Associated Press (February 23, 1935).

39 *Downtown had come back to life with tourists*: Details about Hot Springs' change in fortune are taken from Allbritton, *Leo and Verne*, 400–401 and 408.

40 *Tourists who got off those trains were accosted by cabdrivers*: Collie Small, "The Town Without a Lid," *Saturday Evening Post* (July 20, 1946).

40 *sometimes hitchhiked and even walked*: Allbritton, *Leo and Verne*, 414.

40 *Hazel, and many like her, found fulfillment in strolling down Central Avenue*: The details of life in downtown Hot Springs in this chapter are taken from anecdotes in Allbritton, *Leo and Verne*, as well as from multiple interviews conducted for this book by the author.

41 *a hundred dollars' bond*: Marriage certificate.

42 *It was sometime that summer that Hollis and Hazel met Dr. Petty*: Details about Hazel's relationship with the Pettys are taken from an interview with Ressie Parker (July 20, 2015) unless otherwise noted.

43 *over half of the counties in the state were still dry*: Jay Barth, "Get Rid of Dry Counties," *Arkansas Times* (November 28, 2013).

43 *Most of the restaurants and bars in Hot Springs served liquor in defiance of this law*: Boyden Underwood, "Racing and Liquor Issues Uncertain; Futrell Is Silent," *Hope Star* (April 5, 1934).

OWNEY, DECEMBER 1935

45 *cold December morning in 1935*: Orval Allbritton, *The Mob at the Spa* (Garland County Historical Society, 2011), 214.

45 *joined by Agnes's father and Reverend Kincaid*: Graham Nown, *Arkansas Godfather* (Butler Center, 2013), 280.

45 *"members of the family today shrouded the affair in utmost secrecy"*: "Madden Set for Wedding in Arkansas," *Daily News* (New York) (June 19, 1935).

45 *The ceremony was short*: Nown, *Arkansas Godfather*, 280.

45 *modest room at the Cleveland Manor Apartments*: FBI, memorandum on Owney Madden by Claburn White, File Number 92-2699 (September 23, 1960), 58.

46 *on a deal with Frank Costello*: Nown, *Arkansas Godfather*, 267; Allbritton, *The Mob at the Spa*, 211.

46 *seventeen-room Queen Anne Victorian home*: Orval Allbritton, *Leo and Verne* (Garland County Historical Society, 2003), 561.

46 *"Don't worry about giving Leo a raise. Leo will get his one of these days"*: Orval Allbritton in *City of Visitors: The Story of Hot Springs* (Arkansas Educational Television Network, 2004).

47 *He paid the one-dollar poll tax required of every voter*: Allbritton, *Leo and Verne*, 374.

47 *who had initially recruited McLaughlin to run for mayor*: Allbritton, *Leo and Verne*, 244.

48 *promoted across the country by the surgeon general and the government*: Ray Hanley, *Hot Springs, Arkansas in Vintage Postcards* (Arcadia, 1998), 9–10.

48 *Hot Springs was called a "Mecca of the afflicted"*: Word Mills, "Mantaka," *Daily Arkansas Gazette* (April 5, 1892).

48 *cure 90 percent of all diseases*: Ibid.

48 *bloody shootout in the streets*: "Sheriff Houpt Mortally Wounded; Outlaw Killed in Hot Springs Street," *Daily Arkansas Gazette* (August 18, 1910).

48 *major con artist gangs*: "Bucked Roulette Wheel and Lost," *Times* (Shreveport) (January 10, 1913); "Swindlers Had a Ledger of Their Victims," *Arkansas Democrat* (February 24, 1909).

48 *the city's residents were desperate for a return to the days when Hot Springs was known as the Carlsbad of America*: "Life at the Hot Springs," *Sun* (New York) (August 2, 1896).

49 *owned a controlling interest*: Allbritton, *Leo and Verne*, 266.

49 *Jacobs kept his spot at the top of the action*: The description of W. S. Jacobs and details of his operation are taken from Shirley Abbott, *The Book-maker's Daughter: A Memory Unbound* (University of Arkansas Press, 1991), 22–23, unless otherwise noted.

49 *"You know we'll never be able to come back to Hot Springs if we stiff Bill Jacobs"*: Allbritton, *The Mob at the Spa*, 23.

50 *offered a 25 percent stake in the Belvedere*: Allbritton, *Leo and Verne*, 382–83.

50 *Rival gangsters tried to assassinate Al Capone*: Allbritton, *The Mob at the Spa*, 34–37.

50 *roughing up caddies on the golf course or stiffing clubs and restaurants*: Ibid., 28–29.

51 *donations to McLaughlin's political campaigns*: Ibid., 27.

51 *"If it was known you had any interest in the clubs here, we wouldn't be able to operate"*: Allbritton, *Leo and Verne*, 320.

51 *"Have a good time, stay out as late as you want, spend your money, keep out of trouble"*: Ibid., 279.

51 *At the horse races people would crowd around him*: Nown, *Arkansas God-father*, 301.

52 *The New York* Daily News *called him "love smitten"*: Carl Warren, "Madden Defies New York and Returns South," *Daily News* (New York) (July 14, 1934).

52 *and followed his "bucolic romance with an Arkansas postmaster's pretty daughter"*: "Madden Parole Ends, Arkansas Love Waits," *Daily News* (New York) (June 15, 1935).

52 *And when he and Agnes entertained famous guests, as they did one night in March*: Allbritton, *The Mob at the Spa*, 78.

52 *twelve-million-dollar prostitution racket*: "Luciano Will Fight Against Going to NY," *Clarksdale Register* (April 3, 1936).

52 *Luciano had been there just the year before*: Allbritton, *The Mob at the Spa*, 76.

53 *Luciano and Orlova stayed in town for two weeks*: Details of Luciano and Orlova's time in Hot Springs are taken from Allbritton, *The Mob at the Spa*, 77–78.

53 *was also the head of security at the Belvedere*: Allbritton, *Leo and Verne*, 341.

53 *stealing tourists' cars and offering them back to the owners for a reward, or selling confiscated handguns*: Ibid., 282.

54 *Akers used to take payoff money from Nash*: Allbritton, *The Mob at the Spa*, 80–82.

54 *"Chicago in its Capone era"*: "Former C-J Police Reporter Out to Clean Up Hot Springs," *Courier-Journal* (Louisville) (February 21, 1937).

54 *Akers saw a man check in*: Allbritton, *The Mob at the Spa*, 82.

54 *On April 1, 1936, Orlova told Luciano*: Ibid., 80.

54 *"Lucky, do you realize that Thomas Dewey has an arrest warrant out for you?"*: All of the dialogue and descriptions from the Luciano arrest are taken from Allbritton, *The Mob at the Spa*, 80–99, unless otherwise noted.

55 *"Don't worry about a thing"*: Nown, *Arkansas Godfather*, 291.

55 *"What about extradition?"*: Martin Gosch and Richard Hammer, *The Last Testament of Lucky Luciano* (Dell, 1975), 195.

55 *"the most dangerous and important racketeer in New York, if not the entire country"*: "Luciano Captured as Vice Ring Chief," *Baltimore Sun* (April 2, 1936).

56 *The jailer bolted the doors*: Details of the standoff at the jail are from Allbritton, *Leo and Verne*, 329–30.

57 *dozen deputies with submachine guns*: Ibid., 330.

57 *"Every time a major criminal of this country wants an asylum, he heads for Hot Springs, Arkansas"*: Ibid., 330.

57 *"Arkansas cannot be made an asylum for criminals"*: "New York Vice Leader Wrested from 'Spa' Police," *Hope Star* (April 4, 1936).

58 *"I've appointed too many of my relatives to state jobs and they haven't been earning their money"*: Allbritton, *Leo and Verne*, 368.

58 *at thirty-five was now the youngest county sheriff in the state of Arkansas*: Ibid., 375.

58 *which he stuffed with more than thirteen hundred premarked ballots*: Frederick Collins, "Crime in Hot Springs," *Liberty* (July 29, 1939).

58 *In 1936, Jacobs employed more than eleven hundred people*: "Raiders Strip 8 Swanky Clubs in Hot Springs," Associated Press (January 31, 1937).

58 *He paid a man to camp out at Crow's Station*: Allbritton, *Leo and Verne*, 376.

HAZEL, JANUARY 29, 1937

59 *The Kentucky Club wasn't the fanciest club*: The description of the Kentucky Club is based on Wayne Threadgill, *Gambling in the Spa*, 8th ed. (self-pub., 2015), 47.

60 *The track owners were anticipating crowds of more than fifteen thousand to show up for the "Mayor Leo P. McLaughlin Inaugural Handicap"*: "Oaklawn Park Ready for Annual Meeting," *Palm Beach Post* (February 28, 1937).

60 *Men in moving company uniforms carried a roulette wheel*: "Gaming Devices Taken to Little Rock for Bonfire," *Sentinel Record* (Hot Springs) (January 30, 1937).

61 *Across town at the Belvedere, the guard in the tower at the entrance gate got a phone call that the raiders were on the way*: This description of the Belvedere's security precautions comes from Inez Cline and Fred Palmer, "Belvedere," *The Record* (Garland County Historical Society, 1992).

61 *By the time they entered the club, there were only a handful of guests*: "Gaming Devices Taken to Little Rock for Bonfire."

61 *"Sorry, Mr. Jacobs, I can't let you do that"*: Ibid.

61 *One newspaper described Jacobs*: "Gambling Tables at 'Spa' Seized by State Agents," *Hope Star* (January 30, 1937).

61 *"You can use your own judgment about opening up tomorrow"*: "Gaming Devices Taken to Little Rock for Bonfire."

62 *He was irritated to be called away from his work*: "Spa's Gambling Equipment Fed to Big Bonfire," *Sentinel Record* (Hot Springs) (January 31, 1937).

63 *"Our friends in the gambling industry are willing to provide campaign support for a candidate who is friendly to Hot Springs"*: Orval Allbritton, *Leo and Verne* (Garland County Historical Society, 2003), 378.

63 *"And we can guarantee delivering the vote in Garland County in your next election. You wouldn't want to throw that away"*: Ibid.

63 *"You should appeal to your local courts"*: Ibid., 379.

DANE, MARCH 1939

65 *short, muscular man*: The description of Sam Harris is from an interview with Fred Palmer (January 2017).

65 *He was half American Indian, the son of a white man and a Choctaw woman*: Details of Dane Harris's early life, including dialogue, are from interviews with Marcia Heien (July 2015, October 2017) unless otherwise noted.

66 *He once took an order for a case of booze*: "Two Moonshiners Stage Jail Delivery Yesterday," *Little Rock Daily News* (February 17, 1922).

66 *He operated a notorious still in Hughes County, Oklahoma*: FBI, memorandum on Hubert Dane Harris, File Number LR 92-122 (September 20, 1961).

66 *Sam Harris teamed up with Harry Hastings*: Interview with Fred Palmer (January 2017).

68 *One day in the spring of 1939*: The story about Owney Madden playing golf is based on an interview with Walter "Skip" Ebel Jr. (December 2016).

69 *Each day as Dane passed by the Belvedere Club*: Interview with Marcia Heien (July 2015).

69 *Little did Dane know that the Belvedere*: Inez Cline and Fred Palmer, "Belvedere," *The Record* (Garland County Historical Society, 1992).

HAZEL, JUNE 1939

70 *Hazel's parents had split up, and it wasn't the first time*: Interview with Larry Hill (July 2015).

70 *Hollis was up each morning at three o'clock*: Details about Hazel and Hollis's early married life in this chapter, including dialogue, are based on an interview with Ressie Parker (July 2015).

Part II: Fire

DANE, JUNE 1941

77 *On the weekends he would go to the parties out at Fountain Lake*: Details about Dane and Marcella's courtship and marriage are from an interview with Marcia Heien (July 2015).

78 *One day while Jacobs was driving back from Little Rock*: Orval Allbritton, *Leo and Verne* (Garland County Historical Society, 2003), 434.

78 *Every police officer in Hot Springs*: Ibid., 435.

78 *majority share in six of the eight largest gambling clubs*: Ibid.

79 *He put together a partnership of six men*: Ibid., 439.

79 *It lasted nine months*: Ibid.

79 *renting out the top floor to bookmakers*: Ibid., 448.

79 *He was involved in the trafficking of all kinds of contraband*: Details of Harry Hastings's criminal dealings are from an interview with Bob Douglas conducted by Roy Reed as part of the Pryor Center's *Arkansas Gazette* Project (February 1997).

79 *Sam was all too willing to put Dane into service*: Interview with Fred Palmer (August 2016).

79 *just had enough to fill his trunk*: Ibid.

80 *George was part Cherokee and an elected county commissioner*: 1920 Census; "Gunter Is Chosen as Committee Member in State Relief Plan," *Sequoyah County Democrat* (August 6, 1931).

80 *So much so that when Dane got pulled over*: Interview with Fred Palmer (August 2016).

80 *With the help of the American Legion*: Jere Bishop Franco, *Crossing the*

Pond: The Native American Effort in World War II (University of North Texas Press, 1999), 199.

80 *John was a barnstormer*: Details about John Stover's life and career are from Lewis Stephens, "John Henry Stover, Airport Manager," *The Record* (Garland County Historical Society, 1983); and Allbritton, *Leo and Verne*, 462.

81 *Stover thought Dane would have an easier time*: Interview with Fred Palmer (August 2016).

81 *Soon Dane was carrying Harry Hastings's whiskey*: Ibid.

81 *loading a small plane at Moon Distributors*: Ibid.

OWNEY, JUNE 1942

82 *The ballroom was packed with dancers, black and white alike*: Graham Nown, *Arkansas Godfather* (Butler Center, 2013), 301.

82 *meetings between black underworld leaders*: Robert Raines, *Hot Springs: From Capone to Costello* (Arcadia, 2013), 23.

83 *The federal government's Army and Navy Hospital*: Details in this section about the history of the Army and Navy Hospital are taken from "Army & Navy General Hospital Historic District," National Register of Historic Places Registration Form, U.S. Department of the Interior (February 2007); and "The Old Hospital," *Student Selects* (Arkansas Educational Television Network, 2017).

84 *McLaughlin gave part of Jacobs's share*: Orval Allbritton, *The Mob at the Spa* (Garland County Historical Society, 2011), 131.

84 *"rather dumb individual"*: FBI, Bremer kidnapping files, File Number 7-576, prison interview with Dutch Akers (December 18, 1939).

84 *Jack McJunkins started wearing a top hat and tails*: Inez Cline and Fred Palmer, "Belvedere," *The Record* (Garland County Historical Society, 1992).

84 *McLaughlin arranged for Owney to buy a 25 percent stake*: FBI, memorandum on Owney Madden by Claburn White, File Number 92-2699 (September 23, 1960), 19.

84 *Owney also purchased the Kentucky Club*: Ibid., 14.

85 *The police turned the Kentucky Club over one night*: Ibid., 31.

85 *Hoover ordered his agents to act*: Nown, *Arkansas Godfather*, 302.

85 *A couple of FBI agents dropped in on city hall*: Ibid., 307.

86 *nearly a quarter of a million dollars*: Ibid.

86 *Friend Owen—The preachers had a meeting*: Ibid., 308.

HAZEL, JULY 1944

87 *The plains of Texas in July are hot*: Details about Hollis Hill's time with the threshing crew, including dialogue, are taken from an interview with Ressie Parker (July 2015). Other details about life on a threshing crew are taken from interviews with various wheat harvesters conducted by Claudia Reinhardt for *Living History Farm*, https://livinghistoryfarm.org /farminginthe20s/life_09.htm.

DANE, 1946

92 *One night in 1946, a tourist who had had a bit too much to drink*: Collie Small, "The Town Without a Lid," *Saturday Evening Post* (July 20, 1946).

92 *filled with twelve hundred patients*: Ibid.

93 *He told them slot machines were illegal*: Ibid.

93 *There had never been more gambling in Hot Springs*: Orval Allbritton, *Leo and Verne* (Garland County Historical Society, 2003).

93 *He was rejected, however, because he was color-blind*: Interview with Marcia Heien (July 2015).

93 *Dane was assigned to Arkadelphia, Arkansas, to work as a flight instructor*: "Dane Harris Dies at 62; Rose to Prominence in Hot Springs Heydays," *Arkansas Gazette* (June 11, 1981).

93 *Marcella would come visit Dane at the air force base*: Interview with Marcia Heien (July 2015).

94 *thirty-three dry counties*: "33 Dry Counties May Lose Funds," *Courier News* (Blytheville) (October 25, 1946).

94 *one of Dane's old college fraternity brothers back in Hot Springs had enlisted him*: Roy Reed, *Faubus: The Life and Times of an American Prodigal* (University of Arkansas Press, 1997), 318; "Dane Harris Dies at 62."

95 *One blustery February evening in 1946*: Allbritton, *Leo and Verne*, 482.

95 *"Go home. Discuss with your wives and family what's at stake. Be thinking about if you are willing to put your name on the ticket and run for office"*: Ibid., 484.

96 *He served stateside as a counselor*: Patty Hawthorne Ramsey, "A Place at the Table: Hot Springs and the GI Revolt," *Arkansas Historical Quarterly* 59 (Winter 2000), 414.

96 *Hurst wasn't completely on the outside looking in*: Interview with Q. Byrum Hurst Jr. (December 2016).

96 *Dane wasn't interested in politics*: Interview with Marcia Heien (July 2015).

97 *On the morning of July 4, 1946*: Allbritton, *Leo and Verne*, 489.

98 *About eight hundred people*: Ibid., 494.

98 *"I will protect you against the violation of your civil rights"*: Ramsey, "A Place at the Table," 415.

98 *As Sid McMath held forth, outside the theater*: Shirley Abbott, *The Book-maker's Daughter: A Memory Unbound* (University of Arkansas Press, 1991), 209.

98 *In the weeks leading up to the primary*: Allbritton, *Leo and Verne*, 497.

99 *The GIs prepared for Election Day by rounding up shotguns and ammunition*: Ramsey, "A Place at the Table," 418.

99 *They drove around town on primary day*: Allbritton, *Leo and Verne*, 507.

99 *Jack McJunkins was armed with two thousand poll tax receipts*: Sid McMath interview with Roy Reed, *Arkansas Gazette* Project (March 28, 2001).

99 *The night before the primary*: Sid McMath, *Promises Kept* (University of Arkansas Press, 2003), 172.

99 *3,900 votes to 3,375*: Ramsey, "A Place at the Table," 419.

100 *McMath smiled and shook everyone's hands*: McMath, *Promises Kept*, 172–73.

100 *Birdie Fulton and Otis Livingstone were former football players*: This account of the holdup of Fulton and Livingstone is from Allbritton, *Leo and Verne*, 497.

101 *a local bookie and a member of a nationwide ring of professional con artists*: David W. Maurer, *The Big Con: The Story of the Confidence Men* (Anchor Books, 1999), 23.

101 *"Well, we have some people on our side"*: McMath, *Promises Kept*, 175.

101 *"If anything happens again"*: Joe Alex Morris, "He Wants to Make Something of Arkansas," *Saturday Evening Post* (February 18, 1950).

101 *The judge ruled in favor of the GIs*: "1,600 Garland Poll Taxes Are Ruled Invalid," *Hope Star* (July 11, 1946).

102 *He wasted no time in reaching out*: Graham Nown, *Arkansas Godfather* (Butler Center, 2013), 314.

102 *The 1946 general election was held on a cold, rainy November day*: Allbritton, *Leo and Verne*, 515.

102 *Sixteen thousand people voted. It was a record turnout, more than double*: Ramsey, "A Place at the Table," 420.

102 *Twenty members of the state police*: Allbritton, *Leo and Verne*, 515.

OWNEY, DECEMBER 1946

103 *About two dozen gangsters were called to the meeting*: Details from the 1946 Havana Conference are taken from Gus Russo, *The Outfit: The Role of Chicago's Underworld in Shaping Modern America* (Bloomsbury, 2001);

and T. J. English, *Havana Nocturne: How the Mob Owned Cuba and Then Lost It to the Revolution* (William Morrow, 2008).

103 *In 1941, California Attorney General Earl Warren ordered raids on a number of gambling boats*: Sally Denton and Roger Morris, *The Money and the Power: The Making of Las Vegas and Its Hold on America* (Knopf, 2001), 98.

104 *They opened a number of small casinos*: Ibid.

104 *the Nevada legislature legalized bookmaking by wire*: "Horse Betting Bill Is Now Law Despite Veto by the Governor," *Reno Gazette-Journal* (March 15, 1941).

104 *"There's so much dough to be made in everything else we have"*: Martin Gosch and Richard Hammer, *The Last Testament of Lucky Luciano* (Dell, 1975), 314–15.

104 *Lansky had already invested hundreds of thousands of dollars*: English, *Havana Nocturne*, 16–19.

105 *Lansky had dispatched his partner*: Denton and Morris, *The Money and the Power*, 50–51.

105 *Bookies paid big money, sometimes as much as four or five thousand a week*: U.S. Senate Special Committee to Investigate Organized Crime in Interstate Commerce, *Third Interim Report* (May 1, 1951), 150–60.

106 *gunned down on a Chicago street*: Denton and Morris, *The Money and the Power*, 32.

106 *mercury bichloride tablets in his mouth*: Ibid.

106 *That wire room was controlled by Carlos Marcello*: U.S. Senate Special Committee to Investigate Organized Crime in Interstate Commerce, *Third Interim Report*, 77–80.

106 *For more than thirty years the wire service in New Orleans had been run on the square*: Ibid.

107 *Papa Joe came to Hot Springs*: Details of Joe Poretto's visits to Hot Springs are from various FBI reports on Owney Madden from 1941 to 1961.

107 *fly McMath around the state*: "Dane Harris Dies at 62; Rose to Prominence in Hot Springs Heydays," *Arkansas Gazette* (June 11, 1981).

HAZEL, APRIL 1947

108 *Hazel and the boys huddled together*: The details of the Hill family in Mountain Pine, including dialogue, are based on an interview with Larry Hill (July 2015) except where otherwise noted.

109 *second-largest city in the county*: Wendy Richter, "Mountain Pine," Encyclopedia of Arkansas (January 2017).

109 *shotgun houses for just three dollars a month*: Kenneth Smith, *Sawmill: The Story of Cutting the Last Great Virgin Forest East of the Rockies* (University of Arkansas Press, 1986), 79.

110 *the first black residents the town had ever seen*: Interview with Ressie Parker (June 2015).

110 *Some of the black workers were recruited specifically to play*: Smith, *Sawmill*, 190.

DANE, NOVEMBER 1949

112 *in 1947 that Dane would meet Frank Niemeyer*: Interview with Marcia Heien (December 2017).

114 *In 1949 the Arkansas legislature passed a law*: Tom Hockersmith, "Million Dollar Legal Bootlegging Industry Poised for Quick Action," *Arkansas Democrat* (April 22, 1949).

114 *up to a million cases of whiskey*: Ibid.

114 *The state chose to license three firms*: Ibid.

114 *Wallace Beery would fly his own airplane to Hot Springs to visit Owney*: Graham Nown, *Arkansas Godfather* (Butler Center, 2013), 300–01.

115 *"What's wrong?"*: Details about Dane's golf game with mobsters and dialogue between Dane and Marcella are based on an interview with Marcia Heien (July 2015).

116 *After a meeting of 250 people at the Willow Room*: Orval Allbritton, *Leo and Verne* (Garland County Historical Society, 2003), 551.

116 *"a number of high class clubs operating under strict supervision"*: Ibid.

116 *a leasing fee to the clubs they operated out of*: Interview with Walter "Skip" Ebel Jr. (December 2016).

HAZEL, DECEMBER 1949

117 *"That boy's gone back on his raisin'"*: Interview with Ressie Parker (July 2015).

117 *"You see, back in Matthew, the sixteenth chapter"*: Quotations from Millard Shields are taken from undated audio recordings of his sermons in the author's possession.

118 *squeezed in between a furniture store and a cafeteria*: 1949 Hot Springs City Directory.

118 *at the end of the service there was a full spread*: Interview with Larry Hill (July 2015).

119 *A couple of months earlier*: This story, including dialogue, is taken from an interview with Larry Hill (July 2015).

Part III: Holy Ghost

DANE, 1950

123 *they had been partners in all things, including business*: Interview with Marcia Heien (July 2015).

124 *Marcella often felt at odds with Dane's mother*: Ibid.

124 *They were now leasing space in the Ohio Club and the White Front Cigar Store*: Interview with Walter "Skip" Ebel Jr. (December 2016).

124 *Owney organized a trip to Cuba*: Interview with Q. Byrum Hurst Jr. (December 2016).

125 *The locals would lease space*: T. J. English, *Havana Nocturne: How the Mob Owned Cuba and Then Lost It to the Revolution* (William Morrow, 2008), 96–97.

125 *Lansky brought in dealers from the United States*: Ibid., 98.

126 *There were bingo games and cash drawings, as well as a cheap buffet*: Sally Denton and Roger Morris, *The Money and the Power: The Making of Las Vegas and Its Hold on America* (Knopf, 2001), 56–57.

126 *sawdust on the floors in case somebody missed*: Doug Swanson, *Blood Aces: The Wild Ride of Benny Binion, the Texas Gangster Who Created Vegas Poker* (Penguin, 2015), 167.

127 *While Lansky hedged his bets*: Denton and Morris, *The Money and the Power*, 102.

127 *There wasn't enough housing for everyone*: Eugene Moehring and Michael Green, *Las Vegas: A Centennial History* (University of Nevada Press, March 2005).

OWNEY, MARCH 1951

128 *At Curley Humphreys's suggestion*: Gus Russo, *The Outfit: The Role of Chicago's Underworld in Shaping Modern America* (Bloomsbury, 2001), 61.

128 *In New Orleans, Carlos Marcello pleaded the Fifth 152 times*: U.S. Senate Special Committee to Investigate Organized Crime in Interstate Commerce, *Third Interim Report* (May 1, 1951).

129 *"I was just a goodwill man for them. And I would recommend different acts for the club"*: Peter Carlson, "Encounter: Frank Costello vs. Estes Kefauver," *American History* (November 14, 2016).

130 *Several weeks before Costello's appearance*: Graham Nown, *Arkansas Godfather* (Butler Center, 2013), 321.

130 *It also didn't help that in April 1950, a cabdriver in Kansas City*: "Political Boss and Ex-Convict Slain," Associated Press (April 6, 1950).

130 *The gambling combination would surely wonder*: Orval Allbritton, *Leo and Verne* (Garland County Historical Society, 2003), 585.

131 *his name was brought up time and again*: "Investigation of Organized Crime in Interstate Commerce: Hearings Before a Special Committee to Investigate Organized Crime in Interstate Commerce," United States Senate, Eighty-first Congress, Second Session (U.S. Government Printing Office, 1950).

131 *Owney went from one club in Hot Springs to the next*: Ben Montgomery, "Spoiled by Mobsters, Meyer Lansky's Daughter Recalls Family Men, Not Killers," *Tampa Bay Times* (June 13, 2014).

131 *"What's so bad about gambling? You like it yourself. I know you've gambled a lot"*: Russo, *The Outfit*, 271–72.

131 *Prior to his meeting with Lansky, Kefauver had called Hot Springs, Arkansas*: Nown, *Arkansas Godfather*, 321.

131 *"we don't have time to go to Hot Springs"*: Orval Allbritton, *The Mob at the Spa* (Garland County Historical Society, 2011), 143.

132 *"Gambling is your problem over there . . . until it becomes a statewide problem"*: Allbritton, *Leo and Verne*, 582.

132 *Owney and his partners summoned Frank Costello*: Allbritton, *The Mob at the Spa*, 145–47.

132 *"Costello as Spa Gambling Czar Rumored"*: Ibid.

133 *"I can't believe that Costello has any such plans"*: Ibid.

133 *"I never had the remotest idea of engaging in or being connected with the gambling business in Hot Springs"*: Ibid.

133 *worth about thirty thousand dollars*: FBI, memorandum on Owney Madden by Claburn White, File Number 92-2699 (September 23, 1960), 6.

133 *wooden Chris-Craft ski boat the actor George Raft bought him*: Nown, *Arkansas Godfather*, 260.

133 *"Hey, what say we all eat out tonight?"*: Ibid., 285.

HAZEL, MAY 1951

134 *Comes the plaintiff Hazel Hill*: Hazel Hill v. Hollis Hill, Complaint in Equity, Garland Chancery Court (May 22, 1951).

135 *"We're going to live with Grandpa and Grandma"*: The account of the Hill family in Ashland, Ohio, including dialogue, is based on an interview with Larry Hill (July 2015).

135 *Ashland, Ohio, had around fourteen thousand residents in 1951*: Decennial census of population, Ohio Development Services Agency, https://development.ohio.gov/files/research/plchist.pdf.

OWNEY, MAY 24, 1955

141 *Five years earlier, he had thrown his weight behind Floyd "Babe" Huff*: FBI, memorandum on Owney Madden by Claburn White, File Number 92-2699 (September 23, 1960), 36.

141 *Owney went around and collected fifteen thousand dollars*: Ibid.

142 *According to reports in a local gossip rag called* The Hot Springs Rubdown, *Babe paid the Reverend A. R. Puckett*: "Accuse Arkansas Minister of Selling Votes," *Jet* (October 15, 1953), 20.

142 *nearly a third of the population*: "Most Businesses, Professions Found Among City's 8,000 Negro Citizens," *Sentinel Record* (Hot Springs) (February 18, 1962).

142 *The Negro Civic League, for example, would pay the poll tax*: Janis Kearney, ed., *Conversations: William Jefferson Clinton from Hope to Harlem* (Writing Our World Press, 2006), 92.

142 *Huff filed libel charges against the paper's publishers*: "Judge Brown Hearing Spa Libel Case," *Hope Star* (September 22, 1953).

142 *In 1913, when Babe was ten years old*: Details of the lynching of Will Norman are taken from "Negro Assailant of Girl Lynched," *Arkansas Gazette* (June 20, 1913); and interview with Fred Palmer (January 2017).

143 *Lynchings were relatively uncommon*: David Greaves, "The Lynching List," http://www.ourtimepress.com/view-from-here-never-forget-the-lynchings-list/.

143 *More than twenty people arrested in those raids were hauled into Darnell's municipal court*: "Gambling Charges Are Dismissed," Associated Press (March 6, 1952).

143 *pay 20 percent of their profits to Huff*: FBI, memorandum on activities of top hoodlums by Thomas Emery, File Number NY 92-632 (December 12, 1958).

144 *A week later they shut down the wire*: FBI, memorandum on Owney Madden by Claburn White, File Number 92-2699 (September 23, 1960), 30.

144 *"It is not right to pick on my friends and let Huff's operate"*: "Telephones of Bookies Ousted," Associated Press (November 9, 1954).

144 *The bookies and club owners were feeling the pinch*: FBI, memorandum on Owney Madden by Claburn White, File Number 92-2699 (September 23, 1960), 34.

144 *Babe Huff recruited Dick Galatas*: Ibid., 20.

144 *When Galatas's sentence ended, he moved to California with his wife and found work as a salesman*: 1940 U.S. Census.

144 *Over the next two weeks, police raided*: "State Police Arrest 25 in New Orleans Raids," *Times* (Shreveport) (May 25, 1955).

145 *offered him $140,000*: Graham Nown, *Arkansas Godfather* (Butler Center, 2013), 323.

145 *Faubus and Hastings were close. They took vacations and hunting trips together*: Bob Douglas interview with Roy Reed, *Arkansas Gazette* Project (February 14, 1997).

145 *more pious citizens of the state expressing concern*: Roy Reed, *Faubus: The Life and Times of an American Prodigal* (University of Arkansas Press, 1997), 292.

145 *Hastings was silent partners with Dane Harris*: Bob Douglas interview with Roy Reed, *Arkansas Gazette* Project (February 14, 1997).

145 *it was Dane who arranged the visit through Hastings*: Confidential interview (July 2015).

146 *He had his fingers in more than just gambling*: FBI, memorandum on Hubert Dane Harris, File Number LR 92-122 (September 26, 1958).

146 *He even joined the chamber of commerce*: Robert Boyle, "The Hottest Spring in Hot Springs," *Sports Illustrated* (March 19, 1962).

HAZEL, APRIL 1955

147 *Josie was tired of Hollis*: The account of Hollis Hill's death and the aftermath, including dialogue, is based on interviews with Ressie Parker and Larry Hill (June 2015) as well as from recollections from my father and grandmother when they were alive.

151 "People get sick and die like they did when Lazarus died": Quotations from Millard Shields are taken from undated audio recordings of his sermons in the author's possession.

DANE, JUNE 1956

156 *Early one June morning in 1956*: "Elmer Tackett Ends Own Life with Gunshot," *Hot Springs New Era* (June 7, 1956).

157 *Rumors were flying that Tackett was murdered by gamblers*: Interview with Eutha Corder (June 2017).

157 *Owney and Q. Byrum Hurst organized behind the scenes*: FBI, memorandum on Owney Madden by Claburn White, File Number 92-2699 (September 23, 1960), 33.

157 *Hebert won the election, and within weeks he closed down every casino*: "Truce Reached, Report Gambling Will Be Resumed at Hot Springs," Associated Press (January 7, 1958).

157 *"Huff is out-and-out crooked, but he isn't going to control me"*: Graham Nown, *Arkansas Godfather* (Butler Center, 2013), 323.

158 *He had also been a front for Frank Costello's operation*: Orval Allbritton, *The Mob at the Spa* (Garland County Historical Society, 2011), 130–32.

158 *McJunkins was also partners with Owney*: FBI, memorandum on Owney Madden by Claburn White, File Number 92-2699 (September 23, 1960), 48.

159   *It had been modeled on a home in California*: Descriptions of the Harris home on Trivista are from an interview with Marcia Heien (December 2017).

159   *Tensions between the two women had grown*: Ibid.

161   *"Do you know what causes lightning?"*: Ibid.

OWNEY, MAY 1957

162   *Frank Costello headed home to his Central Park West penthouse*: Ed Reid and Ovid Demaris, *The Green Felt Jungle* (Trident, 1963), 69–70.

162   *Gross casino wins as of 4/27/57 $651,284*: Ibid.

163   *$150,000 a year in the late 1950s*: Personal files of Dane Harris, in the author's possession.

164   *Some gangsters speculated openly*: Hank Messick, *Lansky* (Putnam, 1971), 215.

164   *endorser of donation checks from Owney and Agnes Madden*: Graham Nown, *Arkansas Godfather* (Butler Center, 2013), 11.

164   *decided to deny the New Orleans gangster*: "Nevada Can't Tie Tropicana to Costello," Associated Press (June 29, 1957).

165   *struggling to turn a profit in 1957*: W. L. Russell, "Las Vegas Casinos Hit Record Stride After 'Recession,'" *Pittsburgh Press* (January 15, 1957).

165   *"Las Vegas—Is the Boom Overextended?"*: *Life* (June 20, 1955).

165   *Of the seven resorts that had opened in Las Vegas since 1955*: David Schwartz, "The Long, Hot Summer of '55," *Vegas Seven Magazine* (August 6–12, 2015), 23.

165   *"Many, many persons out over the state feel that Hot Springs and Garland County should have the fate of legalized gambling in their own hands"*: "Joint Committee Rejects Amendment on Gambling," *Sentinel Record* (Hot Springs) (March 12, 1957).

165   *Let's take a look at Reno, Nev.*: L. K. McClure, Letter to the Editor, *Arkansas Gazette* (March 17, 1957).

DANE, JANUARY 1958

167   *They hired a staff of 110 people. They had lobster flown in*: John Hynes, "Open Gambling in Hot Springs Draws Record Crowds to City," *St. Louis Post-Dispatch* (March 29, 1959).

168   *While one crowd watched the first show, the crowd waiting for the next one gambled*: Interview with Wanda Thompson (July 2015).

168   *he had devised a plan to move new machines from Chicago into Arkansas*: FBI, memorandum on Hubert Dane Harris, File Number LR 92-122 (September 20, 1961), 22.

169 *Dane and Owney started holding meetings in the back room of the Crawford Pharmacy*: Maxine Temple Jones, *Maxine: Call Me Madam* (Lily of the Valley, 2011), 109.

169 *The top madam in Hot Springs*: Ibid.

170 *It got so bad that the cheerleaders at the high school*: Interview with Eutha Corder (June 2017).

170 *"Persons who bring bottles are excluded"*: John Hynes, "Faubus Would End Gaming Only if Hoodlums Ran It," *St. Louis Post-Dispatch* (March 30, 1959).

171 *"We don't want undesirables in the operation of gambling establishments"*: Ibid.

171 *They'd raise fifty to seventy-five grand*: Roy Reed, *Faubus: The Life and Times of an American Prodigal* (University of Arkansas Press, 1997), 319.

171 *Faubus would eventually use that money*: Ibid.

171 *his allies would need to come up with at a quarter of a million dollars*: FBI, memorandum on Owney Madden by Claburn White, File Number 92-2699 (September 23, 1960), 46.

172 *"You know, in my day, back in New York, how I'd have handled this"*: Interview with Walter "Skip" Ebel Jr. (December 2016).

172 *The Southern, for example, employed nine "heavy men"*: Hynes, "Open Gambling in Hot Springs Draws Record Crowds to City."

HAZEL, MAY 1958

Details in this section about Hazel's relationship with Jack Cartwright, including dialogue, are based on an interviews with Larry Hill and Ressie Parker (July 2015). "Jack Cartwright" is a pseudonym. All accounts of Jack come from interviews with members of my family. I was unable to locate and speak with any surviving members of Jack's family while researching this book. Because I have no other accounts of Jack and his life other than from my own family, I have chosen to use a pseudonym for him in this book.

175 *They gave a percentage of the Pines to Chicago mobsters Les Kruse and John Drew*: "Gaming Activity Denied by Drew," *Reno Gazette-Journal* (April 2, 1954).

176 *McDonald hired men like Jimmie Green, who was said to be the best palm man in the whole country*: FBI, memorandum on James Henry Dolan by Robert Barrett, File Number 92-292 (November 16, 1962), 16–17.

176 *He also put on Hal Stanger, a carny who ran the razzle-dazzle scam*: Ibid.

176 *He was a grifter who traveled the country*: James Dolan, "My Father's Connection with the Assassination of JFK" (2000), http://lotuseaters.org/jfkdad.shtml.

176 *When Dolan was released*: David Kaiser, *The Road to Dallas* (Harvard University Press, 2009), 333–36.

177 *For his part, Dane wasn't too fond of the Pines, either*: Interview with Tony Frazier (August, 2016).

177 *Dane was now leasing space from the owners*: FBI, memorandum on Hubert Dane Harris, File Number LR 92-122 (September 20, 1961), 9.

177 *Owney bought a small piece of the action*: FBI, memorandum on Owney Madden by Claburn White, File Number 92-2699 (September 23, 1960), 28–29.

DANE, JUNE 1958

179 *Danny Boy's Combo was tearing it up late one Saturday night in June*: Jack Palms, "Hot Springs Steam," *The Citizen* (Hot Springs) (June 1958), 6.

180 *He would eventually set up a separate company, Acme Amusement*: Interview with Tony Frazier (August 2016).

180 *Dane would see to it that three of the black clubs in the Second Ward*: FBI, memorandum on Hubert Dane Harris, File Number LR 92-122 (December 18, 1963).

181 *Fistfights between segregationists and more liberal Faubus supporters*: Roy Reed, *Faubus: The Life and Times of an American Prodigal* (University of Arkansas Press, 1997), 178–81.

181 *"traitors to their own race"*: "Candidates All Touch on Segregation," Associated Press (July 5, 1956).

182 *"A shame is being brought on us because of all this"*: Paul Hendrickson, "Orval Faubus and the Shadow of History," *Washington Post* (January 25, 1993).

182 *nearly eight thousand black residents*: "Most Businesses, Professions Found Among City's 8,000 Negro Citizens," *Sentinel Record* (Hot Springs) (February 18, 1962).

182 *Some white business owners, for example, would allow the more prominent and wealthy black residents*: Tim Spofford, "African Americans Remember the Segregated Way of Life in Hot Springs," *The Record* (Garland County Historical Society, 2010), 197.

183 *over seventeen hundred mostly white fans*: "Hot Springs in Hot Water," Associated Press (May 21, 1953).

183 *one of only six Arkansas school districts*: "The 1957 Crisis, as Governor Faubus Saw It," *Arkansas Democrat-Gazette* (September 26, 1997).

183 *The only Race issue at present seems to be in the Gubernatorial Campaign*: "Editorial Comments," *The Citizen* (Hot Springs) (June 1958), 2.

184 *"treason"*: "Expect Arkansas Governor to Win Primary Race Today," United Press International (July 29, 1958).

184 *"bullet and bayonet"*: "Judge Ward to Be in Runoff Says Loyal Supporters," *The Big Picture* (Paragould) (July 17, 1958).

184 *He despised segregation—so much so, he often said*: "African Americans and the Hot Springs Baths," National Park Service, U.S. Department of the Interior.

184 *They had already raised thirty thousand dollars*: Edna Lee Howe, "Factional Row Threatens to Again Force Shutdown of Spa Gambling," *Sentinel Record* (Hot Springs) (December 18, 1960).

184 *Dane and his allies offered to put up thirty-three thousand dollars to build a brand-new swimming pool at the Webb Center*: Ibid.

185 *"I am in a position now where I have spent nearly $6,000, including Darnell-Huff election"*: Undated letter from Duane Faull to Dane Harris.

185 *there would be no more payoffs*: FBI, memorandum on Hubert Dane Harris, File Number LR 92-122 (September 20, 1961), 8.

186 *"Dane Harris's gambling casino on the Little Rock Highway"*: Clyde Wilson political advertisement, *Sentinel Record* (Hot Springs) (July 28, 1958).

186 *"Shopping Center Ellis"*: Will Lowe political mailer, in the author's possession (1958).

186 *"notorious character from Chicago"*: Ibid.

186 *"In fact," Ellis said from the stage, "he's being sued for not paying for two head of beef"*: Details and dialogue from the competing political rallies are taken from "Second Ward Residents Attend Rallies, Absentee Balloting High," *Sentinel Record* (Hot Springs) (July 29, 1958).

187 *He even represented the notorious madam Maxine Gregory*: Maxine Temple Jones, *Maxine: Call Me Madam* (Lily of the Valley, 2011), 31.

187 *He was a fixture at the Southern Club, a gambler and boozehound*: Ibid.

188 *"Marion says he's sick Dick (Kansas City Massacre) Galatas is gone"*: Plummer Dobbs political advertisement, *Sentinel Record* (Hot Springs) (1958).

188 *Faull hired staff to stuff and mail thousands of envelopes*: Undated letter from Duane Faull to Dane Harris, in the author's possession.

188 *Ellis beat Wilson 6,172 to 5,933*: "Complete, Unofficial Returns from Garland County Democratic Preferential Primary Election," *Sentinel Record* (Hot Springs) (July 30, 1958).

188 *They claimed that Glenn Buchanan*: Wilson v. Ellis, Supreme Court of Arkansas, 230 Ark. 775 (June 1, 1959).

188 *While the Second Ward voted for Ellis and Dobbs by a margin of two to one*: "Complete, Unofficial Returns from Garland County Democratic Preferential Primary Election," *Sentinel Record* (Hot Springs) (July 30, 1958).

188 *Owney and Dane met with the judge and contributed five thousand dollars*: FBI, memorandum on Owney Madden by Claburn White, File Number 92-2699 (September 23, 1960), 42–43.

189 *Leonard Ellis called up Gregory*: Jones, *Maxine*, 39.

189 *His entire trip was paid for by Owney*: FBI, memorandum on Owney Madden by Claburn White, File Number 92-2699 (September 23, 1960), 41.

189 *One of Plummer Dobbs's first acts as the new circuit judge*: "Hot Springs Gaming Bill Is Expected," *Courier News* (Blytheville) (January 17, 1959).

189 *"a risk of the trade"*: Ibid.

HAZEL, JANUARY 1959

190 *Jack and Hazel were dressed to the nines, strolling arm in arm down Broadway*: The account of Jack and Hazel at the auctions is based on a confidential interview with one of Hazel and Jack's contemporaries.

191 *Owney had helped Harry "Dutch" Goldberg*: FBI, memorandum on Owney Madden by Claburn White, File Number 92-2699 (September 23, 1960), 24–25.

191 *The less reputable auction houses worked with some of the less reputable jewelers to appraise phony diamonds as real*: Interview with Wanda Thompson (July 2015).

191 *Years before, in the late 1940s, the Esskay was robbed*: "Man Taken in Raid Here Held for $65,000 Theft," *Boston Globe* (October 25, 1946).

191 *"The thieves are friends of mine"*: Sid McMath interview with Roy Reed, *Arkansas Gazette* Project (March 28, 2001).

191 *The prosecutors even put the Esskay's owner, Samuel Kirsch, on the stand*: "Grand Jurors' Charges Dropped by Circuit Judge," *Courier News* (Blytheville) (May 5, 1948).

191 *"Catskills of the South"*: Details about Jewish life in Hot Springs are taken from the Institute for Southern Jewish Life's Encyclopedia of Southern Jewish Communities, https://www.isjl.org/arkansas-hot-springs -encyclopedia.html.

191 *By 1959, Samuel Kirsch had become one of the most important people in town*: "Aristocrat Manor," National Register of Historic Places Registration Form, U.S. Department of the Interior (November 2016), 12–14.

193 *"Jack doesn't want you around"*: Accounts of Jack and Hazel's life together, including dialogue, are based on interviews with Larry Hill (June 2015).

193 *Jack suggested she try some "medicine"*: Accounts of Jack and Hazel's drug use are based on a confidential interview with a contemporary of Jack and Hazel (August 2016).

194 *before finally wrapping it around a utility pole in front of a hotel*: Interview with Ressie Parker (June 2015).

194 *When Hazel was finally brought before the judge, she begged for mercy*: Details of Hazel's hearing, including dialogue, are based on interviews with Larry Hill and Ressie Parker (June 2015).

OWNEY, JANUARY 1959

196 *A pickup truck pulled up alongside the Ritter Hotel*: Graham Nown, *Arkansas Godfather* (Butler Center, 2013), 332–33.

196 *State Senator Q. Byrum Hurst had put Owney together with Jerry Poe*: FBI, memorandum on Owney Madden by Claburn White, File Number 92-2699 (May 9, 1960), 2.

197 *Poe wanted one hundred dollars per line per month*: Ibid.

197 *Owney fronted Hurst the money*: Ibid., 3.

197 *Then Owney put the phone lines in the name of Walter Metzer*: FBI, memorandum on Owney Madden by Claburn White, File Number 92-2699 (September 23, 1960), 42.

197 *cost a handbook only $150 a week*: Ibid.

198 *Owney flew to Chicago and asked Curley Humphreys*: Testimony of Robert F. Kennedy, Attorney General of the United States, before the House Committee on the Judiciary in Support of Legislation to Curb Organized Crime and Racketeering (May 17, 1961), 10–11; FBI, memorandum on Owney Madden by Claburn White, File Number 92-2699 (September 23, 1960), 50.

198 *"Where do you live in Hot Springs, Mr. Madden?"*: Nown, *Arkansas Godfather*, 284.

DANE, JULY 1959

200 *"There were times I thought I would die in that desert"*: Sally Denton and Roger Morris, *The Money and the Power: The Making of Las Vegas and Its Hold on America* (Knopf, 2001), 27–28.

200 *fewer than half the cars on the road had air-conditioning*: "The Evolution of Automotive Air Conditioning," *HVAC&R Nation* (June 2008), 22.

200 *But in July 1959, Nevada was in the middle of a heat wave*: "Slight Break Is Expected in Heat Wave," *Reno Gazette-Journal* (July 13, 1959).

200 *Dane had been invited to Las Vegas*: Details and dialogue from the Harris family trip to Las Vegas are based on an interview with Marcia Heien (June 2015) except where otherwise noted.

201 *the Last Frontier, which was the second hotel built on the Strip, back in 1942*: Details about the Frontier in this section are taken from Deanna DeMatteo, Las Vegas Strip Historical Site, http://www.lvstriphistory.com/ie/frontier.htm.

202 *"the mob's amateur operation"*: Denton and Morris, *The Money and the Power*, 132.

203 *"Mr. Raft, the Revolution is here. Fidel Castro has taken over everything"*: T. J. English, *Havana Nocturne: How the Mob Owned Cuba and Then Lost It to the Revolution* (William Morrow, 2008), 302–304.

203 *In 1959, the large and much-needed Sunrise Hospital was funded with a million dollars*: Ed Reid and Ovid Demaris, *The Green Felt Jungle* (Trident, 1963), 85–87.

203 *at the suggestion of Chicago mobsters Curley Humphreys and Ralph Pierce*: Drew Pearce, "An Obscure Senator Sits at the Side of Hoffa," *Poughkeepsie Journal* (August 26, 1957).

204 *Drew had once owned a stake in the Pines*: "Gaming Activity Denied by Drew," *Reno Gazette-Journal* (April 2, 1954).

204 *He was rumored to use a blowtorch*: Ed Koch and Mary Manning, "Mob Ties," *Las Vegas Sun* (May 15, 2008).

204 *He cut Greenbaum's head off*: Reid and Demaris, *The Green Felt Jungle*, 47–48.

OWNEY, NOVEMBER 1959

206 *Jimmy Hill was thirteen years old when he laced up his gloves*: The story about Jimmy Hill in the boxing tournament, including dialogue, is based on an interview with Benny Bridwell (January 2017).

206 *the overnight shift workers would pay him to fight bigger kids*: Interview with Larry Hill (June 2015).

206 *snuck off to New York to see Buddy Baer fight Nathan Mann*: Graham Nown, *Arkansas Godfather* (Butler Center, 2013), 303.

206 *watch the Sugar Ray Robinson–Carmen Basilio fight in a movie theater in Little Rock*: FBI, memorandum on Owney Madden by Claburn White, File Number 92-2699 (September 23, 1960), 39.

207 *regularly fronted the money to keep the Boys Club up to snuff*: Orval Allbritton, *The Mob at the Spa* (Garland County Historical Society, 2011), 229.

209 *He had left a girl in New Mexico with child*: Interview with Martha Ann Henry (January 2017).

209 *Jimmy had a friend in school named Judy*: Interview with Judy Horner (January 2017).

210 *"Does anybody need a lift?"*: Interview with Q. Byrum Hurst Jr. (December 2016).

210 *Owney had said before that he didn't see himself as a role model*: "Passed in Review," *Brooklyn Daily Eagle* (February 12, 1932).

210 *"The only way I can help boys is financially"*: Leonard Lyons, "Broadway Medley," Post-Hall Syndicate (February 10, 1954).

210 *"Who told you that?"*: Interview with Q. Byrum Hurst Jr. (December 2016).

DANE, DECEMBER 1959

213 *Over a hundred million dollars had been bet in Hot Springs*: John Hynes, "Open Gambling in Hot Springs Draws Record Crowds to City," *St. Louis Post-Dispatch* (March 29, 1959).

213 *The crowds in Hot Springs during the race meet nearly doubled*: "New Records Set at Oaklawn Track," *Camden News* (March 23, 1959).

213 *The city's "amusement tax" on casinos, bookies, and card clubs raised hundreds of thousands of dollars*: Orval Allbritton, *Leo and Verne* (Garland County Historical Society, 2003), 581–582.

213 *up by more than eight million dollars*: "Bank Deposits, Hot Springs Clearing House Association, 1950–1960," Walter Hebert political advertisement, *Sentinel Record* (Hot Springs) (July 10, 1960).

214 *A grand jury investigation*: "Spa Board Retires Police Chief," *Arkansas Democrat* (February 17, 1960).

214 *And a wave of burglaries and safecrackings*: "Officers Believe Home 'Talent' Responsible for Safecrackings," *Sentinel Record* (Hot Springs) (June 19, 1960).

214 *"I think the people of Hot Springs know that I have no interest in interfering in their affairs"*: John Hynes, "Hot Springs Tax on Gambling, Liquor Quickly Raises $80,000," *St. Louis Post-Dispatch* (March 31, 1959).

214 *"I have made it known through public announcements that we don't want gangsters and racketeers in Arkansas"*: John Hynes, "Faubus Would End Gaming Only If Hoodlums Ran It," *St. Louis Post-Dispatch* (March 30, 1959).

215 *The gambling business was worth billions of dollars in America*: Fred Cook, "Gambling Inc., Treasure Chest of the Underworld," *The Nation* (October 22, 1960).

216 *Casino bosses were already moving their personnel and whatever money*: Scott Deitche, "The Rise of Castro and the Fall of the Havana Mob," The Mob Museum, https://themobmuseum.org/blog/rise-castro-fall-havana-mob/.

216 *Meyer Lansky had escaped, but he left seventeen million dollars in cash behind*: T. J. English, *Havana Nocturne: How the Mob Owned Cuba and Then Lost It to the Revolution* (William Morrow, 2008), 320.

216 *But Castro's economic advisers suggested he reopen them*: Ibid., 310.

216 *He returned to Hot Springs and reported that Havana would soon be back to normal*: "Coinmen You Know: Hot Springs," *Billboard* (March 23, 1959).

216 *lost $750,000 at the Riviera alone*: English, *Havana Nocturne*, 310.

216 *By the end of the year, all the major casinos and hotels were in debt*: Ibid.

216 *The survey results were discouraging. Fifty-one percent were opposed to legalizing gambling in Hot Springs*: Eugene Newsom, "Survey of opinions over the state of Arkansas on issues related to the proposal to make Hot Springs gaming legal," *Mid South Opinion Surveys* (December 15, 1958).

217 *"As it stands we have control"*: Hynes, "Faubus Would End Gaming Only If Hoodlums Ran It."

217 *another quarter of a million dollars for the 1960 campaigns*: FBI, memorandum on Owney Madden by Claburn White, File Number 92-2699 (September 23, 1960), 46.

217 *All of this while Dane invested nearly a million dollars*: "Construction Projects Underway in Hot Springs," *Sentinel Record* (Hot Springs) (August 7, 1960).

Part IV: Repentance

HAZEL, FEBRUARY 1960

221 *Whenever Larry and Jimmy would show up at Jack's house*: Details about Jack and Hazel in this chapter, including dialogue, are based on an interview with Larry Hill (June 2015).

221 *But in 1960, there were only about sixty thousand cases of drug addiction nationwide*: "Illegal Drug Addiction in the United States," *Public Health Reports* 85, no. 12 (December 1970).

221 *that number would balloon to over two hundred thousand before the end of the decade*: Ibid.

OWNEY, MARCH 1960

226 *"How long will you be staying with us, Mr. Poretto?"*: FBI, memorandum on Owney Madden by Claburn White, File Number 92-2699 (September 23, 1960), 22.

226 *schemed with Ralph Pierce*: FBI, memorandum on Murray Humphreys by Marshall Rutland, File Number 92-3182 (July 29, 1960), 89–90.

226 *"the little man at the Southern"*: FBI, memorandum on Owney Madden by Claburn White, File Number 92-2699 (September 23, 1960), 29.

226 *Papa Joe had already made Owney sell him his 5 percent of the Pines Supper Club*: FBI, memorandum on Murray Humphreys by Marshall Rutland, File Number 92-3182 (July 29, 1960) 89–90.

226 *Owney took Papa Joe to dinner at Coy's Steakhouse*: FBI, memorandum on Owney Madden by Claburn White, File Number 92-2699 (September 23, 1960), 22.

227 *When Papa Joe returned to his hotel, the new circuit judge, Plummer Dobbs, was waiting for him*: Ibid., 21.

227 *"take everything"*: The conversation between Poretto and Giancana is taken from a transcript of an FBI wiretap. The transcript censored obscenities, and I have taken the liberty of replacing them with my best guesses. FBI, memorandum on Murray Humphreys by Marshall Rutland, File Number 92-3182 (July 29, 1960), 89–90.

227 *"I wish you'd stay in New Orleans"*: FBI, memorandum on Owney Madden by Claburn White, File Number 92-2699 (September 23, 1960), 23.

228 *boarded a flight to Chicago to talk to Curley Humphreys*: Ibid., 49–50.

228 *Owney wanted Papa Joe eliminated*: Ibid., 45–46.

DANE, JULY 1960

230 *"several hundreds of thousands of dollars"*: "Construction Projects Underway in Hot Springs," *Sentinel Record* (Hot Springs) (August 7, 1960).

230 *In truth it had eclipsed a million*: FBI, memorandum on Angelo Bruno, File Number 92-2717-413 (December 1, 1961), 2.

230 *over a million dollars per year*: Edna Lee Howe, "Factional Row Threatens to Again Force Shutdown of Spa Gambling," *Sentinel Record* (Hot Springs) (December 18, 1960).

230 *He also set aside nearly a half million dollars a year*: Ibid.

230 *seventy-five-thousand-dollar advertising budget*: Ibid.

231 *eighty brand-new slot machines, six dice tables, four roulette wheels, and four blackjack tables*: "No More Alligator Shoes," *Newsweek* (April 20, 1964).

231 *Dane installed shag carpeting throughout his clubs*: Inez Cline and Fred Palmer, "Belvedere," *The Record* (Garland County Historical Society, 1992).

231 *He had the mahogany bar from the Belvedere moved*: Ibid.

231 *expensive steaks*: According to a menu from the Vapors, in the author's possession, steaks were eight dollars—roughly equivalent to seventy dollars today.

231 *hydraulic stage retracted and revealed the polished mahogany dance floor*: "Open Gambling at Hot Springs? Sure, Just Walk Right In and Take a Look," *Arkansas Gazette* (June 17, 1962).

231 *"This fine club the Vapors compares"*: John Longinotti, "'Slapsy Maxie' Would Be Good Subject for Film Spectacular," *Sentinel Record* (Hot Springs) (August 7, 1960).

231 *Rooney liked to gamble, too*: Interview with Walter "Skip" Ebel Jr. (December 2016).

232 *"If you let us have this, it will mean a lot to Arkansas"*: "Arkansas Senate Turns Down Bill on Legal Gaming," Associated Press (March 4, 1959).

232 *The bill was voted down 27–4*: Ibid.

232 *had never served in law enforcement before*: "Whittington, Searcy Win Prosecutor, Sheriff Races," *Sentinel Record* (Hot Springs) (August 9, 1960).

233 *"home talent" with "local connections"*: "Officers Believe Home 'Talent' Responsible for Safecrackings," *Sentinel Record* (Hot Springs) (June 19, 1960).

233 *wrote a letter signed by every member of the jury but one*: "A Message to the Citizens of Garland County," *Sentinel Record* (Hot Springs) (July 21, 1960).

233 *His construction company had won the contract*: Sam Anderson political advertisement, *Sentinel Record* (Hot Springs) (July 10, 1960).

233 *He had a dramatic outburst in front of reporters*: "Dobbs, Anderson Clash Over Information on Poll Taxes," *Sentinel Record* (Hot Springs) (July 6, 1960).

234 *One guy who usually has a kroner or so riding on a primary or election*: Paul King, "Hot Springs Unconfidential," *Sentinel Record* (Hot Springs) (July 10, 1960).

234 *His campaign ads depicted a man in a necktie*: Political advertisement, *Sentinel Record* (Hot Springs) (July 23, 1960).

234 *offering twenty dollars*: "What Are the Odds?," political advertisement, *Sentinel Record* (Hot Springs) (August 8, 1960).

234 *"I am not mad at anybody and I hope no one is mad at me"*: "Whittington, Searcy Win Prosecutor, Sheriff Races."

235 *He canceled all of his upcoming acts*: Howe, "Factional Row Threatens to Again Force Shutdown of Spa Gambling."

235 *Dane quickly put together a partnership corporation*: "Harris, Others Buy Belvedere Country Club," *Hot Springs New Era* (January 14, 1960).

235 *who by then numbered over a hundred*: Ibid.

235 *He enlisted the help of the chamber of commerce*: "Truce Apparently Reached in Spa's Gambling Dispute," *Sentinel Record* (Hot Springs) (December 31, 1960).

235 *In order to keep the Vapors, the Southern, and the Belvedere open, Dane had to agree to sell the Tower*: Ibid.

235 *in over eighty locations*: Ibid.

236 *establishment of a joint fund for advertising*: Ibid.

236 *A week before the 1961 horse racing season began, hotels across Hot Springs were sold out for the entire meet*: "Record Year," *Sentinel Record* (Hot Springs) (February 14, 1961).

HAZEL, JANUARY 1961

237 *Jimmy and Larry came by Hazel and Jack's house*: Details about Jack and Hazel in this section, including dialogue, are based on an interview with Larry Hill (June 2015).

239 *Hollis Jr. showed up on Jack and Hazel's doorstep one day*: Details about Hollis Jr. in this section are based on interviews with Martha Ann Henry (January 2017) and Larry Hill (June 2015).

240 *Jimmy had a paper route*: Interview with Judy Horner (January 2017).

240 *"Like Jimbo"*: Interview with Benny Bridwell (January 2017).

241 *"I don't know what to do"*: This story is based on an interview with Judy Horner (January 2017).

DANE, MARCH 1961

242 *Jack Digby drove Polly Barentine up on Cedar Mountain*: "Officer and Husband Shoot It Out," *Hope Star* (January 16, 1961).

243 *He pimped women*: FBI, memorandum on Criminal Intelligence Program (Little Rock Division), File Number 94-221 (April 4, 1961), 3.

243 *He ran the bingo games*: Interview with Tony Frazier (August 2016).

243 *He and three other men put up twenty-five thousand dollars apiece*: Ibid.

243 *regularly packed in over one hundred planes*: John Hynes, "Open Gambling in Hot Springs Draws Record Crowds to City," *St. Louis Post-Dispatch* (March 29, 1959).

243 *The popular singer Frankie Laine even hosted an episode*: "Hot Springs Club Returns Frankie Laine," *Times* (Shreveport) (October 15, 1961).

244 *In the past year, Dane had started taking a number of alarming precautions*: Interview with Marcia Heien (July 2015).

245 *Marcella had heard rumors*: FBI, memorandum on Hubert Dane Harris, File Number LR 92-122 (November 27, 1963).

245 *"If you're going to be in business, you have to be the same all the time"*: Ibid.

245 *It was, however, an impressive gambling den*: The description of the Bridge Street Club comes from FBI memorandum on Hot Springs clubs, File Number 162-3 (May 22, 1961).

246 *One weekend a group from Dallas*: Interview with Tony Frazier (August 2016).

246 *including the palm man Jimmie Green*: FBI, memorandum on James Henry Dolan by Robert Barrett, File Number 92-292 (November 16, 1962), 9.

HAZEL, JUNE 1961

247 *Larry met a girl in town*: Details and dialogue in the story about Larry stealing the car are based on an interview with Larry Hill (June 2015).

249 *Jimmy and Judy were still together*: Details and dialogue in the story about Jimmy and Judy caring for the dog come from an interview with Judy Horner (January 2017).

OWNEY, MARCH–JULY 1961

252 *"We find their fingers in Texas, and in Mississippi, Alabama"*: Testimony to U.S. Senate Select Committee on Improper Activities in the Labor Management Field (March 23, 1959).

252 *mobsters in Chicago were overheard complaining*: FBI, memorandum by Elliot Anderson on Leslie Kruse, File Number 92-1037 (September 1963).

253 *was shocked to find Senator McClellan*: FBI, teletype from San Francisco office to Little Rock office regarding Sebastian John LaRocca, File Number 92-2940 (October 27, 1961).

253 *"The Justice Department will follow up McClellan's closed-door hearings with swift, vigorous prosecutions"*: Drew Pearson, "Merry Go Round," *Northwest Arkansas Times* (December 27, 1961).

253 *Owney and Dane did all they could to keep the senator happy*: FBI memorandum on Hubert Dane Harris, File Number LR 92-122 (November 7, 1963), 2.

253 *"Look at Hot Springs, it's wide open"*: FBI, memorandum by Frank Hill on Sam Giancana, File Number 92-350 (February 7, 1962).

253 *They kicked in the doors at the Harlem Chicken Shack*: "FBI Men Seize 5 Slot Devices at Hot Springs," *Arkansas Gazette* (March 31, 1961).

254 *filing reports to J. Edgar Hoover complete with photographs*: FBI, memorandum by Claburn White on activities of top hoodlums in the Chicago Area, File Number 62-9-9-641 (March 8, 1961).

254 *twelve buses carrying seven hundred law enforcement officers*: "U.S. Sheriffs Find Spa Disarming," *Arkansas Gazette* (June 13, 1961).

254 *In July of that same year, Paul Kamerick*: "Madden, Pal Plead Fifth as Probers Apply Heat to Hot Springs Gambling," *Arkansas Gazette* (September 1, 1961).

255 *Hurst told Owney not to say a word*: Hearing before the Permanent Subcommittee on Investigations of the Committee on Government Operations, U.S. Senate, *Gambling and Organized Crime* (August 1961), 564.

255 *"Jesus, Mary, and Joseph. I was in partnership with his father"*: Graham Nown, *Arkansas Godfather* (Butler Center, 2013), 339.

255 *"Another example of the type of situation which we are trying to curb"*: Testimony of Robert F. Kennedy, Attorney General of the United States, before the House Committee on the Judiciary in Support of Legislation to Curb Organized Crime and Racketeering (May 17, 1961).

256 *After Kamerick left the Ritter Hotel, he made stops at clubs all over town*: "Racket Probers at Hot Springs," *Arkansas Gazette* (July 25, 1961).

256 *"If you don't stop asking people around here questions about me"*: Charles Samuels, "Owney Madden: Only Gangster Exiled in America," *Cavalier* (November, 1961).

256 *Dane bought out Owney's interest in the clubs and slot machines*: FBI, memorandum on Owen Vincent Madden, File Number 162-74 (August 24, 1961), 5.

256 *Hurst passed Owney on to another lawyer*: Nown, *Arkansas Godfather*, 343.

256 *Owney called a meeting of every bookie in Hot Springs*: FBI, memorandum on Owen Vincent Madden, File Number 162-74 (August 24, 1961), 5.

257 *He told the bookies he expected them to reimburse him*: Ibid.

257 *He insisted that Dane still kick him a piece*: FBI, memorandum on Hubert Dane Harris, File Number LR 92-122 (February 12, 1964).

257 *A few days before Owney's testimony, Senator McClellan was filmed*: "McClellan Tries Rose Colored Glasses, Gets Gambling Eyeful," *Sentinel Record* (Hot Springs) (August 23, 1961).

258 *"Does that light bother you?"*: Details and dialogue from Owney's testimony before the McClellan hearings are from Nown, *Arkansas Godfather*, 346–48.

258 *As he boarded his flight back to Arkansas*: Ibid., 348–49.

DANE, 1962

259 *According to the National Park Service, 5,130,984 people visited the area*: "Hot Springs Counts 5 Million Visitors, Prepares for More," *Times* (Shreveport) (October 29, 1961).

259 *Over eight hundred new hotel rooms were built or under construction in 1962*: Edna Lee Howe, "'School' Trains Residents for Casino Jobs to Meet Need, Avoid Clash with U.S. Laws," *Sentinel Record* (Hot Springs) (November 25, 1962).

259 *including by the Teamsters Central States Pension Fund*: "Aristocrat Manor," National Register of Historic Places Registration Form, U.S. Department of the Interior (November 2016), 18.

259 *Total receipts across all industries were up by more than ten million dollars*: Howe, "'School' Trains Residents for Casino Jobs to Meet Need."

259 *collectively employed over a thousand people*: Theodore Link, "Gamblers Edgy in Hot Springs Over US Inquiry," *St. Louis Post-Dispatch* (December 2, 1962).

259 *When Dane traveled to Las Vegas for the Wine & Spirits Wholesalers of America convention*: FBI, memorandum on Hubert Dane Harris, File Number LR 92-122 (October 26, 1961).

260 *"the most unusual spa in the United States"*: Robert Boyle, "The Hottest Spring in Hot Springs," *Sports Illustrated* (March 19, 1962).

261 *"We are serving notice that any prostitute, hoodlum, or racketeer"*: "Hot Springs to Arrest 'Undesirables,'" *Arkansas Gazette* (January 24, 1962).

261 *When agents checked in on the Vapors in February 1962*: FBI, memorandum on Hubert Dane Harris, File Number 162-232 (February 28, 1962).

261 *the dealers kept check registers*: Ibid.

261 *Using phone records, the FBI built a list*: Ibid.

262 *The FBI agents showed up at many of their places of business*: Ibid.

262 *"Y'all go on ahead and I'll ride up in the ambulance with Bookie"*: Interview with Walter "Skip" Ebel Jr. (December 2016).

263 *the grand jury deliberated for twenty-five minutes*: "Grand Jury Closes Probe of Gaming; Refuses to Indict," *Arkansas Gazette* (December 14, 1962).

263 *won by a single vote*: Ibid.

263 *"delighted to know that the federal laws were not found to have been violated"*: Ibid.

HAZEL, AUGUST 1962

265 *The blackjack tables had three or four customers lined up waiting behind each player*: "Open Gambling at Hot Springs? Sure, Just Walk Right In and Take a Look," *Arkansas Gazette* (June 17, 1962).

265 *On a good night the Southern Club may have pulled in a hundred customers*: "Open Gambling at Hot Springs?"

265 *more than ten thousand dollars a week*: Wallace Turner, "Hot Springs: Gamblers' Haven," *New York Times* (March 8, 1964).

265 *Mickey would stay at Dane's place*: Interview with Marcia Heien (July 2015).

265 *she said the audiences in Hot Springs were sophisticated*: Bill Whitworth, "Mitzi Gaynor Testing Her Act at Hot Springs Before Tour," *Arkansas Gazette* (May 28, 1962); Randy King, "Actress Mitzi Gaynor Praises People of Spa on Last Day Here" *Sentinel Record* (Hot Springs) (June 18, 1962).

266 *Dane's commercials for the Vapors played on radio stations*: Interview with Wayne Threadgill (July 2015).

266 *Virginia loved the Vapors*: David Maraniss, "Clinton Life Shaped by Early Turmoil," *Washington Post* (January 26, 1992).

266 *The Palms booked Sally Rand*: "$16 Million Bet at Spa Race Track," *Hope Star* (March 26, 1962); Orval Allbritton, *Leo and Verne* (Garland County Historical Society, 2003), 590.

266 *Digby chose instead to invest in a juiced craps table*: Confidential interview (July 2015).

267 *purchased their equipment from the same place, Taylor & Company in Cicero, Illinois*: Interview with Wayne Threadgill (July 2015).

267 *He ordered the plans for the slot machines*: Interview with Tony Frazier (August 2016).

267 *His technicians built eighty clones of the Bell slot machine*: Ibid.

268 *A sizable percentage of his casino employees came from out of state*: FBI, memorandum on Hubert Dane Harris, File Number 162-232-6 (February 28, 1962), 2–4.

268 *Dane figured out a workaround*: Ibid.

268 *I hereby certify that I was not requested*: Ibid.

268 *The meeting was attended by a few dozen prospective casino employees*: FBI, memorandum by Henry Oliver on Hubert Dane Harris, File Number LR 166-91 (February 23, 1962), 15.

269 *Fewer than a quarter of those prospective employees*: FBI, memorandum on Hubert Dane Harris, File Number 162-232-6 (February 28, 1962), 2–4.

269 *job at the Crawford Pharmacy*: Interview with Larry Hill (June 2015).

269 *Dane was unhappy with the quality*: FBI, memorandum on Hubert Dane Harris, File Number 162-232-6 (February 28, 1962), 2–4.

270 *first organized school for dealers*: Edna Lee Howe, "'School' Trains Residents for Casino Jobs to Meet Need, Avoid Clash with U.S. Laws," *Sentinel Record* (Hot Springs) (November 25, 1962).

270 *limited to forty people*: Ibid.

270 *About a dozen of the students in the first class were women*: Ibid.

DANE, JANUARY 1963

271 *Early on the morning of January 4, 1963, the first of the dealer training classes was just getting started*: Beverly Longinotti v. Park Realty Co. Inc., 64 Civil 941, 942 (U.S. District Court, Western District, 1964).

271 *a pit boss named W. C. Tucker*: Ibid.

271 *As the alarm clock rang, students in the dealer class could smell something*: Robert Fry v. Park Realty Co. Inc., Civil 942 (U.S. District Court, Western District, 1964).

272 *The plate glass window in the front of the club shattered*: "Mysterious Blast Rips Vapors Club; At Least 12 Hurt," *Arkansas Gazette* (January 5, 1963).

272 *A roulette wheel splintered*: "Vapors Blast Still Unsolved; Work of Fanatics or Rivals?" *Arkansas Gazette* (January 6, 1963).

272 *Chunks of concrete and rebar and slivers of glass were sent hurtling*: Beverly Longinotti v. Park Realty Co. Inc., 64 Civil 941, 942 (U.S. District Court, Western District, 1964).

272 *A meat salesman from Memphis*: "Blast Probe Continues," *Arkansas Democrat* (January 5, 1963); "Explosive Caused Vapors Blast, Says Fire Marshal," *Hot Springs New Era* (January 5, 1963).

272 *sliced through the neck and shoulders*: Beverly Longinotti v. Park Realty Co. Inc., 64 Civil 941, 942 (U.S. District Court, Western District, 1964).

272 *Garland Mitchell, was lifted from his feet*: "Mysterious Blast Rips Vapors Club."

272 *Thirty-seven-year-old Lila Manuel's eardrum*: "Explosive Caused Vapors Blast, Says Fire Marshal."

272 *One of the dealer students, sixty-three-year-old Jack Fry*: Robert Fry v. Park Realty Co. Inc., Civil 942 (U.S. District Court, Western District, 1964).

272 *Mrs. E. E. Dodd was getting her hair done*: "CD Test Helps Spa Handle Real Thing," *Arkansas Democrat* (January 5, 1963).

272 *The blast could be heard all across town*: Interview with Fred Palmer (January 2017).

272 *The explosion lifted the roof*: "Explosive Caused Vapors Blast."

273 *A layer of dust settled onto the surrounding cars*: Ibid.

273 *Ten doctors and nurses tended to the wounded*: "CD Test Helps Spa Handle Real Thing."

273 *Dane was on his way to the club when it happened*: Interview with Marcia Heien (June 2015).

273 *"Where are we supposed to go, Dane?"*: Ibid.

273 *All over town police officers showed up at various schools*: Interview with Walter "Skip" Ebel Jr. (December 2016).

274 *"We've had enough bad publicity"*: "Mysterious Blast Rips Vapors Club."

274 *"The Picture They Didn't Want Taken"*: Ibid.

274 *Jack Fry would later die*: Robert Fry v. Park Realty Co. Inc., Civil 942 (U.S. District Court, Western District, 1964).

274 *Beverly Longinotti was left partially paralyzed*: Beverly Longinotti v. Park Realty Co. Inc., 64 Civil 941, 942 (U.S. District Court, Western District, 1964).

274 *Officially, Dane told the press it was the work of a disgruntled customer*: "Spa Blast Still Mystery," *Arkansas Democrat* (January 6, 1963).

274 *The press speculated that the bomb might have been the work of the mob*: "Underworld Move Seen in Club Blast," *Arkansas Gazette* (January 7, 1963).

274 *He'd even shown up on the runway of the airport*: "Spa Blast Still Mystery."

274 *The new sheriff in Cook County, Illinois, Richard Ogilvie*: "Home-owned? 'No,' Chicago Official Says of Hot Springs Clubs," *Arkansas Gazette* (January 8, 1963).

275 *"saw all that easy money"*: Ibid.

275 *bringing in an estimated $200 million a year*: "Faubus Confirms Probe into Gambling Reports," Associated Press (March 5, 1965).

275 *entire state of Nevada reported only $227 million*: "Casino Gross Revenue 1946–1971," Nevada Gaming Abstract, University of Nevada at Las Vegas Center for Gaming Research.

275 *By 1963, the Teamsters Central States Pension Fund held over two hundred million dollars in assets*: Tom Powers, "U.S. Agents Dig into Teamster Loan Policies," *Chicago Tribune* (June 2, 1963).

275 *almost all in commercial real estate, and much of it in casino projects in Las Vegas*: Ed Reid and Ovid Demaris, *The Green Felt Jungle* (Trident, 1963), 83.

275 *In 1962, the fund had issued a ten-million-dollar construction loan*: Ken Miller, "Mob in Nevada Alive and Well," *Reno Gazette-Journal* (July 14, 1985); Deanna DeMatteo, "Las Vegas Strip Historical Site," http://www.lvstriphistory.com/ie/cae1962.htm.

275 *More than one of Benny Binion's competitors had been killed*: Sally Denton and Roger Morris, *The Money and the Power: The Making of Las Vegas and Its Hold on America* (Knopf, 2001), 30–37.

275 *The Cleveland mob was involved in just such a bombing campaign*: Dick Habien, "File on Numbers Is Thick, Bloody," *Cincinnati Enquirer* (February 23, 1959).

276 *"for just such a jackpot"*: FBI, memorandum by Robert Pearce on Angelo Bruno, File Number 92-444 (March 30, 1962), 6.

276 *The Ginny Tiu Show, a song-and-dance act of four young Chinese siblings, was coming to the Vapors fresh from a performance for President Kennedy*: "Ginny Tiu Show Slated Monday, Tuesday at Southwest Junior High," *Sentinel Record* (Hot Springs) (January 6, 1963).

276 *"We didn't want our Hot Springs children to be disappointed in not being able to see the show"*: Ibid.

276 *A sold-out crowd of more than 350 people turned out that Saturday*: "Vapors Reopening Draws Full House," *Arkansas Democrat* (January 11, 1963).

277 *On February 1 he received an anonymous telephone call*: FBI report on David Whittington car bombing, File Number 157-186 (April 27, 1963), 5.

277 *Dane upped the security on their homes and at the Belvedere*: "Spa Casinos Add 'Muscle,'" *Arkansas Democrat* (January 8, 1963); interview with Fred Palmer (January 2017).

277 *Dane even had guards posted in the ladies' washrooms*: "Gambling Continues as Usual in Hot Springs Despite Inquiry," *St. Louis Post-Dispatch* (February 19, 1964).

277 *"There are always the ins and the outs"*: "Spa Casinos Add 'Muscle.'"

277 *"In a matter of days, people will almost forget it happened"*: "Spa Blast Still Mystery."

277 *crowds in 1963 would break the record set in 1962*: "Race Track Sets Changes for Upcoming Season," *Denton Record-Chronicle* (January 24, 1963).

277 *set new benchmarks for attendance and money wagered*: "Activity Mounts at Oaklawn Park," *Northwest Arkansas Times* (January 17, 1964).

278 *He vowed to veto the bill*: "Faubus Vows to Veto Legal Gambling Bill," *Arkansas Gazette* (January 12, 1963).

278 *A day later Hurst announced he was dropping the bill*: Ibid.

278 *The state-of-the-art convention center, funded entirely by gambling money*: "Garland Jury Blasts 'Amusement' Tax; Drink Sale to Halt," *Arkansas Gazette* (September 21, 1967).

278 *late on the night of April 22, a call came in to the police department*: "Spa Officer Reveals Ruse," *Hope Star* (April 27, 1963).

278 *The person on the other end of the line said someone was on their way to shoot up the house*: Interview with Marcia Heien (June 2015).

279 *across town a bomb went off under the hood of David Whittington's car*: "Bomb Blast at Hot Springs," *Hope Star* (April 23, 1963).

279 *"I just think somebody doesn't care for me very much"*: Ibid.

279 *in connection with a major multistate car-theft ring*: "2nd Trial for Attorney Set," *Hope Star* (December 5, 1963).

279 *The FBI turned its attention squarely to Digby*: FBI report on David Whittington car bombing, File Number 157-178 (May 3, 1963), 2.

279 *The FBI's informants pointed the finger at two hoodlums from Chicago*: FBI report on David Whittington car bombing, File Number 157-178 (April 29, 1963), 1.

279 *word kept coming in that more violence was on its way*: FBI report on David Whittington car bombing, File Number 157-186 (April 27, 1963), 2–6.

280 *"those in political power have used negro votes to influence elections"*: Ibid.

280 *hotel owner Gerald Vanderslice, found two sticks of dynamite*: "Spa Motel Man Gets Dynamite in Front Yard," *Northwest Arkansas Times* (May 30, 1963).

DANE, SEPTEMBER 1963

281 *"island of sporty urban life in an ocean of rural austerity and hominy grits"*: Bern Keating, "A Fresh Look at Arkansas," *Holiday* (September 1963), 55.

281 *I have watched other casino crowds*: Ibid.

282 *continuing a five-year upward trend for Hot Springs*: "Attendance, Wagering Up at Oaklawn," Associated Press (April 10, 1963).

282 *six thousand dollars a month on out-of-state advertisements, and as a result Hot Springs had ranked fourth*: FBI, memorandum on Hubert Dane Harris, File Number LR 92-122 (December 9, 1963).

282 *Governor Faubus and Senator McClellan requested that Dane call a meeting*: FBI, decoded teletype from Little Rock Office to FBI director (October 29, 1963)

283 *"Craps and roulette upstairs!"*: FBI, memorandum on Hubert Dane Harris, File Number LR 92-122 (November 1, 1963)

283 *no living person except himself*: FBI, memorandum on Hubert Dane Harris, File Number LR 92-122 (November 27, 1963).

283 *"What does Dane Harris think about it?"*: FBI, memorandum on Hubert Dane Harris, File Number LR 92-122 (November 20, 1963).

283 *anywhere from twenty-five to thirty thousand dollars a month*: FBI, memorandum on Hubert Dane Harris, File Number LR 92-122 (December 9, 1963).

283 *Eighteen hundred dollars to the mayor*: FBI, justification for continuation of technical or microphone surveillance, File Number 92-3834 (November 27, 1963).

283 *Five thousand dollars to a former Department of Justice staffer*: Ibid.

283 *An envelope full of money to the state police investigator*: FBI, memorandum on Hubert Dane Harris, File Number LR 92-122 (December 18, 1963).

283 *split thirteen ways*: FBI, memorandum on Hubert Dane Harris, File Number LR 92-122 (December 9, 1963).

284 *It began a disinformation campaign*: FBI, memorandum on Hubert Dane Harris, File Number LR 92-122 (December 4, 1963).

284 *He and Owney had their own ideas*: "Officials Take Issue with Speculation over Bomb Blast at Vapors," *Hot Springs New Era* (January 7, 1963); confidential interview (July 2015).

284 *drove down to Fort Worth, Texas, to visit R. D. Matthews*: FBI, memorandum on Russell Douglas Matthews, File Number 166-636 (September 20, 1963).

284 *Matthews was holding thirty thousand dollars for a job*: Ibid.

285 *he told her he didn't want to speak with either of them*: Ibid.

285 *That summer, Virginia Clinton danced*: Virginia Clinton Kelly, K. C. Kelly, and James Morgan, *Leading with My Heart* (Simon & Schuster, 1995).

285 *Bill Clinton visited the White House*: Jeff Kunerth, "Summer of '63 Reunion," *Detroit Free Press* (July 24, 1992).

285 *Dane ordered the police to shut down every casino*: FBI, memorandum on Hubert Dane Harris, File Number LR 92-122 (November 26, 1963).

285 *Meanwhile, Dane wasted little time in making inquiries*: FBI, memorandum on Hubert Dane Harris, File Number LR 92-122 (November 29, 1963).

286 *whose phone number they claimed was in Ruby's pocket*: Doug Swanson, "Blood Aces: The Wild Ride of Benny Binion, the Texas Gangster Who Created Vegas Poker" (Penguin, 2015), 244.

286 *Investigators came to Hot Springs to question Dane*: Warren Commission Document 4, FBI Clements Report on Jack Ruby (November 30, 1963), 395.

286 *"You need to know what your daughter and her boyfriend are saying"*: Interview with Marcia Heien (June 2015).

287 *Since the two bombings, phone calls threatening more explosions*: FBI report on David Whittington car bombing, File Number 157-186 (April 27, 1963).

287 *Three days before Christmas 1963, James Rice's phone rang*: Clay Hermann interview with Elmer Beard, https://www.youtube.com/watch?v=0FAgQFp14ec (August 3, 2015).

287 *"You'll get the same thing President Kennedy got"*: "Fire Destroys Negro Church; Probe Started," United Press International (December 23, 1963).

287 *But Rice and other leaders had been performing "checks" at the federally owned bathhouses*: "Integration of Bath House Asked," *Hope Star* (December 18, 1963).

288 *"Now we want you to look out the door"*: Clay Hermann interview with Elmer Beard.

288 *local police and fire officials claimed they could find no evidence of arson*: "Arson Dismissed in Hot Springs Church Blaze," *Northwest Arkansas Times* (December 24, 1963).

288 *"a simple, unadulterated case of arson"*: "What About Roanoke?," *Arkansas Citizen* (Hot Springs) (December 22–30, 1963).

Part V: Pentecost

DANE, MARCH 1964

291 *The crew working on Dane's house were sweating in the midday sun*: The story about Dane's fence is based on an interview with Tony Frazier (August 2016).

292 *when he got an envelope in the mail from Missouri with thirty-four dollars in chips*: FBI, memorandum on Hubert Dane Harris, File Number LR 92-122 (March 2, 1964).

292 *Kennedy dispatched two U.S. assistant attorneys general to Hot Springs*: Orval Allbritton, *Leo and Verne* (Garland County Historical Society, 2003), 592–594.

292 *At each club the men witnessed packed houses and furious action*: Orval Allbritton, *Lawman: The Story of Clay White, A Life of Service* (Garland County Historical Society, 2014), 121–22.

292 *"It seems awfully hard for me to comprehend that gambling of this scope could be self-contained"*: Ibid.

292 *"Biggest Non-Floating Dice Game in the Land"*: Jerry Greene, "Biggest Non-Floating Dice Game in the Land," *Daily News* (New York) (March 9, 1964).

292 *"Gambler's Haven"*: Wallace Turner, "Hot Springs: Gambler's Haven," *New York Times* (March 8, 1964).

293 *"On behalf of your children and yourselves, remove this cancer from your county"*: "Calls Gambling Cancer of Spa," *Hope Star* (January 15, 1964).

293 *where he had moved in 1953 in order to secure a quick divorce*: "Rockefeller Divorce Action Is Shrouded in Deep Secrecy," *Miami News* (October 15, 1953).

293 *Winthrop was supportive of civil rights, which made him an attractive candidate to the liberal Democrats*: John Kirk, "The Election That Changed Arkansas Politics," *Arkansas Times* (March 28, 2012).

294 *a bill requiring that blood for transfusions be labeled*: William Shelton, "Will Faubus Fire Rockefeller? Will Gambling Stay Alive? What Will Legislature Do Next?," *Arkansas Gazette* (February 24, 1963).

294 *A group of Baptist ministers organized vigilantes from all over Arkansas*: "CUAG Planning Gambling Drive," *Arkansas Gazette* (March 13, 1965).

294 *"We must be taught the truth—that it is evil"*: "Faubus Vows to Veto Legal Gambling Bill," *Arkansas Gazette* (January 12, 1963).

295 *"We're forty-ninth and fiftieth in everything"*: "Legal Gambling Backers Explain Their Defeat," *Northwest Arkansas Times* (November 7, 1964).

295 *"When you visit us in New York, we're not going to be able to show you anything like this"*: Leroy Donald, "Operator of Vapors Says Gambling Good for Arkansas Image," *Arkansas Gazette* (March 29, 1964).

295 *"The truth is that the flourishing rackets industry at Hot Springs is an anachronism"*: "The Relief That Lies Just an Election Away," *Arkansas Gazette* (February 22, 1963).

295 *"The way this Federal thing looks, the only thing for me to do is close up"*: FBI, memorandum on Hubert Dane Harris, File Number LR 92-122 (February 19, 1964).

295 *At the start of 1964 there were over a thousand people*: "1,000 Casino Employees Jobless in Hot Springs," AP (March 30, 1964).

296 *more than two thousand applicants*: FBI, memorandum on Hubert Dane Harris, File Number LR 92-122 (February 12, 1964).

296 *his payroll was over a million dollars a year*: Ibid.

296 *More than eighteen million dollars in new construction loans*: "Hot Springs Gambling Is Immoral, House Says; Vote Bill Is Approved," *Arkansas Gazette* (March 27, 1964).

296 *The gambling clubs spent more on out-of-state advertising*: "Spa Casinos Close amid Record Business," *Sentinel Record* (Hot Springs) (March 29, 1964).

296 *possibly as high as a billion dollars*: "State Officials Deny Charge That Illegal Gambling Take Reaches $1 Billion a Year," *Arkansas Gazette* (September 24, 1964).

296 *"the big boys"*: FBI, memorandum on Owen Vincent Madden by Claburn White, File Number 92-2699 (July 24, 1964), 3.

297 *"last fling night in the most luxurious gambling houses east of Las Vegas"*: "Casinos Crowded for One Last Fling Before Shutdown," *Arkansas Gazette* (March 29, 1964).

297 *The Vapors was filled with over a thousand revelers*: John Hynes, "Gambling Clubs in Hot Springs Will Shut Down After Tonight," *St. Louis Post-Dispatch* (March 28, 1964).

297 *"The gambling won't be going quite as fast tonight"*: Donald Janson, "Hot Springs Blue After Final Fling," *New York Times* (March 30, 1964). This article mistakenly identifies the comedian as Dick Van Dyke.

297 *A writer from* The Saturday Evening Post *witnessed a man*: John Skow, "No Dice in Hot Springs," *Saturday Evening Post* (September 19, 1964).

298 *"Only a few people get the money"*: Leroy Donald, "People in the Know Aren't Worried, Says One Business Leader," *Arkansas Gazette* (March 28, 1964).

298 *Dane gathered his employees together*: Donald Janson, "Hot Springs Blue After Final Fling," *New York Times* (March 30, 1964).

298 *they were met by more than a thousand men and women*: Wick Temple, "Chips Clatter, Slots Whirl in Final Fling," *Arkansas Democrat* (March 29, 1964).

298 *"The Old Rugged Cross"*: According to numerous accounts of this yearly event, this hymn was traditional during the procession.

HAZEL, DECEMBER 1964

299 *Jimmy called them seizures*: The details in this chapter, including dialogue, are based on an interview with Judy Horner (January 2017) as well as on Jimmy Hill's recollections to me.

DANE, APRIL 1965

303 *Dane tried to keep the Vapors open*: Leroy Donald, "Operator of Vapors Says Gambling Good for Arkansas Image," *Arkansas Gazette* (March 29, 1964).

303 *In one eight-block stretch, fourteen stores had gone out of business*: Frank Morgan, "The Big Spenders Flee Hot Springs as Voters Bar Gambling Revival," *Wall Street Journal* (December 8, 1964).

303 *"The period of depression is going to be with us a long time"*: Ibid.

304 *"My friend, this is what you call a plush hotel"*: James Campbell, "Battle over Legalizing Hot Springs Gambling," *St. Louis Post-Dispatch* (October 7, 1964).

304 *thirty-two of the hotels and motels in Hot Springs banding together*: Edna Lee Howe, "Private Club Projects Pay Off for Spa Hotels, Motels," *Camden News* (March 5, 1966).

304 *The participating hotels paid the Vapors three dollars per room per month*: Ibid.

304 *Five hundred locals*: Ibid.

304 *wheeled in thirty-six of his Super Bell slot machines*: "Slots Return to Hot Springs," *Arkansas Gazette* (March 4, 1965).

304 *The crowd never arrived*: Wallace Turner, "Gambling Back at Hot Springs," *New York Times* (March 31, 1965).

OWNEY, 1965

305 *He demanded his agents follow Owney*: Graham Nown, *Arkansas Godfather* (Butler Center, 2013), 349–50.

305 *same routine almost every single day*: Ibid.

306 *Ellis groused that Owney was "old and senile"*: FBI, memorandum on Hubert Dane Harris, File Number LR 92-122 (February 12, 1964).

306 *"You know they watch like a hawk"*: Ibid.

306 *Agnes brought Owney to the hospital with chest pains*: Nown, *Arkansas Godfather*, 353.

306 *On the day of Owney's funeral it poured down rain*: Ibid.

306 *"Page after page of sensationalism has been written about him"*: Ibid., 354.

307 *They told her the money was tainted*: Ibid., 355.

EPILOGUE

309 *The water in Hot Springs is hot*: Details about the hot springs are from Jeffrey Hanor, *Fire in Folded Rocks: Geology of Hot Springs National Park*, Eastern National Park and Monument Association (1980).

310 "To everything there is a season": Quotations from Millard Shields are taken from undated audio recordings of his sermons in the author's possession.

311 *made ten dollars a day*: Interview with Benny Bridwell (January 2017).

311 *she and her coworkers drove to Las Vegas*: Details about Hazel's trip to Las Vegas are based on a confidential interview with one of her contemporaries (August 2016).

311 *The owners of the massive resort were already under investigation*: "Gaming Board Approves Florida Group Purchase of Vegas Caesars Palace," *Nevada State Journal* (August 14, 1969).

311 *operating budget was forty thousand dollars a day*: "Las Vegas Hosts Conventions," *Nevada State Journal* (January 29, 1967).

312 *left in a coma for twenty-nine days*: Robert Green, "A Daredevil's Life Ends," *National Post* (Canada) (December 1, 2007).

313 *word was that the going rate was one thousand dollars*: "Gambling Still Issue in House," *Hope Star* (March 8, 1967).

313 *Hurst had secured a pledge from Rockefeller*: "Governor Promises to Veto Bill, Garland Legislators Tell Colleagues WR Gave Assurance Against Veto," *Arkansas Gazette* (March 7, 1967).

313 *The raiding party started at the Bridge Street Club*: "Gambling Devices Worth $70,000 Seized at Resort," *Arkansas Gazette* (August 18, 1967).

314 *Dane's house on Trivista was bombed*: "Bombers Strike Two Targets at Hot Springs," *Northwest Arkansas Times* (March 31, 1966).

314 *Circuit Judge Dobbs had a bomb go off at his house*: Ibid.

314 *Dane and Marcella would play golf until it got dark outside*: Interview with Walter "Skip" Ebel Jr. (December 2016).

314 *Marcia and Dane Jr. would explore the rolling hills*: Interview with Marcia Heien (December 2017).

314 *It was eventually purchased by Jack Digby*: Hot Springs National Park City Directory (Polk, 1977).

315 *1985, 1996, and 2000*: Benjamin Hardy, "Arkansas Becomes Casino Country," *Arkansas Times*, https://arktimes.com/news/cover-stories/2018/11/15/arkansas-becomes-casino-country-2 (November 15, 2018); "Work Underway on $100 Million Dollar Expansion at Oaklawn," *U.S. News*, https://www.usnews.com/news/best-states/arkansas/articles/2019-05-13/work-underway-on-100-million-expansion-at-oaklawn (May 13, 2019).

315 *A new hotel is under construction*: Beth Reed, "Oaklawn Unveils $100 Million-Plus Expansion," *Sentinel Record*, https://www.hotsr.com/news/2018/nov/20/oaklawn-unveils-100-million-plus-expans/ (November 20, 2018).

315 *"If this pretty little thing can win, you sure can!"*: Confidential interview (August 2016).

ACKNOWLEDGMENTS

This book would not have been possible without the support and encouragement of my wife, Katie Gerken, who not only picked up so much of my slack when I was in the thick of writing and research but also agreed to move our family from Brooklyn to Arkansas for an entire year. Her late-night pep talks and her nonjudgmental audience to my manic writer's-block-induced rants and raves are proof that she truly loves me. She's always my first reader; it is her opinion that matters above all others. I am eternally in her debt.

Thank you to my agent, Jim Rutman, for his patience, advice, and willingness to be a shoulder to cry on as I learned how to write a book. Thank you to my editor, Colin Dickerman, not only for his brilliant notes, ideas, and edits, which made this book so much better, but for his belief in this project and his willingness to see it through to the end. I am lucky to have had the opportunity to work with him. Thanks as well to Ian Van Wye at FSG and James Melia at Flatiron for their hard work and their thoughtful insights.

I am grateful beyond words to the people who sat down with me for interviews, sometimes for several hours, sometimes revealing painful memories: Marcia Heien, Larry and Nelta Hill, Ressie Parker, Martha

Ann Henry, Judy Horner, Benny Bridwell, Tony Frazier, Fred Mark Palmer, Skip Ebel, Steven and David Mitchell, Mary Loye, Wanda Thompson, Orval Allbritton, Wayne Threadgill, Chris Hendrix, Lanny Beavers, Donald Christiansen, Q. Byrum Hurst Jr., Eutha Corder, and others who wished not to be named.

I stand on the shoulders of a small and talented group of local historians who have spent years researching Hot Springs' history of gambling, and working to solve the town's many mysteries. I want to particularly highlight Orval Allbritton, whose books and advice and encouragement were invaluable to me; and Wayne Threadgill, whose kindness and willingness to open up his home, his files, and his collection of gambling obscurities to me, and to show a complete stranger so much hospitality, was appreciated. Wayne helped make introductions and pointed me in the right direction whenever I was lost. Without his guidance I might never have found my way.

My family spent a year in Hot Springs while I researched and wrote this book, and during that time we were embraced and made to feel welcome by so many in that community. In particular, the organization Low Key Arts and the collection of creative geniuses who run it were like a second family to us, and this book wouldn't have been possible without their friendship and assistance.

Matt Rowe and Adam Webb were the two people I most trusted to understand what I was trying to do with this book and to help me with my research, both in Hot Springs and in Little Rock. Their willingness to drop everything and spend hours staring at microfilm for me was the truest expression of friendship. I thank them both for sticking with me through the years and for not giving up on this project. Midnight Madness forever.

The folks at the Garland County Historical Society went over and above the call of duty any time I came in with unusual or seemingly impossible requests. Renee Lucy, Clyde Covington, Liz Robbins, Dan Anderson, and all of the many volunteers and board members who hauled out boxes and files for me to pick through, thank you.

Thank you to my mother, Pamelia Hill, and my sister, Jamie Hill, for always being willing to help out in ways great and small. I wrote this book to honor the life and preserve the memory of my father, and in that respect this book is as much theirs as it is mine.

So many others have been helpful in making introductions for me, or pointing me toward people who had good stories to tell, or otherwise doing whatever they could to help with the book: Randy Hill, Zac Smith and Cheryl Roorda, Shea Childs and Bill Solleder, Chuck Dodson, Agnes Galeka and Kevin Rogers, Bobby Missle, Ashley Hill, Josh Small, Jaime Keeling, Karen Shafer, Arlene Cox, Zainab Zaheer, Karla Parker, Richard Parker, Lance Hill, Randy and Kathy Muse, Clayton Blackstock, Olympia Pakis, Pete D'Amato, David Schwartz, and many others I'm sure I've forgotten. It's been a long five years.

Lastly, I want to thank my children, August, Adeline, and Harry. My decision to quit my job and spend five years writing a book has affected their lives in ways they don't understand, but that are profound and important all the same. I have dragged them across the country and put them into three different schools, and we have all lived by the seat of our collective pants in service of this book. I hope one day when they read it they will think it was worth it. But just in case they don't, hopefully a trip to Disneyland will absolve me.

INDEX

A NOTE ABOUT THE AUTHOR

David Hill is a writer from Hot Springs, Arkansas. His work has appeared regularly in *The Ringer* and has been featured in *The New Yorker, Esquire, GQ,* and *New York* magazine, as well as on *This American Life.* He lives in Nyack, New York, with his wife and three children, and serves as vice president of the National Writers Union.